PENGUIN B̶O̶O̶K̶S̶

A DUTY O̶

'At the heart of the author's th̶
the British people during the pan̶d̶
to be much better than their rule̶
to mobilise our true national spir̶.̶ ̶.̶ ̶.̶ ̶.̶ ̶.̶ ̶.̶ ̶nobler politics'
Max Hastings, *Sunday Times*

'A timely examination of how the lessons of the past can help build a
new post-Covid society, Lord Hennessy's latest book is both compelling
and remarkable . . . Peter Hennessy understands just how Britain
ticks. . . . There is no one better acquainted with those who have pulled
the levers of power. In this latest short, but compelling, book he brings
all that knowledge and sense of perspective to a remarkable analysis'
Lord Cormack, *The House Magazine*

'In *A Duty of Care*, Peter Hennessy draws a link between the
history of the postwar welfare state and the post-pandemic case
for a new settlement . . . Admirably concise, it is proof that
a strong political case does not require hundreds of
pages to make its point' Robert Shrimsley, *Financial Times*

'Compelling' Jay Elwes, *Spectator*

'The Hennessy ethos is an engaging and warm moderation . . .
A passionate call for a new social settlement covering
everything from elderly care to vocational training'
Tom Clark, *Prospect*

'*A Duty of Care* is much more than just an appeal for a politics of
sanity and mutual respect. It is also, no less importantly, and more
interestingly, a Confucian appeal for a politics of benevolence'
Oliver Letwin, *The Tablet*

ABOUT THE AUTHOR

Peter Hennessy, one of Britain's best-known historians, is Attlee Professor
of Contemporary British History at Queen Mary, University of London
and an Honorary Fellow of St John's College, Cambridge. He was elected
a Fellow of the British Academy in 2003. He is the author of the classic
'post-war trilogy', *Never Again: Britain 1945–1951* (winner of the NCR
and Duff Cooper Prizes), *Having it So Good: Britain in the Fifties* (winner of the Orwell Prize) and *Winds of Change: Britain in the Early
Sixties*, the bestselling *The Prime Minister* and *The Secret State: Preparing For The Worst 1945–2010*. He was made an independent crossbench
life Peer in 2010.

States of Emergency (with Keith Jeffery)

Sources Close to the Prime Minister
(with Michael Cockerell and David Walker)

What the Papers Never Said

Cabinet

Ruling Performance (edited with Anthony Seldon)

Whitehall

Never Again: Britain 1945–1951

The Hidden Wiring: Unearthing the British Constitution

*Muddling Through: Power, Politics and the Quality
of Government in Postwar Britain*

The Prime Minister: The Office and Its Holders since 1945

The Secret State: Whitehall and the Cold War

Having It So Good: Britain in the Fifties

*The New Protective State: Government,
Intelligence and Terrorism* (edited)

Cabinets and the Bomb

The Secret State: Preparing for the Worst, 1945–2010

Distilling the Frenzy: Writing the History of One's Own Times

Establishment and Meritocracy

*The Kingdom to Come: Thoughts on the Union
Before and After the Scottish Referendum*

*The Silent Deep: The Royal Navy Submarine Service
since 1945* (with James Jinks)

*The Complete Reflections: Conversations with
Politicians* (with Robert Shepherd)

Winds of Change: Britain in the Early Sixties

*The Bonfire of the Decencies: Repairing and Restoring the British
Constitution* (with Andrew Blick)

PETER HENNESSY

A Duty of Care

Britain Before and After Covid

PENGUIN BOOKS

PENGUIN BOOKS

UK | USA | Canada | Ireland | Australia
India | New Zealand | South Africa

Penguin Books is part of the Penguin Random House group of companies
whose addresses can be found at global.penguinrandomhouse.com.

First published by Allen Lane 2022
Published in Penguin Books 2023
001

Printed and bound in Great Britain by Clays Ltd, Elcograf S.p.A.

A CIP catalogue record for this book is available from the British Library

The authorized representative in the EEA is Penguin Random House Ireland,
Morrison Chambers, 32 Nassau Street, Dublin D02 YH68

ISBN: 978–0–141–99566–3

www.greenpenguin.co.uk

MIX
Paper from
responsible sources
FSC® C018179

Penguin Random House is committed to a
sustainable future for our business, our readers
and our planet. This book is made from Forest
Stewardship Council® certified paper.

For my beloved grandsons
Joe and Jack Cromby,
Paddy and Tom Coupar-Hennessy.
In the hope that their country and its people
will do good and great things
on the road to 2045.

Contents

List of Tables and Figures

List of Illustrations

Photographic acknowledgements are shown in italics

1. Sir William Beveridge completes his report, London, 20 October 1942. *Popperfoto/Getty Images.*

2. *'WANT is only one of the five giants on the road to reconstruction'*. Cartoon by George Whitelaw for the *Daily Herald*, 2 December 1942. *Daily Herald/Mirrorpix.*

3. Clement Attlee after a speech to his constituents, Limehouse, London, 5 July 1945. *Popperfoto/Getty Images.*

4. John Maynard Keynes with his wife Lydia, Southampton, 17 December 1945. *Hulton-Deutsch.*

5. Winston Churchill, Anthony Eden and Rab Butler after the election defeat, London, 1945. *Press Association.*

6. A mother picks up her first family allowance payment, Stratford, London, 6 August 1946. *Hulton-Deutsch/Getty Images.*

7. Aneurin Bevan speaking at the Labour Party conference, Margate, 4 October 1950. *Popperfoto/Getty Images.*

8. Tenement housing in Camden Street, the Gorbals, Glasgow, 1956. *Topical Press/Getty Images.*

9. Harold Macmillan visiting a new housing development, Manchester, April 1952. *Mirrorpix/Alamy.*

10. Kidbrooke Comprehensive school, Greenwich, London, 1954. *PA Images/Alamy.*

11. Harold Wilson and frontbenchers at the State Opening of Parliament, Westminster, 21 April 1966. *Keystone/Alamy.*

12. Claimants for unemployment benefit outside the employment exchange, Newtownbreda, Belfast, 1974. *PA Images/TopFoto.*

Acknowledgements

This is a book I neither planned nor wished to write. None of us wanted our country or our world to be blighted by Covid-19. My usual heartfelt thanks to those who have helped me acquire an even higher level of intensity because the preparation of *A Duty of Care* coincided with a period of ill health on my part (mercifully, not Covid).

First my family. My wife, Enid, provided crucial support, editorial and statistical. My younger daughter, Polly, read my words with a specially discerning eye, as did my agent and friend David Godwin.

Fortunate is the author who has the Allen Lane Penguin team on their side. Stuart Proffitt has been looking after me for over thirty years now. He knows just how much I value his wisdom and friendship, way beyond our professional relationship. Penguin's duty of care to me was unstintingly shown by Alice Skinner, Corina Romonti and Rebecca Lee.

I was delighted that the prince of copy editors, Trevor Horwood, was persuaded to take me on again. Working on the photographs with Cecilia Mackay was, as always, a delight.

Special thanks to Nick Timmins, a very old friend from newspaper days and author of that classic work of post-war British History *The Five Giants: A Biography of the Welfare State*, for his help with facts, figures and analysis. Thanks too for the briefing paper prepared for me on the economic consequences of Covid-19 by Nick Macpherson, Lord Macpherson of Earl's Court, the former Permanent Secretary to the Treasury.

My former student Matt Lyus was, as always, positively Sherlock Holmesian in his pursuit of details and quotes that I could not find.

My workplace, the House of Lords, was a boon throughout the writing of the book even though I could not turn up physically. The librarians and researchers were a gleaming asset to me as they have been, and are, for so many others. I am ever grateful to them, as I am to my colleagues on the House of Lords Select Committee on the Constitution, superbly chaired by Baroness Taylor of Bolton, from whose wisdom and stimulus I have benefited every week that we have met (virtually) and from the tremendous support we receive from the committee's secretariat and legal advisers.

It may be that I shall need everyone again if I can summon the blood and stiffen the sinew sufficiently to carry the story on through the Covid-19 recovery period and beyond. I certainly hope so. In fact, I feel another volume coming on, and not just because I am writing this in the Orkney Islands, where my elder daughter, Cecily, and her family live.

There is nothing like picking up a fountain pen of a morning and gazing out of the window at the moodily beautiful and history-soaked waters of Scapa Flow with its fast and fickle weather systems and sea states to stimulate the old cortex . . .

Introduction: It Took a Virus

The wind of before and after.
      George Mackay Brown, 'An Old Man in July'[1]

On the morning of Tuesday, 17 March 2020, six days before Britain's first lockdown, I decided to keep a 'Covid Britain' diary. There were three reasons: contemporary historians like me can fall victim to the temptation of tidying events up excessively once they have unfolded. Diaries can also help us to think about what is happening as we traverse a baffling, disturbing arc in our collective and individual histories. Thirdly, and more prosaically, the Department of Health and Social Care had instructed me to stay at home initially for twelve weeks along with 2.5 million other self-shielders deemed to be especially vulnerable.

I had scarcely finished page one of the diary when a producer from BBC Radio 4's *World at One* rang and asked me to give a historical perspective on the pandemic. I did so, and suggested to Sarah Montague that the impact of the virus on Britain would ensure that future historians would henceforth divide post-war UK history into BC (Before Covid) and AC (After Covid).

In a strange way, as the weeks went on, I could not just hear but also *feel* the linkage between the winds of early post-war reconstruction and those of Covid. And each Thursday evening at eight, the cacophony of clapping, cheering, singing and pots-and-pans rattling that resounded round the country in support of the NHS and all those in the front line of the Covid-19 battle sounded like a people rediscovering themselves.

It was also the sound of a 'never again' impulse: the conviction that there had to be a better Britain to come out of it – a refreshed and renewed duty of care both between the government and the people and among the people themselves. My mind turned to the need for a new consensus, of the kind laid out by the greatest social arithmetician of his age, Sir William Beveridge, in his report of November 1942. There has never been another social report as popular, not least because of the vividness of his language and the boldness of his ideas, and it sold 695,000 copies. There are, he wrote, five giants on the road to recovery: 'Want, Disease, Ignorance, Squalor and Idleness'.[2] Beveridge's argument was that all five giants had to be struck simultaneously if the crust of deprivation were to be cracked. Over seventy years later, the questions, inequalities and possibilities about Britain that Covid-19 immediately cast into a sharper relief suggested to me that this just might be a new Beveridge moment – if only we could conjure up a political class capable of finding the right words to express the kind of consensus the UK so desperately needs.

This book is an attempt to capture the two winds of 'before and after' and to try to make sense of the gale of events that struck our islands after the pathogen reached our shores during the first weeks of 2020.

As the diary progressed and this book took shape through the spring and summer of that year, I came to feel increasingly that the Covid-19 experience was turning all of us into contemporary historians. It was as if we were living through a period of continually breaking news. Covid-19 became a bulletin item we could not ignore as it reached into every home, leaving us to sift the magnitude and significance of events as they flew at us in an unrelenting stream. In this sense we became participant/analysts in the biggest collective experience since the Second World War.

One consequence is that we have rediscovered a shared duty of care, in an intense form between government and people, and also between individuals. Hence the title of the book. It's a phrase and concept we all understand, yet it's a fairly recent one in UK history. We owe its entry into our mainstream language to a Scottish lady, a bottle of ginger beer, a dead snail and a Law Lord carving a roast for Sunday lunch (though I can find no trace of Beveridge himself using it).

I invite my friend of decades, Sir Richard Aikens QC, former Lord Justice of Appeal, to explain with his characteristic precision:

Ms M'Alister had bought a bottle of ginger beer and claimed that when she had drunk it there was a decomposed snail in the bottle and she suffered injuries (gastro-enteritis and shock) as a result. She brought an action (in the Scottish courts) against the manufacturer of the ginger beer, not the seller. The issue, which went to the House of Lords, was whether the manufacturer was under any legal duty to the ultimate consumer of the ginger beer to take reasonable care (that is not to be negligent), to ensure that there was nothing in the product that might cause harm to the ultimate consumer. As English and Scottish law stood in 1932, the general rule was that (fraud apart) there was only such a legal duty to another if you were in a contractual relationship. There were a few exceptions for 'dangerous activities', but that category was very narrow. In the courts below, Ms M'Alister had lost on this preliminary legal question of whether there was a general 'duty of care' outside contract. By a 3 to 2 majority in the House of Lords, she won. The case then settled I think.

Lord Atkin gave the leading speech of the majority and it has become one of the most celebrated judgments in the English legal world and is followed in all other common-law jurisdictions in the Commonwealth and beyond. Atkin recognized the importance of the issue – 'I do not think a more important problem has occupied Your Lordships in your judicial capacity' – and described the question as being 'whether, as matter of law in the circumstances alleged, the defender owed any duty to the pursuer to take care'. He considered the point from first principles, before looking at all the cases to see whether they were consistent with his proposed formulation:

At present I content myself with pointing out that in English law there must be, and is, some general conception of relations giving rise to a duty of care, of which the particular cases found in the books are but instances. The liability for negligence, whether you style it such or treat it as in other systems as a species of 'culpa', is no doubt based upon a general public sentiment of moral wrongdoing for which the offender must pay. But acts or omissions which any moral code would censure cannot in a practical world be treated so as to give a right to every person injured by them to demand relief. In this way rules of law arise which limit the range of complainants and the extent of their remedy.

The rule that you are to love your neighbour becomes in law, you must not injure your neighbour; and the lawyer's question, Who is my neighbour? receives a restricted reply. You must take reasonable care to avoid acts or omissions which you can reasonably foresee would be likely to injure your neighbour. Who, then, in law is my neighbour? The answer seems to be – persons who are so closely and directly affected by my act that I ought reasonably to have them in contemplation as being so affected when I am directing my mind to the acts or omissions which are called in question.

It is said that Lord Atkin first formulated this concept at a Sunday lunch (when carving the roast) at his house in Wales during the vacation between the hearing of the submissions and the delivery of the speeches some months later. Quite what his family made of it is not related![3]

A Duty of Care is divided into two parts. Part One, 'The Road from 1945', examines how the Beveridge-shaped duty of care played out in the hands of successive post-war political generations. It finishes with the Brexit experience, which, in my judgement, contributed powerfully to a general coarsening of our politics and our national conversation, leaving us in a diminished and psychologically poor state by the time the virus struck. In Part Two I examine the questions facing the public inquiry, the ingredients of what I think could be a new Beveridge and the political spirit and language that would be required to achieve it.

Peter Hennessy,
Walthamstow, South Ronaldsay and Sheffield
March 2020 to August 2021

PART ONE

The Road from 1945

I

Nye's Perambulators

*. . . a revolutionary moment in the world's history is a time for
revolutions, not for patching.*

Sir William Beveridge, 1942[1]

*Society becomes more wholesome, more serene and spiritually
healthier, if it knows that its citizens have at the back of their
consciousness the knowledge that not only themselves but all
their fellows, have access, when ill, to the best that medical
skill can provide.*

*Aneurin Bevan, Minister of Health, while preparing what
became the National Health Service Act 1946*[2]

Serenity was one of Aneurin Bevan's favourite words.[3] Seventy-four
years later, I remembered his love of it more than once during the far
from serene Covid experience. Bevan, universally known as Nye, was,
in the words of the great Welsh Labour historian Kenneth O. Morgan, 'an artist in the uses of power',[4] and the NHS was his masterpiece.
William Beveridge, whom nobody called 'Bill', was dry, prickly and
difficult but a genius when it came to the social arithmetic of welfare
options and costs on people's life chances. A Liberal in his personal
politics (he entered the House of Commons as MP for Berwick-upon-
Tweed in 1944, losing his seat at the 1945 general election), his 1942
report nonetheless resonated with both the major parties.

His social arithmetic, for a Britain when Hitler was no more, changed
the country for ever. It is a story tinged with irony. He had only been
given the job of tidying up social insurance to get him out of the hair

of Ernest Bevin, the Minister of Labour (another 'artist in the uses of power' but sculpted from the granite of the Trade Union movement). Beveridge disappeared into the dry world of social insurance and actuarial calculations to return in a blaze of publicity (much of it self-generated) with a manifesto for future generations. The Beveridge Report remains the most comprehensive and striking document of political anthropology* the country has ever seen. It was built on two arguments: first, that the thick outer crust of deprivation would not yield unless the five giants were struck hard and simultaneously; second, that the cost would not be bearable without the maintenance of full employment. The most famous phrase associated with it was not actually Beveridge's but Winston Churchill's, when he talked in a radio broadcast on 21 March 1943 of 'National compulsory insurance for all classes for all purposes from the cradle to the grave'.[5]

The equivalent from the lips of Nye Bevan is much less well known. Bevan's parliamentary private secretary when he was Minister of Health was Barbara Castle. In 1948, about the time the NHS came into being, he said to her, 'Barbara, if you want to know what all this is for, look in the perambulators.'[6] I was in one of Nye's prams when he said that and, in a sense, I have been ever since (though I am now far closer to the grave than I am to the cradle).

Beveridge created a blueprint for a society and a political economy remade. First the wartime coalition and then the Attlee government turned it into welfare and unemployment benefits, health treatments, bricks and mortar, classrooms and schoolbooks, university grants and, using the techniques outlined in the Keynes-infused White Paper of 1944,[7] the pursuit of a new macroeconomics to see off major economic slumps and depressions. All of this was powered by a palpable 'never again' impulse that dominated that reform-minded era and it was all the more impressive because its implementation began even before the grim audit of the British war losses had reached their final tally (see Table 1).[8]

Blows on that scale would take some recovering from, but the Beveridge and Keynes-inspired reconstruction plans brought huge extra aspirations and obligations that meant far, far more than a mere

* I.e. where people, systems and social arithmetic meet.

return to 1939. It would take a cornucopia of production and a surge in productivity to pay for it, especially with a third of the nation's wealth gone in the pursuit of victory. As a future Chief Economist to the Treasury, Sir Kenneth Berrill, would put it nearly forty-five years after the 1945 election, 'We had won the war and we voted ourselves a nice peace.'[9]

Table 1: The cost to Britain of the Second World War.

POPULATION	
– Total	46 million
– Armed Forces (Pre-1939 0.5 million)	5 million
– Civil Defence and Munitions Workers	5 million
DEATHS	
– Military and Merchant Navy	380,000
– Civilian	60,000
HOUSING	
– Destroyed	500,000
– Severely Damaged	250,000
ASSETS DISPOSED OF	
– Gold Reserves	33%
– Overseas Assets	33%
DEBTS INCURRED	£305 billion
INCREASE IN TAXATION 1939–45	
– Direct	+300%
– Indirect	+160%

The general election of 1945 is one of the defining ballots in British history. Labour went to the polls offering what might be called 'the full Beveridge'. Nearly half a century later I asked Michael Young, the sociologist and draughtsman of Labour's manifesto *Let Us Face the Future*[10] (and later also author of the fabled satire *The Rise of the Meritocracy*[11]), what had been the key to Labour's programme: He thought for a moment and said, 'Beveridge plus Keynes plus socialism.'[12]

By socialism he meant the proposed nationalization of what Nye Bevan liked to call the 'commanding heights' of the British economy[13] – railways, coal, the water/gas/electricity utilities, the Bank of England, iron and steel and a substantial part of road transport. This was the battlefield of party politics. There wasn't – and has never been – a consensus on nationalized industries. There was mostly consensus on health and social policies, though there were differences of emphasis here too. But it is often forgotten that the post-war consensus also embraced foreign and defence policy, especially once the victorious Allies fell out, the Cold War chilled and the great forty-year East–West confrontation began.

It was a winning prospectus for Labour that delivered them a 146-seat overall majority – the first ever in the party's history. A surprised Clem Attlee turned up to Buckingham Palace for an audience with the equally surprised King George VI shortly after Churchill resigned on the evening of 26 July 1945. The two desperately shy men stood before each other in silence. Finally, Attlee said, 'I have won the election.' George VI stammered back, 'I know, I heard it on the six o'clock news.'[14] So began one of the greatest reformist governments ever. Like the coalition that preceded it, in which several senior Labour figures had shone, the new administration had taken on a monumental duty of care for the British people on a scale unprecedented in peacetime.

The Labour Party picked up the Beveridge Report and ran with it from the start, the coalition government having shrunk from giving it an unequivocal pledge. It fell to Sir John Anderson, the dry but highly dutiful and intelligent War Cabinet minister and ex-civil servant, to face the heat of the great Beveridge debate in the House of Commons in February 1943. He said that there could be 'at present no binding commitment. Subject only to that . . . I have made it clear that the government adopt the scheme in principle.'[15]

From the Labour Party backbenches, Jim Griffiths (who would become a crucial figure in the post-war Attlee government as Minister of National Insurance) pressed for an immediate government commitment to Beveridge in full. When the House of Commons divided on 18 February 1943, 121 MPs (out of 650), ninety-seven of whom were Labour, voted against the coalition's refusal to give such a pledge. (The other twenty-four included three MPs from the Independent Labour Party, eleven independents and one Communist. They were joined by nine Liberals, including the First World War leader David Lloyd George, who came in to cast his vote for the last time in the chamber he had once dominated.[16])

The public were overwhelmingly with Griffiths and the rebels. In early 1943 a survey carried out by the British Institute for Public Opinion showed 86 per cent of the population were in favour of the full Beveridge, a mere 6 per cent against.[17] I have always thought that was the moment Labour won the 1945 election, twenty-eight months ahead of the poll.

For all the coalition's unwillingness to make the commitment Griffiths and the rebels wanted, work started on tackling some of the five giants. Education reform was particularly advanced and it was the Conservative President of the Board of Education, R. A. Butler (known to all as 'Rab'), and his Labour deputy, James Chuter Ede, who put through the landmark 1944 Education Act providing for the first time free secondary education for all, the eventual raising of the school leaving age from fourteen to fifteen, and grants and fees for university students. The Family Allowances Act, which provided a non-means tested benefit to mothers for second and all subsequent children, became law on 11 June 1945 under Churchill's caretaker government, after Labour had left the Coalition ahead of the general election due on 5 July (the result was not declared until 26 July, to give time to count the votes of the armed forces deployed across the world).

A ready-reckoner way of capturing the statutory paving of the 1940s version of the duty of care is to chart the legislative flow:

1944 Education Act
1945 Family Allowances Act
1946 National Health Service Act
1946 National Insurance Act
1946 Housing Act
1946 New Towns Act
1947 Town and Country Planning Act
1948 National Assistance Act

1949 Legal Aid and Legal Advice Act
1949 National Parks Act

The legislation required an extraordinary combination of social obligations and extra state power to make it work. The idea – beyond Nye's perambulators – was to create a benign cycle that undid, at last, the inequalities and deprivations bequeathed by the Industrial Revolution of 1750 to 1850. Out of it would come a happier, healthier, better-educated, more productive workforce with a higher level of social harmony.

But Beveridge's social arithmetic came instantly face-to-face with the hard arithmetic of finance. The coalition ministers knew it would. The finest mind and the most fluent pen the economics profession has ever produced, John Maynard Keynes, had told them in a memorandum to the War Cabinet on 15 May 1945, just one week after the war in Europe ended, that Britain faced a 'financial Dunkirk'. Keynes, whose biographer Robert Skidelsky called him 'Whitehall's greatest intellectual charmer',[18] knew how to write in a manner that would attract ministerial attention. In his paragraphs on Britain's deep-set industrial problems, his pen, this time I suspect, alarming rather than charming his readers:

> The available statistics suggest that, provided we have never made a product before, we have the rest of the world licked on cost. For a Mosquito, Lancaster, Radar, we should have the business at our feet in conditions of fair and free competition. It is when it comes to making a shirt or a steel billet that we have to admit ourselves to be beaten both by the dear labour of America and by the cheap labour of Asia or Europe. Shipbuilding seems to be the only traditional industry where we fully hold our own. If by some sad geographical slip the American Air Force (it is too late now to hope for much from the enemy) were to destroy every factory on the north-east coast and in Lancashire (at an hour when the directors were sitting there and no one else) we should have nothing to fear. How else we are to regain the exuberant inexperience which is necessary, it seems, for success, I cannot surmise.[19]

Keynes placed great faith in the United States continuing to pour financial assistance into the UK. 'The sweet breath of Justice between partners in what had been a great and magnanimous enterprise' was how he put it.[20] It was not to be. The US cut off wartime Lend-Lease as soon as Japan surrendered in August. Keynes, as leader of a Treasury team, dashed to Washington in October 1945 in search of a loan. He got one – but on terms far tougher than he was seeking. Instead of $5 billion interest-free he got $3.75 billion at 2 per cent over fifty years. The immediate post-war dollar lifeline would be highly precarious, yet the government had no choice but to accept what became known as the American Loan.

The strain on Keynes was very great. He died on Easter Sunday 1946, 21 April, from a heart attack, after one last walk on the Sussex Downs the day before. He was only sixty-two. The country lost one of the most luminously productive and silky minds ever placed at the service of government. He was already worrying about the problems of wage inflation in a full-employment society (the 1944 White Paper on Employment, deeply infused with Keynesian thought, had argued the new policy model would crack without 'wage moderation'). Sadly, he left no envelope containing a paper on how to deal with it, to be opened when inflation surged as it did in the late sixties.

Nor was there a posthumous Keynes paper on how to undertake economic planning in peacetime once the instruments of the wartime siege economy began to be dismantled. Planning was Labour's big idea. A Central Economic Planning Staff was set up in 1947 to service an Economic Planning Board drawing together government, business and unions. It produced worthy, exhortatory annual Economic Surveys, prototypes of what we would today call industrial strategies, but transformational it was not.[21]

A far greater problem was the Attlee government's failure to grasp the technical education provisions in the 1944 Education Act, which allowed for a network of new county colleges. Butler had envisaged that these would provide day-release courses for fifteen- to eighteen-year-olds in work to supplement their apprenticeships, but they were never built. Nor did the existing technical schools increase their intake of the secondary-school population (4.7 per cent in 1946; 4.3 per cent in 1950).[22] Technical education seventy years later is still waiting for the transformation reformers have been seeking since the 1860s.

Housing was in a poor state post-war. In 1947/8 only 46 per cent had a bathroom,[23] in 1951 15 per cent had to share a WC with another household,[24] and even in 1961 7 per cent did not have a toilet in or attached to their home, although this was mainly in rural areas.[25] The government did not reach its housing target primarily because of a lack of materials and labour, but a million new homes were built between 1945 and 1951.[26]

The more immediate problem was the overriding need just to get by. The crunch year was 1947. The terms of the American Loan of December 1945 had a sputtering fuse attached. The US Congress finally approved the loan on 15 July 1946 (not quite two months after Keynes's death), but it laid down that the pound would have to become freely convertible against the dollar in the currency markets a year later. Inevitably, on 15 July 1947, the holders of sterling ran for the dollar, placing immense strain on the fixed rate of £1 to $4.03 US established under the Bretton Woods system. The first of the great currency crises of the post-war years hit hard and fast. On 20 August convertibility was temporarily suspended; it was another eleven years before it was restored.

The desperation of Britain's position as it tried to sustain military and imperial commitments across the globe while restoring its export capacity at home and building a new welfare state at the same time, is captured in one of the most extraordinary files I have ever read in The National Archives. On the day that sterling became freely convertible into dollars, an intensely secret document began to circle among a tight group of senior officials in Whitehall. It was a contingency plan lest the American Loan run out and so-called Marshall Aid (a plan for west European economic recovery outlined by US Secretary of State George Marshall on 5 June) failed to materialize.

Drawn up by the Treasury's Richard Clarke (known as 'Otto'), one of the most fertile minds in post-war Whitehall and father of Charles, a future Home Secretary in the Blair government, it sketched out a siege economy for the coming three years more austere than anything the UK had experienced in wartime. Here is a taster of what one of the insiders called Otto's 'If Marshall fails (hush-hush) group':

The crucial questions would be:
    1. Agriculture. In the 1947–48–49 harvests to run no risks of insuffi-
       cient labour; this might mean radical interference with educational

arrangements. We should go forward with a 'famine' food programme and, if necessary, direction of Labour to agriculture.

2. Building. The building and investment programmes generally
should be drastically cut down, to save timber and steel and manpower. We should not have resources for satisfying elementary
consumption needs plus exports plus investment.

3. Textiles. Woollen textiles would be of prime importance.

4. Coal. As always, fundamental.[27]

The abyss was avoided. Marshall Aid flowed from 1948 until 1951.
In July that year the Treasury's top economist, Robert Hall, calculated
that 'We have had [from the USA] an average of over a billion dollars
a year one way and another since 1946 ... In fact our whole economic life has been propped up in this way.'[28] Without those dollars
the new post-war duty-of-care measures would not have been fundable. Even so, the pound came under renewed strain in 1949, and in
September that year it was devalued from $4.03 to $2.80. After the
Korean War erupted in June 1950, the substantial Cold War rearmament programme put further strain on the recovering UK economy
and led to Nye Bevan's resignation from the Cabinet (as well as Harold Wilson's) over the imposition of health service prescription
charges to ease the pressure on public expenditure.

New housing suffered from the lack of materials and labour, renovation of bomb-damaged buildings was prioritized and 125,000
prefabs were built by 1948.[29]

By 1951 the NHS had already acquired its talismanic status
throughout the UK population. This was, I think, because since its
inception on 5 July 1948 (the date deliberately chosen to mark the
third anniversary of Labour's election victory) it has been the closest
we have ever come as a country and a people to institutionalizing
altruism. As Peter Calvocoressi wrote in the late 1970s:

> For its customers it was a godsend, perhaps the most beneficial reform
> ever enacted in England, given that it relieved so many not merely of
> pain but also of the awful plight of having to watch the suffering and
> death of a spouse or a child for the lack of enough money to do any-
> thing about it. A country in which such a service exists is utterly
> different from a country without it.[30]

Calvocoressi's words convey probably the most fundamental duty of care of them all. At the time it was institutionalized Clem Attlee's version was very similar: speaking in the House of Commons, this time on the National Insurance Bill (the new benefits system) in 1946, he said:

> The question is – can we afford it? Supposing the answer is 'No', what does that mean? It really means that the sum total of the goods produced and the services rendered by the people of this country is not sufficient to provide for all our people at all times, in sickness, in health, in youth and in age the very modest standard of life represented by the sums of money set out in the Second Schedule to this [National Insurance] Bill. I cannot believe that our national productivity is so slow, that our willingness to work is so feeble or that we can submit to the world that the masses of our people must be condemned to penury.[31]

Attlee, famously, was a study in understatement, a master of brevity with no trace of Bevan's silver tongue or Bevin's physical presence. But there he found the pith of the 1940s duty of care.

Statutes are licences for reform; they do not guarantee the funds needed for their implementation. It would take every ounce of the British productivity Attlee evoked to pay for this new settlement by sustained investment for decades to come. Finest hours come with a price tag. But the prior question was, would it survive a change of government intact? Had we been capable of such anxieties in the run-up to the 1951 general election those of us in Nye's perambulators would have been worried.

2

The Pursuit of Consensus

It is 38 years ago since I introduced [as a member of Asquith's Liberal Cabinet] the first Unemployment Insurance scheme, and 22 years ago since as a Conservative Chancellor of the Exchequer I shaped and carried the Widows' Pensions and reduction of the Old Age Pensions from 70 to 65. We are now moving forward into another vast scheme of national insurance, which arose, even in the stress of war, from a Parliament with a great Conservative majority.

Winston Churchill, addressing the Conservative Party Conference in Blackpool on 5 October 1946[1]

Rarely in the field of political pamphleteering can a document so radical in effect have been written with such flatness of language or blandness of tone. This was not wholly unintentional. We were out-Peeling Peel in giving the party a painless but permanent face-lift: the more unflamboyant the changes, the less likely were the features to sag again. Our first purpose was to counter the charge and the fear that we were the party of industrial go-as-you-please and devil-take-the hindmost, that full employment and the Welfare State were not safe in our hands.

R. A. Butler recalling the making of the Conservative Party's Industrial Charter of 1947 in 1971[2]

Winston Churchill's brain was built to produce grand sweeps of thought clothed in the richest robes of language. Butler's grey cells, also considerable, were distinguished by the serpentine irony with which they conveyed his thoughts. In many respects the two men made a formidable combination, but they were not close. Rab as a Foreign Office minister in the late 1930s had been a convinced appeaser. This to Churchill was a near mortal sin, but he nevertheless appreciated Rab's gifts. Butler recalled that in 1941, when Churchill offered him the job:

> I then said I had always looked forward to going to the Board of Education if I were given the chance. He appeared ever so slightly surprised at this, showing that he felt in wartime a central job, such as the one I was leaving [no. 2 in the Foreign Office], is the most important. But he looked genuinely pleased that I had shown so much satisfaction and seemed to think the appointment entirely suitable. He concluded the conversation by saying 'Come and see me to discuss things – not details but the broad lines.'[3]

Churchill, in Paul Addison's nice phrase, was 'a freelance who resented the restraints imposed by parties'.[4] He was a natural consensualist, telling his principal private secretary, Jock Colville, in 1952 that 'four-fifths of the people of the country were agreed on four-fifths of the things to be done'.[5] When it came to welfare economics, he had his pet phrases: such as 'the magic of the averages' must be brought to 'the rescue of the millions'.[6] But his mind did not stretch to the precise metrics.

Rab's strategy of tedium paid off. The Keynesian and Beveridgian infusions flowed into mainstream Conservative Party policy without Churchill having read *The Industrial Charter*, even though he had commissioned the review and put Butler in the chair. At the heart of the charter lay the so-called 'post-war settlement': an acceptance of the Keynesian full-employment notions and Beveridgian welfare prescriptions, plus a relatively interventionist approach to industry and a recognition that most of the Labour government's nationalizations would not be reversed. All had been designed to capture the middle ground of British politics. As Rab Butler wrote in his memoirs, the draft went to the Shadow Cabinet, under Anthony Eden's chairmanship, and then was submitted to Churchill:

Silence ensued. Though Churchill was to tell the party conference in October [1947] that the Charter 'was officially approved by me at what we call a Consultative Committee, six months ago', his ultimate imprimatur was not so much obtained as divined. At a dinner party for his senior colleagues at the Savoy, he placed me on his right hand, plied me with Cognac, and said several agreeable and no disagreeable things about my work. Emboldened by this prodigality, I gave instructions that the Charter should be published on 12 May, though none of us at the time was one hundred per cent certain whether it was to be regarded as official or even whether it had received the leader's detailed scrutiny. It was not well designed to captivate his attention.[7]

Indeed it hadn't.

Reggie Maudling, one of a cluster of bright young men in the late 1940s Conservative Research Department (the others were Iain Macleod and Enoch Powell), had the job of helping Churchill prepare his closing speech for the party conference in Brighton

> . . . and we came to the topic of the Industrial Charter. 'Give me five lines, Maudling,' he said, 'explaining what the Industrial Charter says.' This I did. He read it with care, and then said, 'But I do not agree with a word of this . . .'
>
> 'Well, sir,' I said, 'this is what the Conference has adopted.'
>
> 'Oh well,' he said, 'leave it in,' and he duly read it out in the course of his speech . . . [8]

In such an eccentric fashion was the post-war consensus given life by the grandest political figure of the age. For those of us who benefited so hugely from it, thank God Churchill never read the text with which Butler lubricated the crucial shift in his party's stance.

Rab was quite a connoisseur of the faintly ludicrous scenes that seemed to accompany his meetings with Churchill. When the Conservatives returned to power in October 1951 Churchill made him Chancellor of the Exchequer, a pivotal position for the new conservatism. Churchill liked to work from his bed in the mornings if there was no Cabinet meeting. Butler was often called in to brief him on the stresses and strains upon the British economy. Rab's presence would excite Toby, Churchill's beloved budgerigar. The bird would fly noisily round Churchill's bedroom, opening his bowels at just the right moment to reach his target – Rab's bald head. 'The things I do for England,' Rab would mutter, as he wiped his pate with a white silk handkerchief.[9]

Butler was also an instinctive consensualist – a pursuer of what Bismarck called 'the art of the possible'[10] (indeed, he made it the title of his memoirs). Yet in preparing his first budget he oversaw a secret plan which, had it been adopted, would have ruptured the consensus perhaps terminally. Codenamed ROBOT, its centrepiece was a floating of the pound – a 'limited' rather than a 'clean' float, to use the technical language – between $2.40 and $3.20, i.e. approximately 15 per cent either side of the $2.80 figure that, after the 1949 devaluation, was the fixed rate in the so-called Bretton Woods system, the currency regime established in 1944.

Butler was persuaded that a floating pound would take the strain off the seemingly permanent balance-of-payments pressures and very largely remove the burden of the £3 billion of 'sterling balances' (the reserves kept in London by countries in the sterling area and the debts the UK had accumulated with them during the war) by freezing them.

ROBOT, much of which came out of the fecund mind of Otto Clarke, was a temptation – at one bound, the UK economy would be free. Its boldness captured Butler's mood. When it hit an unsuspecting Cabinet, the downsides became all too evident. Cherished spending programmes (not least housing) would have to be cut. Unemployment would soar from 400,000 to between 700,000 and 900,000. Bang would go the essentials of the 'British New Deal' (though nobody at the time called it that) built upon the new mixed-economy/welfare-state model and all for a currency policy that might not work. Eden would not have it and threatened resignation; nor would Macmillan. Churchill, heavily influenced, as so often, by his close adviser Lord Cherwell, rowed back and ROBOT was abandoned.

The usually staid Cabinet minutes capture the anguished spirit of the still fledgling post-war consensus as it flitted anxiously round the Cabinet Room:

Under democratic government with universal suffrage such violent reversals of policy were hardly practicable. Even if the case for this change were made abundantly clear on the merits, there would be very great difficulty in persuading the public to accept it. Moreover, the adoption of this policy would create an unbridgeable gap between the Government and the Opposition; and, if it were thought possible that an even more grave economic crisis might develop later in the year, it would be unjustifiable to take at this stage a step which might exclude all possibility of forming a National Government to handle that situation.[11]

Hugh Gaitskell, Shadow Chancellor in 1952 (he had been the serving one 1950–51) heard no whisper of ROBOT for two years, such was the tightness of official secrecy in those days. And when he did so, he was strongly opposed to the idea.[12]

Butler's personal prestige was sapped by the ROBOT experience within the private world of early fifties Whitehall. Somehow, the story did not leak. It would have inevitably done so today, especially after the very rough Cabinet meetings of 28–29 February 1952. But his clout remained considerable. At any time and in any circumstances, Chancellors of the Exchequer are crucial to duties of care. For without the bloodstream of finance they remain either aspirational or, at best, skeletons of the full-bodied promise and purpose they were intended to be.

It was housing, not Rab's beloved education or health, that made the pace in the early-to mid-fifties version. This was not of Butler's choosing. The Conservatives had made much of Labour's failure to build 300,000 houses a year while campaigning prior to the 23 February 1950 general election, which reduced Attlee's majority to five. It became obvious that another poll would not be long delayed and the Conservatives sensed victory. Butler recalled the 'famous wave of hysteria which swept the party conference in Blackpool' in the autumn of 1950.

'Lord Woolton [party chairman], who was sitting beside me as the figure began to be picked up by representatives with the mounting excitement once customarily associated with an auction, whispered, "*Could* we build 300,000?" I replied, "The question is *should* we? And the answer: it will make it that much more difficult to restore the economy."'[13] (The argument being that such an ambitious housing drive would divert resources from the re-equipment of manufacturing industry crucial to economic recovery and the export drive.)

But the conference prevailed – 300,000 it was and Churchill, when the Conservatives won a seventeen-seat majority in the election of 25 October 1951, placed the energetic and ambitious Harold Macmillan in the new Ministry of Housing and Local Government to achieve it. He duly did so, paving the way for his rapid advance up the Cabinet hierarchy and eventually to the premiership. Butler was right. The housing programme did put serious strain on the economy. It also left less public expenditure for the slaying of the other of Beveridge's five giants.

Rab Butler has gone down in history as the epitome of the post-war consensus because of a vivid piece of journalism that flowed from the pen of *The Economist*'s brilliantly mercurial Norman Macrae, convinced free marketer, critic of consensus and foe of economic planning. In the 13 November 1954 edition of the magazine he invented probably the most famous composite character in British political history under the heading 'Mr Butskell's Dilemma'.

> Mr Butskell is already a well-known figure in dinner table conversation in both Westminster and Whitehall, and the time has come to introduce him to a wider audience. He is a composite of the present Chancellor [Butler] and the previous one [Gaitskell] ... Whenever there is a tendency towards excess Conservatism within the Conservative party – such as a clamour for too much imperial preference, for a wild dash to convertibility [highly ironic this, given Rab and ROBOT], or even for a little more unemployment to teach the workers a lesson – Mr Butskell speaks up for the cause of moderation from the Government side of the House; when there is a clamour for even greater irresponsibilities from the Labour benches, Mr Butskell has hitherto spoken from the other. Poor Butler. It's almost as if he existed to be misunderstood.

There is a characteristically plaintive, *Economist*-inspired passage in Rab's memoirs:

> If the pound had been set free in 1952 the word 'Butskellism' might never have been invented ... Gaitskell was known to be ... violently opposed to the 'disastrous turn in our policy' which the Cabinet had

resisted and rejected. Despite our friendship, which became warm, we never discussed the 'doctrine' that united our names and each of us would, I think, have repudiated its underlying assumption but, though sitting on opposite sides of the House, we were really very much of a muchness . . . But I shared neither his convictions, which were unquestionably Socialist, nor his temperament, which allowed emotion to run away with him rather too often, nor of his training which was that of an academic economist. Both of us, it is true, spoke the language of Keynesianism. But we spoke it with different accents and with a differing emphases.[14]

In Butler's last sentence lies one of the plumb lines for fathoming the post-war consensus and its version of the duty of care: Labour and Conservative agreed on the essentials, but spoke in different accents and with different emphases.

In terms of welfare, an early example of this was a Conservative emphasis on a more streamlined, needs-adjusted system based, where possible, on means testing in work undertaken jointly by Iain Macleod and Enoch Powell, both future health ministers and among the most potent political orators of their generation. They were members of the One Nation group, a cadre of highly promising young Conservative MPs, including the future prime minister Ted Heath, who came into Parliament at the 1950 general election. In January 1952 Macleod and Powell published *The Social Services: Needs and Means*. One Nation, in essence, ran with the idea of a British version of the social market which the Christian Democrats made the basis of their political economy in West Germany – the symbiosis of a vibrant free-market economy whose dividend would fund a generous welfare safety net.

Within months, Churchill replaced Harry Crookshank with Macleod as Minister of Health, having, by chance, seen Macleod (a backbencher at the time) eviscerate the great Nye Bevan in a Commons health debate.[15] Health is a great department of state but also always a beleaguered one – central to any notion of the duty of care while at the same time a perpetual target for Treasury control. From the start the Treasury was deeply sceptical about its forecast costings of £134 million for the first year of the NHS. It turned out to be £225 million in 1948–9 and £272 million for 1949–50.[16] Bevan himself acknowledged this eighteen months into the life of the NHS when he famously said, 'I shudder to think of the ceaseless cascade of medicine which is pouring down British throats at the present time.'[17] He believed the torrent would ease after an initial catch-up.[18] It didn't.

Butler's Treasury was after Macleod's health budget from the start. Macleod skilfully headed them off by appointing his old Cambridge economics teacher, Claud Guillebaud, to head a review.[19] Guillebaud came up with exactly what the Treasury did not want. Reporting in January 1956, Guillebaud showed that the share of GDP absorbed by the NHS had actually fallen and that its capital spending needed to treble if there were to be a new hospital building programme.[20] Macleod would never manage to squeeze the money he needed from the Treasury for those desperately needed new hospitals. That had to wait until Enoch Powell's tenure at the Ministry of Health in 1960–63. ('The people have willed it therefore they must have it,' the arch free marketeer Powell would tell his biographer, Simon Heffer.[21]) As the NHS passed its tenth anniversary, a Harvard professor, Harry Eckstein, wrote that it had become 'almost a part of the Constitution'.[22]

The post-1945 duty of care took on another important – and again largely consensual – form in the shape of foreign, defence and intelligence policies. Indeed, it is one of the fundamental and oft-repeated truths of British politics that defending the realm is the first duty of government. The Cold War unsurprisingly kept defence spending high. It surged from 6.5 per cent of GDP in 1949 to 9.9 per cent in 1952 thanks to the general rearmament triggered by the Korean War.[23] This put an immense strain on the British economy as it absorbed skilled and scarce resources, especially in the country's engineering capability, and snuffed out many of the benefits of the 1949 devaluation of the pound. All the main political parties were stalwart supporters of NATO and of the UK as a nuclear weapons state. In January 1947 a small, highly secret Cabinet committee, chaired by Attlee and dominated by his formidable Foreign Secretary, Ernest Bevin, authorized the making of a British atomic bomb. This was made public only in May 1948, slipped out quietly in a pre-arranged parliamentary answer.[24]

The Attlee governments also began the building of a top-secret Cold War state which included detailed planning for a post-nuclear attack on Britain, continued by the Conservatives. This was accompanied by a substantial intelligence effort against the USSR and its satellites abroad, and a matching counter-effort against Soviet intelligence activities in the UK. The UK also enjoyed global reach in signals intelligence, the legacy of the Second World War codebreaking triumphs of Bletchley Park, sustained by a secret SIGINT agreement with the USA and the territorial bequest of empire which left many a remote island or bleak mountainside on which to plant a suite of aerials. Much of the secret state remained just that until the 1990s, when the Cold War was over.[25]

An intriguing tribute was paid to this foreign policy and defence alignment by Normal Tebbit, a great admirer of Attlee and Bevin, many years later. Though regarded as a fairly fierce breed of Conservative with no love for social aspects of the post-war consensus, in 2013 he recalled how he and Margaret Thatcher would talk about those early post-war years in the late 1970s while waiting for evening votes in the House of Commons. I asked him about the distaste he and Mrs Thatcher shared for the Butskellite years.

> TEBBIT: Yes, I found that very refreshing, that I found somebody else who felt that way about the post-war consensus. But also, of course, I think we both felt the same way about some of the things which that early Labour government, the '45 government, did, which were absolutely right, and which it would have been much more difficult for a Conservative government to do at that time.
>
> HENNESSY: Tell me. Such as?
>
> TEBBIT: Membership of NATO. It was not Churchill that created NATO, it was Attlee.
>
> HENNESSY: Ernie Bevin . . .
>
> TEBBIT: Ernie Bevin in particular, one of the truly great men of British politics, in my judgement. And the British nuclear deterrent; again, how difficult would that have been if it had been a Conservative government trying to take that through against the Labour Party?[26]

Another aspect of the UK's place in the world for which Lord Tebbit would retrospectively wish to praise Attlee and Bevin would be that great vexer of the country's politics since 1945, the question of Britain and Europe. Apart from a few enthusiasts for the idea of European integration, even fewer of whom were anywhere near the levers of power (Harold Macmillan being a lonely exception), it was almost as if the senior political figures of both the main parties in the late 1940s and 1950s vied with each other to deride the idea of Britain in Europe:

If you open that Pandora's Box, you never know what Trojan 'orses will jump out.

Ernest Bevin, 1948, on the proposal to create
a Council of Europe[27]

It's no good. We cannot do it. The Durham miners won't wear it.

Herbert Morrison, 1950, on being shown the French
Schuman Plan for a European Coal and Steel Community[28]

I never contemplated Britain joining in this plan on the same terms as the continental partners. We should, however, have joined in all the discussions and, had we done so, not only a better plan would probably have emerged, but our own interests would have been watched at every stage. Our attitude towards further economic developments on the Schuman lines resembles that which we adopt about the European Army [A French plan which did not materialize]. We help, we dedicate, we play a part, but we are not merged and do not forfeit our insular or Commonwealth-wide character. I should resist any American pressure to treat Britain as on the same footing as the European states, none of whom have the advantages of the Channel and who were consequently conquered.

Winston Churchill, paper for the Cabinet, 1951[29]

The American and British people should each understand the strong points in the other's national character. If you drive a nation to adopt procedures which run counter to its instincts, you weaken and may destroy the motive force of its action ... You will realize that I am speaking of the frequent suggestions that the United Kingdom should join a federation on the Continent of Europe. This is something which we know, in our bones, we cannot do.

Anthony Eden, 1952, in a speech
at Columbia University in New York[30]

The Common Market. The so-called Common Market of six nations.*
Know them all well. Very recently this country spent a great deal of
blood and treasure rescuing four of them from attacks by the other two.

Clem Attlee's last speech (in full) before he died in 1967[31]

Thus associated with the early post-war consensus was a shared
belief that for all its economic problems, Britain had a demonstrable
claim to continuing great powerdom. Both main parties agreed that
ours was a special nation, one that had stood with its empire against
seemingly overwhelming peril between the fall of France in June 1940
and Hitler's invasion of the Soviet Union in June 1941, and which
could not possibly contemplate – let alone settle for – the status of a
middle-ranking power tucked inside an ever-integrating western
Europe.

Besides, the Coal and Steel Community and the planned next step
into a common market, bored them all rigid. As Rab Butler would tell
Michael Charlton many years later about the Messina talks of 1955,
which led to the Treaty of Rome in 1957 and the Common Market
the following year, 'Anthony Eden [by this time prime minister] was
bored with this. Frankly, he was even more bored than I was.'[32]

Eden was far more interested – obsessed, even – with the Middle
East and shoring up Britain's position against the rising tide of Arab
nationalism personified by the Egyptian leader, Colonel Gamal Abdul
Nasser, who nationalized the Anglo-French Suez Canal Company in
July 1956. When Britain and France put troops down the canal in the
invasion of Egypt in November 1956 and were halted in the most
humiliating fashion by US economic pressure just days later, Eden's
already shaky health broke and British public opinion split in twain.
There was nothing consensual about the Suez affair and the relationship with the US was put under intense strain. But it was soon restored
by Prime Minister Macmillan and President Eisenhower the following
year.

Despite this, the Conservatives kept their political grip on fifties
Britain. Eden had raised Churchill's 1951 majority of seventeen to

---

* The original members of the European Economic Community when it came into
existence on 1 January 1958 were West Germany, France, Italy, the Netherlands, Belgium and Luxembourg.

fifty-nine in May 1955. Macmillan triumphed with a majority of a hundred in October 1959. Rab Butler would never make it to the premiership. Macmillan denied him the prize when Eden resigned in 1957 and Alec Home did the same in 1963. But apart from the top office itself he had got what he wanted – the electoral reward of a country sufficient of whose voters had indeed come to believe 'that full employment and the welfare state' was 'safe' in the Conservatives' hands, both burnished by the first bloom of a mass-consumption affluent society. Britain had gone for Butler's version of Mr Butskell rather than Gaitskell's. The Conservatives claimed victory for it in this paragraph of their 1959 election manifesto:

> We have provided over two million new homes and almost two million new school places, a better health service and a modern pensions plan. We have now stabilised the cost of living while maintaining full employment . . . By raising living standards and by social reform we are succeeding in creating One Nation at home.[33]

The political competition of late-fifties Britain was driven by the question of which party could bring an even greater burst of economic affluence and social welfare. There was a shared assumption that the shell of deprivation had been cracked and that poverty was on the run. Nye Bevan's disciple Barbara Castle was chairman of the Labour Party in 1959. At its post-election conference (Bevan's last, he was struck down by cancer in 1960, dying at the age of sixty-two), she declared that 'the poverty and unemployment which we came into existence to fight have been largely conquered'.[34]

But had they? As both major parties competed to take the credit for a healthier, richer Britain, an influential group of largely Labour supporting intellectuals and policy analysts set to work on the social arithmetic of the 1950s. Their work, published in 1964, led to what was termed 'the rediscovery of poverty'. The father of this 'rediscovery' was Richard Titmuss, Professor of Social Administration at the London School of Economics. With Brian Abel-Smith and Peter Townsend (future co-authors of 'The Poor and the Poorest'[35] and known as 'The Tit-Mice') they argued that 1950s Whitehall's definitions of poverty – living on less than supplementary benefit – had not kept up with rising living standards and masked a grimmer reality.

The official figures showed 5 per cent were living in poverty, but Abel-Smith and Townsend argued that 140 per cent of supplementary benefit was a more realistic poverty benchmark. If that test were applied to the statistics for 1954–60, in fact 14 per cent of the population, 7.5 million people, were living in poverty. What Nick Timmins called 'the dynamite' in their findings was that the figures included nearly 2.5 million children, and that half a million of these were in households where the man was in work but earning less than the family would have received had he been unemployed and on benefits.[36] Thanks to the establishment in 1965 of a highly effective pressure group, the Child Poverty Action Group, the nature of the welfare debate changed and the illusion that the giant Want had perished was itself slain.

The fifties had seen about 15 per cent of GDP allocated year on year to the social services as Beveridge reforms ran in.* By the end of the sixties, that figure had crept up relentlessly to 20 per cent, and to 25.7 per cent by 1975.[37] The early sixties became ever more preoccupied with the great overarching question of the later years of the post-war settlement. Could the mixed-economy/welfare-state model – built on the Keynesian and Beveridgian architecture – continue to pay for a generous and improving duty of care amidst worsening industrial relations and a faltering economic performance compared to the country's international competitors? It was a question that would dominate the next two decades.

* Social services are defined here as social insurance and assistance, other social transfers, health, housing, education and science.

3
No Satisfaction

Firstly, basic principles. Do we, or do we not, set out to control the pattern of events, to direct development, to plan growth, to use the instruments of government to influence and determine private decisions? Believe that this is inevitable. Forces at work now too complicated, risks of setback too great to leave to market forces and laissez faire. Dirigisme. But it must be creative dirigisme. This is the thread which should run through our policy and by which new proposals should be judged.

Harold Macmillan's notes on 'modernisation' for Cabinet meeting on 25 October 1962[1]

For socialism for us means humanizing what can so easily become a harsh, even brutal, technological revolution ... Socialism in our New Britain will provide that leavening we never had in the first Industrial Revolution.

Harold Wilson, Brangwyn Hall, Swansea, 25 January 1964[2]

The alternative to expansion is not, as some occasionally seem to suppose, an England of quiet market towns linked only by trains puffing slowly and peacefully through green meadows. The alternative is slums, dangerous roads, old factories, cramped schools, stunted lives.

Ted Heath, message to Conservative Party workers, 30 September 1973[3]

All we can do is to press every button we've got. We do not
know which, if any of them, will have the desired results.
Anthony Crosland on the UK's relative economic decline at a
special strategy session of the Wilson Cabinet, Chequers,
17 November 1974[4]

In its political and its economic life, Britain became a jumpier, more anxious place in the 1960s and a positively fraught one in the 1970s. There is a set of figures that haunts me to this day[5]:

GNP, Annual Rate of Growth 1951–73

Japan	9.5%
West Germany	5.7%
Italy	5.1%
France	5.0%
Netherlands	5.0%
Canada	5.0%
Denmark	4.2%
Norway	4.2%
USA	3.7%
UK	2.7%

Relative economic decline is not a bringer of the serenity that Nye Bevan wished for his country. Quite the reverse. It is a carrier of scape-goating and mutual recrimination, a cup-bearer of pessimism. How we longed for a British 'economic miracle'. It never came. And yet, a Britain with that disappointing level of growth could – and did – sustain a flow of social betterment, as the 'social' and the 'market' jostled fruitfully, with general elections sometimes producing an extra helping of one rather than the other.

When he wrote 'Health care, pensions, education, unemployment insurance cascaded from legislation into changed lives',[6] the economist Paul Collier was talking about post-1945 western Europe generally, and it certainly applied powerfully to the early post-war UK in which, like me, he grew up. Collier was born in Sheffield in 1949 and his *The Future of Capitalism* is a cry of scholarly and human rage against the rise of inequality and differential life chances after the deindustrialization of the 1980s.

But the generation of politicians and civil servants for whom 'Keynes and Beveridge had provided the elements of a public philosophy governing political action,' as one of them, Alec Cairncross (who rose to be the Chief Economic Adviser to the Treasury), put it,[7] faced a daily – sometimes, when sterling crises hit, hourly – struggle with how to pay for it. Far from travelling a benign, self-sustaining arc of economic vitality created by a wealthier, better educated and ever more productive workforce as Beveridge's menacing giants diminished in the late fifties and early sixties, a shared sense of 'no satisfaction' increased.

This was made still more dispiriting by poor industrial relations. The problems of wage restraint to avoid inflation in a full-employment society (unemployment averaged just over 300,000 throughout the 1950s), anticipated but not remedied by Keynes, also grew more acute. Full employment lasted into the 1970s, when, in Alec Cairncross's words, 'a world in which it was politically unthinkable that unemployment could remain above 600,000 had given way to a world in which for years unemployment reached over twice that level'.[8]

Successive governments of the 1960s and 70s struggled to inject new life into the mixed-economy/welfare-state model until Mrs Thatcher won her first election in 1979. The memoirs, the diaries, the files at The National Archives, the political speeches crackle with attempted solutions, the hopes, the growing fears. Listen, for example, to Harold Macmillan in May 1962 talking to his Cabinet about politics after the by-election at Orpington in the Kentish suburbs of south-east London a few weeks earlier, which saw a safe Conservative majority of 14,000 turned into an 8,000 Liberal one. He is referring to the new, tripartite (i.e. government/industry/trade unions) National

Economic Development Council and the National Incomes Commission he wished to build alongside it.

> We have ... the NEDC ... it is a tender plant and we must be careful with it. Still the NEDC has decided whether 4 per cent gross [sic] per annum is what we ought to try to aim for ... It [4 per cent growth] is not a thing you get by waiting, like a child that just grows as long as it eats enough ... If we got the stability out of the general acceptance of the incomes policy ... some increase in government expenditure for the things we know are necessary – the housing, the slums, the universities, the schools, – would follow.[9]

Singing out of that Macmillan soliloquy (which, most unusually for a Cabinet meeting, was tape-recorded) is the key theme of the 'no satisfaction' years – how to adapt and modify Keynes to fund and save Beveridge. This was the main melody of the political competition in the 1960s and 70s – how best to invigorate the British economy to pay for an extended duty of care for the well-being of the British people.

Harold Wilson's chance to fulfil this mission rested on his assertion that his was the party that really believed in economic (or indicative) planning – that his team of meritocrats was the one to implement it rather than the Conservatives, the party of privilege and heredity. A new National Plan was to be their instrument involving, like the NEDC, a partnership of government, employers and trade unions.[10]

But there was something deeply stubborn about the UK's growth rate. Whatever successive governments did to unleash its dynamics, it refused to budge from its 2.5 to 2.9 per cent range. The problem was that ministers could not apparently wish into being the British economic miracle but they certainly could wish the expansion of public expenditure as if they had.

The classic example of this was during the Wilson governments of 1964 to 1970. The reality was an average annual growth of 2.6 per cent, *lower* than the 2.9 per cent achieved over the period 1950–64, let alone the 4 per cent planned and hoped for. In February 1965, however, a trajectory of 4.5 per cent growth in public spending over six years was put in place, which would have strained the economy even if the National Plan's economic growth figure had been met.[11] As a result, Alec Cairncross later put it, 'Such a commitment of resources to the public sector, unaccompanied by any similar commitments by the private sector, which was merely offered targets, added to the strain on the balance of payments and made the achievements of industry's targets more rather than less difficult.'[12]

An air of desperation befell successive governments in their attempts to sustain the 'post-war settlement' against the glare of those unforgiving statistics as, month by month, the country waited anxiously for the latest balance-of-payments figures and the pressure on the pound in the days of fixed exchange rates that each poor set would bring. As the formidable Labour thinker Tony Crosland reflected on that gloomy day at Chequers in 1974, they had pressed every button and none of them had worked. Not one had brought satisfaction, let alone Nye Bevan's 'serenity'. It had instead produced a politics of pessimism. Such a belief is always corrosive to the upholding of a duty of care, which needs to be fuelled by the conviction that betterment is possible.

As the fifties moved into the sixties and a growing sense of the country's relative economic decline came more and more to make the political weather, there was a high level of agreement on the mode of production the UK needed to sustain its domestic, overseas and defence spending aspirations. The so-called 'stop-go' cycle of reflation and balance-of-payments crises followed by deflation to see off the resulting sterling crises had to be broken. Alec Cairncross described the arc that defined what his fellow economist Colin Clark called 'growthmanship'.[13]

> The conclusion drawn by those who attributed slower growth to stop-go was that the government should adhere to an expansionist policy, whatever the deficit in the balance of payments, and give more time for investments to respond. The higher productivity that was expected to result would then improve Britain's competitive position and wipe out the deficit, completing a virtuous circle of expanding output, higher investment, higher productivity, and further growth.[14]

Had the UK managed to draw that virtuous circle of self-sustaining investment, productivity and growth, it would have described an ever better-funded Beveridge whose own virtuous circle would have facilitated an ever healthier, better educated and trained and, therefore, ever more-productive and well-rewarded workforce.

This is not the place to write an economic history of post-war Britain, but it's worth itemizing some of the policy instruments – Tony Crosland's 'buttons' – that were applied in the multiple attempts to quicken its pulse, some of which are still relevant today.

INCOMES POLICIES

There was a long line of incomes policies under both Labour and Conservative governments from Stafford Cripps's prototype in 1948–50 to the Callaghan government's pay policy that broke down in the 'winter of discontent' in 1978–9. Some were statutory, others voluntary. Their purpose was to complete Keynes's unfinished business of how to achieve wage restraint in a full-employment society. They had some effect, but it was always short-lived and they built up a reservoir of pay claims that would rush in whenever the sluice-gates were reopened.

CURRENCY POLICIES

Rates of exchange were a near-perpetual anxiety and central to the competitiveness of British exports. There were two devaluations in the era of fixed exchange rates: from $4.03 to $2.80 in 1949 and from $2.80 to $2.40 in 1967. The pound floated in 1972 (and has floated ever since as a daily barometer of international market opinion of the state of the UK economy). In recent times it has been around $1.40. The sterling balances were finally transferred into a basket of other currencies in 1977 following the so-called IMF crisis of late 1976, when the Labour government had to seek a substantial loan from the International Monetary Fund.

INDUSTRIAL STRATEGIES

Attempts were made by successive governments to tackle the deep-set underlying investment/productivity problem (and the difficulty of commercializing Britain's often superb science) by instituting a series of plans and planning organizations from the Central Economic Planning machinery of the Attlee years through the National Economic Development Council in the early sixties, the National Plan of the mid-sixties and Labour's industrial strategy in 1976. Mrs Thatcher had no time for such efforts but they have enjoyed a revival under all governments since until the idea of a formal industrial strategy was abandoned yet again in Boris Johnson's second year of office.

TRADE UNION REFORM

With the rise of industrial disputes in the late 1960s (unofficial strikes especially), the Wilson government proposed legislation in its *In Place of Strife* White Paper of 1969, but it was dropped in the face of fierce trade union and Labour Party resistance.

The Heath government's trade union legislation floundered with his administration in 1973–4 because of the industrial emergency caused by a miners' strike which led to a 'three-day week' and was repealed by the incoming Labour government. Not until Mrs Thatcher's succession of statutes was trade union power curbed – a process greatly accelerated by high unemployment, deindustrialization and the privatization of nationalized industries.

DEFENCE REVIEWS

There was a regular sequence of defence reviews, starting under Labour in 1949, which were designed to ease the pressure on public expenditure of substantial Cold War and (until 1971) east-of-Suez commitments together with the ever-rising cost of defence equipment. The ending of the Cold War during 1989–91 enabled substantial reductions in the proportion of national wealth devoted to defence (a fall from 4.5 to 2.4 per cent in 2007–8, according to the House of Lords Library records).

For all these efforts to unlock and unleash new energies within the British economy, the funding engine for the duty-of-care state continued to struggle and the much-craved economic miracle remained elusive – those crucial relative productivity figures remaining stubbornly inadequate (see Table 2).

Table 2: Real GDP per hour worked, 1950–1973 (relative productivity; UK = 100).[15]

	UK	USA	FRANCE	GERMANY	ITALY	JAPAN
1950	100	171	71	57	57	24
1960	100	174	86	89	70	34
1973	100	145	108	106	102	64

There was a would-be, wished-for transformer – this time a geo-political one – from the early 1960s which was and still is in a class of its own (albeit a deeply controversial and later, profoundly destabilizing one) – which is why I have left it till the end.

EUROPE

After the nearly universally churlish British reaction in the decade after the Second World War to the suggestion that the UK might wish to join first the European Coal and Steel Community and then the fledgling European Economic Community, Whitehall opinion (both ministerial and official) began to shift in the late 1950s for a number of reasons. High among them was the need to invigorate the UK economy by exposing it to competition and free trade from the booming EEC 'Six'. In the early 1960s Harold Wilson, who wasn't pro-Europe until 1966–7, when his government was recoiling from spiralling economic disappointment, used in private to call this the 'cold-douche' theory.[16]

For pro-European enthusiasts inside the UK, British membership

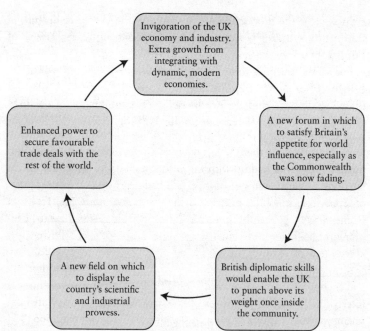

Figure 1: The optimistic case for membership of the European Community.

held out the prospect of another one of those attractive virtuous circles. I think that its shape would be something like the geometry I have drawn in Figure 1.

UK membership would strengthen western Europe in the Cold War struggle while also reducing any future risk of war between the European powers. The price of some element of national sovereignty lost or 'pooled' with the supranational EEC would be worth paying, as would be the hurt within the British Commonwealth, which, it was argued, would eventually benefit from a more economically vibrant UK.

As a transforming instrument for an economically underperforming state overloaded with its welfare and defence commitments, Europe, therefore, brought the biggest and most sustainable prospect of breakthrough. From the Macmillan government's first application (failed) in 1961, through the Wilson government's second application (also failed) in 1967, to the Heath government's (successful) application, this was the kind of map of Europe the pro-Europeans held in their minds. The UK joined the EEC on 1 January 1973 and the vision was sustained at the first referendum on membership in 1975.

But there were three main problems with this benign conception of Britain's place in an ever more integrating Europe. First, there were a number of gifted and extremely eloquent politicians who spoke for those on both the Right and the Left who could never be reconciled to this new position in the world (Enoch Powell and Michael Foot especially in the early days). Second, there were many who accepted the free-trade/cold-douche theory but had no wish for further political or monetary union, let alone a United States of Europe, and had never embraced the notion of 'ever closer union' as outlined in the first paragraph of the Treaty of Rome 1957. Significantly, the idea that membership might come to affect immigration policy never impacted anyone except for Enoch Powell. In a speech to a press lunch in Brussels on 28 September 1972 he declared, 'Every common policy, or attempted common policy, of the Community will encounter a political resentment in Britain . . . These resentments will intertwine themselves with all the raw issues of British politics: inflation, unemployment, balance of payments, the regions, even immigration . . .'[17] Third, we finally joined just months before war in the Middle East led to a quadrupling of world oil prices in 1973–4 and a substantial recession in Western economies that seriously affected the bloom of growth in the original EEC, leaving its attractiveness diminished and its irritations increased. And still no economic lift-off occurred. It really did look as if Tony Crosland was right – every button had been pressed, but to no avail.

Although few appreciated the possibility in the early 1970s, these fragilities underlying our joining the EEC in 1973 expressed them-selves with loud, dramatic and enduring consequences in 2016 when we narrowly voted for the exit, the benign image of the virtuous circle of the early seventies long faded.

Compared to the two great geopolitical shifts of the fifties and early sixties – one largely achieved: disposing of the largest territorial empire the world had ever known; the other hoped for: entry into the EEC – the Conservatives were steady rather than spectacular on the Beveridge front, and mainly managerial rather than innovatory. This is in no way to diminish the boost to the duty of care and significant attack on the giant Disease by Enoch Powell's 1962 White Paper *The Hospital Plan for England and Wales* – £500 million over ten years to build ninety new hospitals and seriously remodel 134 more.[18]

One initiative, however, stands out – the 1963 plan to dramatically expand higher education following the Robbins Report,[19] which did for the universities what the 1944 Education Act had done for the schools. It represented a real and sustained thumping of the giant Ignorance with a squadron of new universities to grace the landscape of learning.[20]

Labour arrived in government in October 1964 promising a better Beveridge – always the piece of policy terrain on which the party was most united. Denis Healey (Defence Secretary 1964–70; Chancellor of the Exchequer, 1974–79) had an intriguing theory about this. We were talking about the Attlee governments in 1993, shortly after my book *Never Again* had been published. Denis memorably said, 'Clem Attlee wanted to end the class war, not to win it,' before observing that by 1951 Labour had implemented the Beveridge Report – the one thing every section of the party was agreed upon. Thereafter, they had a tendency to fall out over things (which they did twice in Denis's lifetime – the Bevanites versus the Gaitskellites in the 1950s; the Militant tendency/hard left versus the mainstream in the 1980s; and once more in the Corbyn years). There has always been something ironic in it being the Liberals – J. M. Keynes and Beveridge – providing Labour with the wherewithal of its greatest historical unity.

As a young Oxford don Harold Wilson had worked for Beveridge on his late-1930s study of employment and the trade cycle. But Wilson had none of the 'filial devotion' towards Beveridge that he felt towards Clem Attlee.[21] Quite the reverse. He wrote later of Beveridge's 'arrogance and rudeness to those appointed to work with him and his total inability to delegate'.[22] Beveridge had asked Wilson to be secretary of his great social insurance inquiry: Wilson declined. Yet, as Wilson's biographer, Ben Pimlott, wrote:

> the imprint of Beveridge upon Wilson was deep . . . Wilson had obtained much from a man of great intellect, energy and ingenuity as well as of personal selfishness, coldness and conceit . . . (He was fond of claiming later that he had learnt from Beveridge 'that a great man does his own work. His own essential work at any rate . . .')

Finally, and perhaps most important, Beveridge gave him a sense of possibility ... The enormous success and popularity of the Beveridge Report over a year after they had parted company increased Wilson's sense of what was within reach.[23]

Beveridge, a man who never knowingly undersold himself, told Wilson when the report was published, 'This is the greatest advance in our history. There can be no turning back. From now on Beveridge is not the name of a man; it is the name of a way of life, and not only for Britain, but for the whole of the civilized world.'[24]

Despite his dislike of the man, Wilson carried the Beveridgian model with him into Number 10 in October 1964. He then sought to embellish and fund it more generously from the dividend of the hoped-for economic growth, but not to reshape it dramatically. There were, however, elements of innovation. One early example was the Redundancy Payments Act 1965, a necessary and humane addition to the statutory armoury for an economy undergoing labour-saving technological advance and the (hopefully temporary) unemployment that went with it.[25]

The most important duty-of-care innovation of the 1964–70 Labour governments was the transformation of local authority social services following the Seebohm Report of 1968, which can be seen as an application of Beveridgian universalist principles. As Nick Timmins put it, a passion for reorganization was in the air and one of its most significant results was:

Seebohm ... with its recommendation to create unified social services departments with complete responsibility for the needs of their areas, covering not just statutory requirements but any needs which might arise. Thus social services were to become, if not a universal service (not everyone would need social work), at least a universalist service; in the words of the report 'a door on which anyone could knock'. Departments would be there not only to help individuals and families but to work with groups and communities, stimulating voluntary activity but in turn using voluntary activity to stimulate councils into action.[26]

Seebohm was launched on a sea of economic gloom following the devaluation of the pound in November 1967. The following year began with a desperate search for public spending cuts as Roy Jenkins, who had replaced Jim Callaghan as Chancellor of the Exchequer after the devaluation, sought to find the resources to boost exports and ease the balance-of-payments deficit using the more competitive exchange rate.

Wilson sought to preserve the Beveridgian duty of care through thick and thin, and steered cuts away from certain programmes. His – and his Cabinet's – priorities were revealed in the House of Commons on 16 January 1968. He recalled in his memoirs:

> On the civil expenditure side I began with social security. Total expenditure in the year (1967–8), at £2,909 million was forty-eight per cent above 1963–4. It was to rise to £3,106 million in 1968–9. There were no cuts. Instead, our pledge to shelter the less well-off families against the effects of post-devaluation price increases, was to be honoured by a second increase in family allowances, and a further increase in the next reconsideration of supplementary benefits [with which Labour had replaced national assistance in 1966].[27]

Wilson's Commons speech was a vivid illustration of how Labour had spent as if the National Plan *had* worked its magic on economic growth. As if to ram the point home, Wilson went on:

> In health and welfare, where expenditure was running at £1,619 million – an increase of forty-five per cent over the figure of four years earlier – our problem was to continue our overriding priority for the record hospital-building programme. This would continue without cuts. But ... we announced the reinstallation of the prescriptions charge at 2s 6d per item.[28]

The cuts fell on housing, roads and above all defence, with a planned withdrawal of British forces from east of Suez by the end of 1971.[29]

The sixties, under Conservative and Labour governments, saw a move away from the Beveridgian principle of flat-rate universal benefits to what Roy Jenkins called 'civilized selectivity' – a concentration of welfare payments on those in the greatest need,[30] reviving the thrust of the argument advanced by the One Nation group in the early 1950s. As Minister of Pensions, John Boyd-Carpenter had started the move with a graduated pension scheme in the early sixties.[31] He was attempting to head off a 'big idea' developed by the brilliant if mercurial Labour MP Richard Crossman for a state-funded earnings-related pension scheme, to take Beveridge a stage further in an age when the expansion of occupational pensions was creating a growing inequality among the retired. Crossman's hour came when Wilson appointed him Secretary of State for Health and Social Security in a new mega-ministry in 1968. But his unfinished plan was swept away by the general election of June 1970, which, to the surprise of everybody except Ted Heath, the Conservatives won with a comfortable majority of thirty.

Heath was a man formed by 1930s Britain, which left him with a powerful 'never again' impulse. Indeed, his description of the formation of his views on the duty of care is one of the most eloquent passages in his memoirs:

> More than anything else ... it was two books which came to prominence during my time at Oxford that convinced me, once and for all that neither socialism nor the pure free market could provide the answer to the problems which beset us. The first was John Maynard Keynes's *General Theory of Employment, Interest and Money*, published in 1936. Inspired by a world depression which had been caused by laissez faire policies, it put forward a wholly new view of economics, which Keynes and his followers used to demonstrate that full and stable levels of employment could be maintained if government intervened counter-cyclically in the economy.[32]

The second was *The Middle Way*, written by his boss-to-be, Harold Macmillan, in 1938. This book was, in Macmillan's words, 'a plea for planned capitalism',[33] arguing that a degree of economic planning could make commerce and industry more efficient and generate the resources that would help protect the needy in society without any threat to individual liberty. This, Heath recalled, was the 'philosophical basis'[34] of the One Nation group when he was a young MP.

Heath was a famously difficult man who gave the impression of being an Easter Island statue-made-flesh, incapable of expressing emotion except through music. Yet Ted at work was shaped by a particularly practical form of Christianity too: 'My Christian faith also provided foundations for my political beliefs,' he wrote, adding, 'In this I was influenced by the teaching of William Temple. Temple's impact on my generation was immense. He believed that a fairer society could be built only on moral foundations, with all individuals recognizing their duty to help others.' Heath also wrote warmly of the Christian Democratic tradition of policies in mainland Europe, sharing 'the view that the individual can be truly fulfilled only as part of a social unit'.[35] Out of Balliol College, Oxford, through the Army during the war and into politics thereafter, he brought a comprehensive sense of duty, a set of values well within the post-war settlement. But unfortunately for Heath, by the time he entered No. 10 in June 1970, his public image had altered. He was seen as very much the brisk free marketer, the would-be breaker of the post-war consensus. Part of this was of his own making; another part was Harold Wilson's brilliance in painting him so.

Over a weekend in early February 1970 Heath took his shadow cabinet away for a manifesto-planning session at the Selsdon Park Hotel near Croydon in south London. The impression was given that its fruits would be a consensus-busting, free-market-driven break with the past. To the fury of Heath:

> Harold Wilson made a savage attack on us, claiming that we had made a cynical move to the right. He came up with the name 'Selsdon Man', and tried to portray us all as right-wing extremists … In later years, some members of my party have talked about Selsdon Park as if Wilson was right all along and that it did signal a move away from traditional Conservative politics. Norman Tebbit has even written of 'the Selsdon declaration', which allegedly marked my conversion to 'the new liberal economics'. There was no such thing. He has rewritten history.[36]

Quite a historical battle has raged over the cadaver of 'Selsdon Man'. I have always shared the view of Heath's biographer, John Campbell, that he 'never intended to break the post-war settlement accepted by Churchill, Eden, Macmillan and Home. His proposed "revolution" was all about trying to change attitudes and remove obstacles to growth within the existing economic and social structure.'[37]

Occasionally there can come a moment in the life of a historian when he or she gets the chance to put a historical debate directly to the subject of it. I had such an opportunity when interviewing Ted Heath for *What Has Become of Us?* in 1994:

> HENNESSY: A debate about when you become prime minister has happened in recent years about whether you were a proto-typical free marketer with Selsdon and so on, but others have argued that your premiership was designed to make Britain more efficient so that the virtues of that consensus could be sustained through the rest of the century ... Am I right in thinking that you always were a consensus man and all the modernization plans for Britain you put in place in 1970 – 'no more lame ducks' and so on – were designed actually to get an economy to sustain that rather than changing ... towards something that we might now call 'Thatcherism'?
>
> HEATH: Yes, I've always said that what I wanted was a balance, and it's very important to achieve that, otherwise you get into difficulties in all sorts of ways – technically and with people. What we wanted to do was modernize. We'd done tremendous work as a shadow government planning all of this ... so we had all of this on which to base our attitudes and work when we took over. And you're quite right, we wanted to increase the efficiency of this country enormously ... and if you can do it jointly with everybody else, so much the better. It avoids all the rows and you also avoid the dogma which has been the curse of recent years – that we know this and we're going to do this because it's our dogma and let's get on with it; all those who aren't with us are against us. That's not the way to run a country. You can't run a business like that either (can't run anything like it) and you certainly can't run a government like it. So yes, I wanted to modernize, I wanted to do it as far as possible on a consensus. But one always recognizes there are some issues on which it might not be possible to get a consensus. Well, then you have to take your own line in the best possible way.[38]

Unbeknownst to Wilson, a free-market approach to the NHS *had* briefly floated in 1968 as a way for the next Conservative government to curb spiralling health costs. It came from Keith Joseph, as Heath recalled in his memoir:

In the autumn of 1968, Keith Joseph circulated a paper to the shadow cabinet . . . He wanted to find ways of encouraging people to take out private insurance for health requirements such as visits to their GPs, out-patient care and boarding charges after more than a few days in hospital. Tax concessions would be granted to those taking out such insurance. At first, I supported these ideas in principle, but the costings made it clear that the financial saving would not have warranted the probable political damage. Moreover, at the Selsdon Park summit Iain Macleod showed that it might also cause distress for many people, potentially doubling the cost of compulsory insurance for those on average wages. We therefore dropped the idea.[39]

Macleod, the shadow Chancellor, ex-health minister and the most powerful man in the shadow cabinet after Heath himself, saved the Beveridge principle. He died in July 1970 at the age of 56, just weeks into the new government, which was greatly weakened without his political gifts, his word power and presence in the Treasury.

With Keith Joseph (an energetic though always a somewhat anguished figure) at the DHSS, health spending grew at about 4 per cent a year in real terms, ahead of the annual economic growth rate.[40] 'One Nation' Heath also took great pride in his government's 'massively' expanding the social services:

> so that when the new integrated healthcare [a closer relationship between health and social services] began in April 1974 [by which time the Heath government had fallen in the February election], those on the medical side had enough professionals working in the community to support them . . . Finally, we made the contraceptive pill, the symbol of personal freedom in the 1960s, available to all on the NHS, free from prescription charges.[41]

All in all, these were refinements of and extensions to the standard model of post-war duty of care. In one area in particular where the Conservatives were expected to at least partially roll back existing practice – comprehensive schools – change did not materialize. This was surprising, not least because the Secretary of State for Education was a woman of intense determination in her first Cabinet post: Margaret Thatcher.

In 1965 Tony Crosland, then Wilson's education secretary, had issued a circular requiring local education authorities to submit plans to reorganize schools along non-selective lines.[42] He told his wife, 'If it's the last thing I do, I'm going to destroy every fucking grammar school in England. And Wales. And Northern Ireland.'[43]

His circular 10/65 (no new law was needed – Crosland would do it under section 13 of the 1944 Education Act) was anathema to Mrs Thatcher, a grammar-school girl to her last fibre. Within days of taking office she issued circular 10/70 countermanding Crosland's. But the comprehensive tide was flowing. It was, she later wrote, 'a time when even Conservative education authorities were bitten with the bug of comprehensivisation'.[44] Her new circular declared, 'The Secretary of State will expect educational considerations in general, local needs and wishes in particular and the wise use of resources to be the main principles determining the local pattern.'[45] In a paragraph tinged with regret, even pain, she wrote in *The Path to Power*:

> For all the political noise which arose from this change of policy, its practical effects were limited. During the whole of my time as Education Secretary we considered some 3,600 proposals for reorganization – the great majority of these proposals for comprehensivisation – of which I rejected only 325, or about 9 per cent.[46]

Mrs Thatcher was education secretary from start to finish of the Heath administration. During what turned out to be her last days in the job, I, as a young reporter on *The Times Higher Education Supplement*, spent a day and an evening shadowing her during the February 1974 election campaign. She had a private lunch engagement so I shared some sandwiches with her agent, Roy Langstone, in her Finchley constituency, where I had spent my boyhood in the 1950s. To his eternal credit, this is what he said to me:

> Normally, women in politics are a bloody menace. But she is the most fantastic person I've ever worked for in twenty-seven years as an agent. She gets more done in one day than most MPs do in a week. The greater proportion of this constituency would be very proud to see Mrs Thatcher as the first woman Prime Minister of this country. I know she's got the capabilities. One of these days, maybe; one never knows.[47]

I simply couldn't see it. Chancellor of the Exchequer, yes; but not PM. Yet almost exactly a year later Mrs Thatcher was leader of the Conservative Party; four-and-a-half years later she was prime minister. The fall of Ted Heath after the loss of a second election in October 1974 made her and what became her 'ism' possible. In the course of eleven-and-a-half dramatic years those 'capabilities' that Roy Langstone had told me about over those sandwiches in Finchley played out.

In the meantime, what one might call the 1940s duty of care plus refinements had one last hurrah, albeit in dire economic circumstances and in the hands of a Labour Party without a majority in the House of Commons (apart from a brief period between October 1974 and April 1976). Intriguingly, the last Wilson government's proposed new big idea was a 'social contract' with the wider labour movement that had cut down the Heath government – the miners' strike of 1973 being its blade. Wilson and his ministers (few of whom had foreseen the Conservatives losing in February 1974) saw improved welfare as the key to a new deal on pay restraint with the trade unions.

The basis of the agreement with the TUC was that unions would moderate their wage demands in return for a 'social wage' in the form of extra spending on health, pensions, a new child benefit to replace family allowances, control of council-house rents, price controls and food subsidies.[48] The 'social wage' idea came out of the fertile mind of Professor Brian Abel-Smith of the LSE, special adviser to the fiery Barbara Castle, whom Wilson had made his Secretary of State for Health and Social Security. As she recorded in her diary on 1 March 1975, 'I despair at the Government's failure to orchestrate a firm exposition of what is necessary for the Social Contract to succeed.' Later she added a footnote:

> I believed we were failing to get across to working people the cash value to them of the social services and how wrong it was for them to think of the taxes they paid as a pure loss ... We [Mrs Castle and Professor Abel-Smith] estimated that this 'second wage' was worth about £20 a week for every member of the working population.[49]

As Mrs Castle feared, it ended in tears. Yet again Labour had spent on the basis of a growth rate that never materialized. This time, it had absolutely no chance of doing so as the economy was being daily battered by the inflationary consequences of quadrupling oil prices following the Yom Kippur War of 1973 that ended the gilded phase of the post-war years. Joel Barnett, Chief Secretary to the Treasury and one of the most warm-hearted and affable politicians I have known, wrote bitterly of the supposedly give-and-take social contract in his memoirs, 'the only give and take in [it] was that the Government gave and the unions took'.[50]

In 1975, one final consensus was achieved between Labour and the Conservatives on the state earnings-related pensions scheme, which, in Nick Timmins's words, 'mixed a flat-rate basic pension which would rise in line with earnings with an earnings-related pension top up which was to be inflation-proofed [and] based on "the best twenty years" earnings; contributions were to be earnings related, and the whole thing would be phased in over twenty years.'[51]

More widely, there was precious little to celebrate as inflation soared to 26 per cent in June 1975, the economy stagnated and the pound came under pressure. Jim Callaghan, a classic man of '45, steeped in that generation's duty of care, succeeded Wilson in April 1976. He always regretted his age (sixty-four) and his lack of a Commons majority. His room for initiative was highly circumscribed. His formidable political gifts were almost entirely devoted to economic fire-fighting, apart from one foray into education policy. In a speech delivered at Ruskin College, Oxford on 16 October 1976, Callaghan tried to shift the terms of the educational debate from the fixation with comprehensivization to the question of standards. He larded it with scepticism about 'new informal methods of teaching' and suggested that the possibility of a 'core curriculum' should be examined. In so doing he enraged his left wing and affronted progressive opinion.[52]

By the time he rose to speak at Ruskin, Callaghan was caught in the coils of a severe and worsening economic crisis that led him and Denis Healey, now his formidable Chancellor of the Exchequer, to seek a loan from the IMF. Callaghan was, as he told me later, determined above all to avoid a rerun of the great financial crisis of 1931, which had destroyed Ramsay MacDonald's second minority Labour government. He 'knew it was quite possible for the government to break up, and [that it] could have been another 1931'.[53] Avoiding a '1931' meant two things for Callaghan: keeping the Cabinet together and rejecting cuts in benefits to meet the spending reductions demanded by the IMF (the issue on which the government foundered in 1931). He succeeded in both. As his biographer Ken Morgan noted, 'Social benefits had been protected. In 1931 they had been the first target for attack.'[54]

Jim Callaghan was shot through with the spirit of trade unionism – as a young man he had been an official in the Inland Revenue Staff Federation – but it was trade union power wielded in the 1978–9 'winter of discontent' that effectively broke his government and with it the post-war settlement. Callaghan sensed this. In a famous exchange with his senior policy adviser, Bernard Donoughue, during the 1979 election, he said, 'You know there are times, perhaps once every thirty years, when there is a sea-change in politics. It then does not matter what you say and do. There is a shift in what the public wants and what it approves of. I suspect there is now such a sea-change – and it is for Mrs Thatcher.'[55]

It was. As Ken Morgan wrote, 'James Callaghan ... represented more clearly perhaps than any other living politician the full force of the post-1945 creed of moderation. He was the classic consensus man.'[56] The remains of the post-war consensus went with Jim Callaghan to Buckingham Palace to resign on 4 May 1979.

The 'no satisfaction' years were dripping with disappointing metrics as the post-war settlement came under increasing strain. Yet there was one statistic that did shine through the gloom, though it was little talked about. The Gini coefficient, named after the Italian statistician Corrado Gini, who invented it in 1912, has become the most commonly used measurement of inequality of incomes. A country that had 'perfect' equality of income would possess a Gini coefficient of 0. A society where one person enjoyed every scrap of income would be rated at 1.[57]

Anthony Heath, Director of the Centre for Social Investigation at Nuffield College, Oxford, who traced the fate of Beveridge's five giants in his *Social Progress in Britain*, concluded that 'the general trend in our peer countries [Canada, France, Germany, Italy, Japan and Sweden], up until the 1970s, had been towards greater equality. There was then a reversal and income inequality began to rise. At the start of 1977, and among the peers, Britain's inequality was low with a Gini coefficient 0.23 and similar to Germany, Sweden and Japan.

From then until 1990 it had the largest and most rapid increase in inequality, from 0.23 to 0.34. However, by 1990 the Gini coefficient had started to rise in the others, albeit more slowly. By 1998 the coefficients were as follows: Britain 0.35, Italy 0.34, Canada 0.31, Sweden and France 0.28, Germany 0.25 and Japan 0.24[58] (of which more in the next chapter).

The creation of a more equal society was central to the wider Beveridgian philosophy. Until Mrs Thatcher's arrival in power its cumulative achievement could be celebrated as one of the happier outcomes of the post-war settlement.

By the end of the 1980s, excessive inequality, a source of resentment and disquiet, had become a sixth giant (of which more in Chapters 4 and 5).[59] There was another giant just discernible in its menace, in 1969. For in November and December that year the ecologist Frank Fraser Darling delivered the 1969 BBC Reith Lectures on the theme of 'Wilderness and Plenty'. I have a vague memory – no more than that – of reading extracts in the newspapers over the six weeks in which the lectures were delivered but I must confess that their long-term importance did not enthuse me. In his final lecture 'Where does responsibility lie?' Fraser Darling said:

> Such qualified pessimism as I have voiced in these lectures allows no relaxation in our ease for the fate of the planet in a problematic future ... I have expressed my doubts whether we shall have a long posterity if we continue as we are doing, living off the capital of the world's ecosystems that evolved long before we were consciously men, throwing our poisonous refuse into air and water arrogantly as well as in ignorance.[60]

To his great credit, the Prince of Wales, on 19 February 1970, did pick up Fraser Darling's theme in a speech delivered at Cardiff:

> Dr Frank Fraser Darling recently said that he was afraid 'people will get tired of the word ecology before they know what it means [but] we are faced at this moment with the horrifying effects of pollution on all its cancerous fronts. There is chemical pollution discharged into rivers from factories and chemical plants which clogs up the rivers with toxic

substances and adds to the filth in the seas. There is air pollution from smoke and fumes discharged by factories and from gases pumped out by endless cars and aeroplanes.[61]

Throwing poisonous refuse up into the air and down into the oceans is exactly what Britain and the world continued to do until the seventh giant, Climate Change, assumed the most menacing character of them all. The time is now long past when we could plead ignorance, and perhaps our experience of living through Covid-19 is finally dispelling our arrogance with regard to the planet we inhabit and the environment in which we live.

In 1979, a decade after Frank Fraser Darling's Reith Lectures and Prince Charles's address to the Welsh conservationists, James Lovelock published his famous *Gaia: A New Look at Life on Earth*.[62] (Gaia is the Greek Goddess of the Earth. The name had been suggested to him by the novelist William Golding as they walked through the village of Broad Chalke in Wiltshire, where they both lived.) Gaia, wrote Lovelock, if it 'does exist, then we may find ourselves and all other living things to be parts and partners of a vast being who in her entirety has the power to maintain our planet as a fit and comfortable habitat for life'.[63] The book was published in the year that Mrs Thatcher became prime minister. One of the diplomats she most admired, Crispin Tickell, aroused her interest in this on a flight back from Paris after a meeting with President Mitterrand in 1984. He gave her Lovelock's book to read and arranged for them to meet.[64] They got on well. As her authorized biographer, Charles Moore, put it, 'Mrs Thatcher was very impressed by Lovelock, a man who had come from humble beginnings,'[65] and Lovelock was the star of her 1989 Downing Street Seminar on 26 April. Thatcher was the first head of any British political party to show serious environmental concern, giving her, in Moore's judgement, 'something close to global leadership on it'.[66] She spoke as if it were part of her personal duty of care.

4

Safe in Her Hands?

This century [the twentieth] has seen an unprecedented political and economic experiment. The centrally controlled model has been tried in various forms – ranging from the totalitarianism of communism and Nazism, through various brands of social democracy or democratic socialism, to an un-ideological technocratic corporatism. So has the decentralized liberal model – most notably in Britain and the United States in the 1980s. The balance sheet of this century which can now be drawn up conveys the irresistible message: whether judged on political, social or economic grounds, collectivism has failed. By contrast, the application of classical liberal principles had transformed countries and continents for the good. The tragedy is, of course, that this great experiment was unnecessary. State monopoly and the command economy could never in the end mobilize human talent and energy. And nor could their milder coercive equivalents.

Margaret Thatcher 1995[1]

Margaret Thatcher: Do you know, Tony, I'm so proud I don't belong to your class.

Sir Anthony Parsons, Diplomat, and her foreign affairs adviser 1983–4: What class would that be?

Margaret Thatcher: The upper middle class who see everybody's point of view but have no view of their own.

Sir Anthony Parsons, reporting an exchange
with Mrs Thatcher, The Thatcher Years,
Part 1, BBC One, 6 October 1993

You always knew where you were with Mrs Thatcher. 'There was no difference between her front of house or her private persona,' as a senior civil servant once explained to me. Margaret Thatcher had plenty of her own giants to slay – most of them wielding their clubs and patrolling the border of what she called the 'progressive consensus'. Forty years later Nigel Lawson told me in a BBC Radio 4 interview, 'I was not anti-consensus. Margaret was. Margaret hated the idea of consensus *in itself*. I just hated the idea of the consensus we'd had before, which clearly was mistaken.'[2] Two words never failed to launch her into an orbit of denunciation: 'consensus' was one; 'equality', the other.

This was evident from the first months of her era. In a speech in New York in 1975 (the year in which she succeeded Ted Heath as leader of the Conservative Party) she asked:

> What lessons are to be learned from the last thirty years? First, the pursuit of equality is a mirage. Far more desirable and more practicable than the pursuit of equality is the pursuit of equality of opportunity. Opportunity means nothing unless it includes the right to be unequal – and the freedom to be different ... Let our children grow tall – and some grow taller than others, if they have it in them to do so.[3]

It was vividly plain – the post-war settlement was in for a hammering. She also put the Gini coefficient on notice. Mrs Thatcher's first job in 1961 had been at the Ministry of Pensions and National Insurance. She was always grateful to Harold Macmillan for appointing her but she did not share his instincts for planning, his devotion to the middle way and his romantic side ('Disraeli's style was too ornate for my taste, though I can see why it may have appealed to Harold Macmillan ... Things looked very different from the perspective of Grantham [where she grew up] than from that of Stockton [which Macmillan had represented in Parliament during the slump]'[4]).

Sensing, one suspects, her persistent mixture of keenness and earnestness, Macmillan plainly couldn't resist teasing her: 'I wanted to begin as soon as possible and asked him how I should arrange things with the department. Characteristically, he said: "Oh well, ring the Permanent Secretary and turn up about 11 o'clock tomorrow morning, look around and come away. I shouldn't stay too long."'[5]

She immediately displayed some of the characteristics that the country would come to know in abundance during her eleven-and-a-half years as prime minister: 'It was not just a matter of avoiding being caught out in the House of Commons. If one was to make any serious contribution to the development of policy one had to have mastered both the big principles and the details. This I now set out to do.'[6]

With this combination of fine print and big picture, Mrs Thatcher was, perhaps surprisingly, a kindred spirit of Beveridge. She reread him soon after she became a junior minister; thirty-five years later, she wrote that 'the Beveridge Report's rhetoric has what would later be considered a Thatcherite ring to it', and quoted her favourite bits:

> The State should offer security for service and contribution. The State in organizing security should not stifle incentive, opportunity, and responsibility; in establishing a national minimum, it should leave room and encouragement for voluntary action by each individual to provide more than the minimum for himself and his family [Paragraph 9].
>
> The insured persons should not feel that income for idleness, however caused, can come from a bottomless purse [Paragraph 22].
>
> Material progress depends upon technical progress which depends upon investment and ultimately upon savings ... It is important that part of the additional resources going to wage-earners and others of limited means should be saved by them, instead of being spent forthwith. [Paragraph 376].[7]

She was also critical of Beveridge: 'He greatly underestimated the cost of his proposals, though this was partly because the post-war Labour Government introduced full-rate old-age pensions immediately without the twenty-year phasing in period which Beveridge had envisaged.'[8]

Despite this, Mrs Thatcher respected Attlee: 'I was an admirer. He was a serious man and a patriot. Quite contrary to the general tendency of politicians in the 1990s [when she was writing], he was all substance and no show.'[9] Overall, however, his government (pushed on, perhaps, by more radical members) had pursued 'a root and branch assault on business, capitalism and the market'.[10]

Her early views on Beveridge stayed with Mrs Thatcher when the electorate put her so decisively into No. 10 on 5 May 1979. As a member of her Downing Street Policy Unit between 1984 and 1986, David Willetts advised her on social security and remembers 'she would pepper me with questions . . . She had the Beveridge contributory principle very much in mind.'[11] But it was not the Beveridge elements of the post-war settlement that Mrs Thatcher had her sights on, as David Willetts told Nick Timmins in an interview:

> She had a sense that it [the welfare state] cost a lot. She asked why the budget rose all the time, and 'how the hell do we get a grip on it?' She suspected, or feared, that quite a lot of it was inefficient. And she did have a feeling that individual initiative and the drive for self-improvement could be undermined by too extensive a welfare state; that it could rot people's moral fibre. She did have a set of instincts. But she had no clear programme. In the early 1980s, social policy featured relatively little on the No. 10 agenda. She was concerned with the economy, industrial relations, the unions and the nationalized industries – not with health, or social security, or education.[12]

The Thatcher years were lived as if her government were engaged in a perpetual spending review, but the welfare state always had the air of unfinished business, even at the end of her long tenure as prime minister.

Many years later in a BBC Radio 4 *Reflections* interview I asked one of her keenest supporters, Norman Tebbit, about his priority had he become prime minister.

HENNESSY: If you had made it, what statute can I give you?
TEBBIT: I think it would have been welfare reform, because I think that welfarism has become the curse of this country. When I like to pull the leg of left-wing audiences, I speak about it. I always pop in those words of Professor Beveridge in which he says that the period of time for which a man may draw unemployment benefit should be limited lest men become habituated to idleness* . . . and that of course raises the most terrible shouts and yells, and I say, 'Well, not my words, Beveridge's words.' And had we enacted the original

* He was referring to Paragraph 22; one of Mrs Thatcher's favourites, as we have seen.

reforms in Attlee's day more in line with Beveridge, they would have stood the test of time better, because we've created a dependency culture, and that has really been a curse.[13]

Earlier in the interview, we had talked about the human and the parliamentary limitations experienced even by governments with ample majorities:

TEBBIT: I think one of the things I learned in government was that in a Cabinet of twenty-odd people, it's unlikely that you're going to have more than half a dozen real drivers, a lot of competent people, but people who really drive reform are in short supply. Parliament can only accept a certain amount of great reform at any time, and we had to concentrate on the most urgent issues: the trade-union problem was one of the great issues, the problem of the nationalized industries, which instead of creating wealth, actually consumed it; and the problems of the economy more broadly ... So we simply didn't have the manpower or the parliamentary time to conduct as many reforms as I would have liked. Indeed, probably the electorate would have said, no, no that's too much ... [14]

Norman Tebbit did not mention it in our conversation, but there was one policy area – housing – where the first Thatcher government *did* move swiftly and radically and with a high degree of acclaim from council house tenants. This was the 'right to buy' policy energetically pursued by her environment secretary, Michael Heseltine. It turned out to be the biggest single privatization of the Thatcher era, raising £28 billion over thirteen years. By 1983 half a million households had bought their council houses on generous terms. The figure rose to nearly 1.5 million by 1990. It was one of the most significant shifts engineered by the Conservative governments of the 1980s in terms of both political economy and social policy, and Mrs Thatcher certainly reaped the political reward in the 1983 and 1987 general elections. The downside was that local authorities were forbidden to spend the money raised by the sales on building new social housing.[15]

By the 1990s, council house building had virtually ceased, while contributions from housing associations never replaced the earlier council level. This combined with low private housebuilding in the early 1980s and private renting falling to 8 per cent of households by 1989, was possibly associated with a rise in homelessness.[16] If there was a moment when the country stopped building sufficient homes for its growing population this was probably it.[17] However, on the upside, by 1991 in England only 1 per cent of households lacked a basic amenity of washbasin, shower/bath or WC.[18] While renovation in the public and private sector had improved the quality of the housing stock in the 1980s, by 1988 the proportion of homes that were unfit for human habitation* was only down to 5 per cent from 7 per cent a decade earlier.[19]

This substantial change to the welfare status quo would most definitely not have been electorally replicated if the wind of radical privatization had blown through health care as well as housing. Nigel Lawson, Mrs Thatcher's Chancellor of the Exchequer from 1983 to 1989, had long believed the National Health Service was – and remains – in a class of its own: 'The National Health Service is the closest thing the English have to a religion, with those who practise in it regarding themselves as a priesthood. This made it quite extraordinarily difficult to reform.'[20]

Lawson's (rueful) observation became even more evident during the pandemic. No other British institution has brought people in large numbers out on the streets week after week to clap and rattle their pots and pans in an act of devotion. For me, the NHS has always been and will always remain the greatest gift a nation ever gave itself.

Mrs Thatcher was particularly sensitive to the place of the NHS in the nation's affections. As David Willetts expressed it, 'She was aware of the political appeal of institutions like the NHS. People don't realize it. But she was very cautious.'[21] One of the most famous lines of her long premiership was delivered to the Conservative Party Conference on 8 October 1982: 'Let me make one thing absolutely clear. The National Health Service is safe with us.'[22]

It did not always feel like that at the time – particularly for those on the NHS and the public service front lines. Those wedded to the NHS's 1948 principles of a service free for all at the point of delivery

* Unfit definition according to 1957 and 1985 Housing Acts.

were right to be suspicious of Mrs Thatcher's instincts. For here there *was* something of a difference between her front of house and her back of house. She believed in it for the poor and for everybody, whatever their means, if they encountered what she had called 'the great accidents and the terrible diseases'.[23] For other treatments, those who could afford it should take out private insurance.

Sir Roy Griffiths, the businessman she brought in to review NHS management structures in 1983, knew her private mind very well. His 1983 report began with an unforgettable claim: 'If Florence Nightingale were carrying her lamp through the corridors of the NHS today she would almost certainly be searching for the people in charge,' earning him an entry in *The Oxford Dictionary of Political Quotations*.[24] Later he became her Downing Street health service management adviser.

Griffiths told Nick Timmins:

> She would have liked to have got away from it. If it hadn't been there she would never have invented it ... There was always the feeling that if anything went right with the health service it was because of this magnificent welfare state which the Labour Party had set up in the 1940s – and if anything went wrong it was all the fault of those damn Tories.

Had it been politically possible, said Griffiths, 'she would have got rid of it. But Maggie's great strength was that even if she didn't like something – and this may fly in the face of the popular perception – she was a realist. She knew she couldn't do it.'[25]

Griffiths himself was a great believer in the NHS. He had grown up in a mining community in North Staffordshire and had memories of the 1930s slump. He had worked down the pits as a 'Bevin Boy' during the war and remembered what he called the 'great and glorious days' when Beveridge was published.[26] He had been a scholarship boy at Exeter College, Oxford, where he had met Sir Ken Stowe, Permanent Secretary to the DHSS at the time of his inquiry.

Sir Geoffrey Howe's Treasury took aim at the education, housing and welfare budgets from the start of the first Thatcher government. For the first three years, health was protected from the cuts in line with a Howe-approved pledge made by Patrick Jenkin, the shadow health and social security spokesman, during the 1979 general election campaign.[27]

But health was to become the most fissile element in one of the most explosive leaks of the Thatcher years in September 1982 when details appeared in *The Economist* from a long-range study of public expenditure prepared by the Central Policy Review Staff (CPRS), the Cabinet's 'think tank'. I was working on the magazine at the time and have a vivid memory of the afternoon a colleague brought the story back from Whitehall to the Economist Tower in St James's. In one of the strangest passages of *The Downing Street Years*, Mrs Thatcher sought to downplay the whole exercise and the Cabinet meeting on 9 September 1982 at which it was discussed (described by Nigel Lawson as 'the nearest thing to a Cabinet riot in the history of the Thatcher administration'[28]):

[The CPRS] prepared its own paper to accompany the Treasury paper, which contained a number of very radical options that had never been seriously considered by ministers or by me. They included, for example, sweeping changes in the financing of the National Health Service and extensions of the use of charging. I was horrified by this paper. As soon as I saw it, I pointed out that it would almost certainly be leaked and give a totally false impression. That is exactly what happened.[29]

The CPRS itself, she said, 'had become a freelance "Ministry of Bright Ideas", some of which were sound, some not, many remote from the Government's philosophy'.[30]

The paper trail, when it was declassified, suggested a different story. As Howe put it in the opening paragraph of his paper for the key Cabinet meeting on 9 September, 'The issues we are to discuss on 9 September are among the most important we shall consider at any time in this Parliament. The way we handle them will crucially affect the policies we put forward at the next election, and the performance and shape of the economy for many years to come.'[31]

Howe invited his colleagues to consider ways of breaking free of the mire in which previous administrations had found themselves sinking:

The record of the past two decades has shown all too clearly the dangers of formulating or accepting policy commitments on the assumption of a continuing economic growth which in the event has not been achieved. It has been a failure of successive Governments that they have assumed growth in the economy without taking the steps necessary to make it possible. Successive expenditure reviews have thus followed a dreary cycle of over-optimism followed, inevitably, by retrenchment.[32]

To aid the Cabinet's thinking, the CPRS 'has been asked to examine some of the long-term options open to the Government, especially as regards the possibilities for major structural changes affecting the larger expenditure programmes'.[33]

The CPRS was asked to paint two pictures of a Britain in 1990, as Howe explained to the Cabinet in that September 1982 meeting: a high GDP growth scenario of 2.5 per cent per year between 1980/81 and 1990/91; and low-growth scenario of 0.75 per cent between 1981/2 and 1984/5 followed by 0.5 per cent between 1985/6 and 1990/91.[34] The team that produced the study was led by Alan Bailey, one of the finest minds on the spending side in post-war Whitehall, on secondment to the CPRS.

It was the low-growth portrait that burnt the pages of the report and seared across the nation's imagination when it was leaked. It is of particular interest for the present study, because if the options of deep structural change to the welfare state had been followed it would have led to a significantly different and much diminished duty of care in Britain. The key elements in its depiction of the removal of the jewel from the crown of the post-war settlement, the National Health Service, were as follows:

PRIVATE HEALTH INSURANCE
Proposal
The working population would be obliged by law to obtain insurance to cover the costs of health care for themselves and their dependants. Premiums would relate to the family's risks, not their means, and so the poor would need help with meeting the costs . . .

Arguments in favour
- This proposal offers the prospect of a very large cut in the costs of health care to the tax payer.
- The public would have its horizons of choices and of responsibility greatly widened . . .

- Although initially at least NHS hospitals could remain in state hands, trading like nationalized industries, they could be progressively privatized . . .

Problems

Even though a free state service would be retained for the uninsured and possibly for the non-working population, for the majority the change would represent the abolition of the NHS. This would be immensely controversial.[35]

The last sentence is one of the greatest Whitehall understatements I have ever encountered.

Add to this large cuts in teacher numbers and £1 billion a year out of the five- to sixteen-year-olds' budget, charging wealthier parents fees for their children's schooling, charging students for their degree courses (there were at this time no fees), plus holding social security payment increases below the levels of inflation,[36] and this was a prospectus that truly undid the post-war settlement and dramatically reduced the state's duty of care. *The Economist* appropriately illustrated its scoop with a collage of the key 1940s statutes, the cutting edge of the attack on the five giants, with a cross scored through them.[37]

The Cabinet discussion was deemed so sensitive that the Cabinet Secretary, Sir Robert Armstrong, placed its minutes in a 'limited circulation annex'. We don't know which minister said what because the Cabinet Secretary's notebook for 1982 still hasn't been declassified. But we do know that the veteran Lord Chancellor, Lord Hailsham, said 'my hair stood on end, and at my age that takes some doing'.[38] As Quintin Hogg, the young MP for Oxford during the war, Hailsham had been a central figure in the Tory Reform Committee set up to nudge the Conservative Party towards a warmer response to the Beveridge Report.[39]

Thus invited to contemplate tearing up the post-war settlement, several ministers in Mrs Thatcher's Cabinet recoiled. For others, as David Howell told me nearly forty years later, 'it was one day, one day we will come to do something like this'.[40] Student fees apart, they still haven't. Here's a flavour of that heated Cabinet discussion as captured in the ever-cool language of the Cabinet Secretary:

Government must not seem to be adopting a purely negative stance . . . public expenditure and taxation lay within the Government's control; industrial performance did not . . . Considerable change could be achieved through greater efficiency. [This sounds very much like Michael Heseltine.] . . . It was likely that unemployment would remain at high levels for many years. The Government should devise policies to deal with this situation. Otherwise the social consequences, particularly among young people, would be extremely serious.[41]

Hugo Young, political editor of *The Sunday Times*, Thatcher-watcher and her early biographer, recorded that 'when the voices were collected she said, in what one minister called a petulant huff, "All right then, shelve it." '[42]

It was one of those rare might-have-been moments, like the decision on whether to float the pound in February 1952, when ministers are presented with the possibility of a truly fundamental change, a breakthrough into a new landscape in which longstanding constraints are severed and things are never the same again.

That Cabinet meeting had consequences. Not only was the essential architecture of Britain's welfare state preserved in recognizable form, but also Mrs Thatcher very swiftly had to deliver her 'safe in our hands' pledge on the NHS. What was abolished right after her election victory in May 1983, however, was the CPRS think tank. In producing that eminently leakable report-too-far it had signed its own death warrant.

The Beveridge model was not torn up, but as the fortieth anniversary of the report approached a case could be made for re-examining it. On the very day of that landmark, 4 December 1982, *The Times* published a first leader headlined 'WANTED: A NEW BEVERIDGE' written (anonymously, of course) by David Walker and myself. We talked of the 1940s faith that 'could move mountains. Forty years on that faith has evaporated. Welfare has become discredited both among those who depend on it and those who pay for it.'

Unbeknownst to David and me, Norman Fowler, who had replaced Patrick Jenkin as Secretary of State for Health and Social Services in September 1981, shared our belief in the need for a new Beveridge. Following the election in June 1983, rightly anticipating that the new

Chancellor of the Exchequer, Nigel Lawson, would mount raids against his budget, Fowler headed him off by setting up a cohort of reviews on pensions, supplementary benefits, housing benefit and child benefit. In April 1984 he told the House of Commons that together they amounted to the biggest review of social security since Beveridge.[43]

Fowler regarded the social security system as 'a Leviathan almost with a life of its own'.[44] Even Mrs Thatcher, the diligent junior pensions and national insurance minister in the early 1960s, had failed to keep up with the spread of benefits. As a senior DHSS official told Nick Timmins:

> We had a lot of trouble educating her on how much the whole thing had grown since she had been there. She had only been concerned with pensions and national insurance – not with the poor, because in her day that was still being run by the National Assistance Board. The benefits had proliferated madly between then and 1979 when she came in. So we had great problems getting her to take on board that there were now, I think, thirty-four social security benefits and she was probably familiar with four or five.[45]

For her part, Mrs Thatcher told the *New York Times*, just before the Fowler reviews started, that social security was 'a time bomb' that had to be defused 'before it is too late'.[46]

The reviews turned out to be less than bomb-disposal squads, though some of the resulting changes were significant, especially the ending of the formerly consensual state earnings-related pension scheme (SERPS) in its original form. Incentives would be offered to encourage its members to opt out into private provision. It worked. By 1993 five million people had left, and only a shrivelled remnant of SERPS survived for those who remained. This represented 'the one large part of the welfare state where the Thatcher government did succeed in rolling back the frontiers'.[47] Changes, too, were made to supplementary benefit.[48]

Mrs Thatcher's 'time-bomb' ticked on. And in November 1990, the fuses she had lit beneath her own premiership (the poll tax and that PM-slayer, Europe) saw her losing No. 10 after a leadership challenge from Michael Heseltine had rendered her fatally wounded. Her successor was not Heseltine (of whom more in a moment) but John

Major. In the very year the CPRS had imagined the possible demise of the NHS she was replaced by a One Nation politician to his last fibre who, on the very first page of his memoirs, declared that what attracted him 'from the very first moment I truly thought about politics' was '[t]he Conservatism of Harold Macmillan, Iain Macleod and Rab Butler [who] understood and spoke the language of compassion.'[49]

There is one recitative from the Thatcher years that, with its distinctive dissenting tone, jarred with her own unmistakeable melodies and sprang from the mind and voice of her nemesis Michael Heseltine – all captured in perhaps the most remarkable Cabinet submission of the 1980s. In early July 1981, after three weeks pacing the streets of Liverpool following the disturbances in Toxteth, Heseltine wrote a memorandum to Thatcher with the subject line 'IT TOOK A RIOT'. Although he didn't explicitly say so, he was walking the streets where, as in many of the inner cities of Britain, the five giants still stalked nearly four decades after Beveridge had identified them. Although there had been strides made in housing, medicine and education, unemployment from a low in 1945 (1.6 per cent) had been steadily increasing until 1970, and more steeply to a peak of 13 per cent in 1982.[50] In addition there was a problem in that the 1980 changes to the supplementary benefit system left both staff and claimants confused and families with children in real hardship.[51] Heseltine told me years later that he wrote the report, 'to shock as well as inform'.[52] In that he certainly succeeded. I've never read a Cabinet memo opening quite like this:

PRIME MINISTER
IT TOOK A RIOT

No sentiment [i.e. it took a riot to gain attention] was more frequently expressed to me during the time I spent with Tim Raison* in Merseyside. There is no escaping the uncomfortable implications.[53]

It's hard to remember today quite how shocking the worst disturbances of 1981 were at the time (Brixton 11–14 April; Southall, Toxteth and Moss Side 3 July and 4–8 July), with lesser but still

---

* Minister of State in the Home Office

disturbing incidents in other towns and cities. Riots were, sadly, all too familiar in Northern Ireland since the 'Troubles' had re-erupted in 1968, but they were rare on the mainland. The spring and summer of 1981 shook that part of our national self-image we labelled 'social peace'.

It really concerned Michael Heseltine, as he recalled in 2016:

> . . . that's what everybody said, everywhere I went, 'You've only come because of the riot' . . . And that's why I did come. That's why I said to Margaret . . . 'Look we can just treat this like yobs on the street, we can say public law and order demands backing the police, and we all under-stand and feel the importance of that. But I think there's something worse there, I think there's something more profound and I want your permission to walk the streets of Liverpool and come back and tell you what I think it is.' She gave me permission to do that. I spent three weeks doing it.[54]

On 16 July the Cabinet approved Heseltine's proposal that he visit Merseyside to fact-find.[55] He sent his report to Mrs Thatcher and their colleagues on 13 August. Beveridge's giants walked its twenty-one pages.

I first met Michael Heseltine in May 1982 in Liverpool on one of his weekly visits to Merseyside. I was on the staff of *The Economist* at the time, and he drove me (it was just the two of us) around Tox-teth in his big blue Jaguar. It was plain to me that Liverpool and its singular spirit had come to captivate him, which I understood; it was my father's home city. Michael breathed optimism as he showed me the projects underway and improvements planned.

'IT TOOK A RIOT', however, reads bleakly – as a prick to con-science and a spur to action. He painted a portrait of a once-great commercial, trading and manufacturing city that the national and international economies were increasingly passing by.

> There are 75,000 fewer jobs [in Merseyside] than in 1976. Unemploy-ment rates have been consistently well above national figures since before the last war, and are now [at] 18% . . . In Liverpool alone 55,000 are without a job – 18,000 of them concentrated in the core of the city . . . Nor are prospects good.

Among the people who have left the area have been middle managers who have gone to the suburbs for better homes, schools and surroundings. More significant still has been the loss to Liverpool of the headquarters of its major firms ... and decisions are made elsewhere by the nationals and multinationals ...

Local government – 'the Corpy' – is remote, and much of its housing indescribable. There are 38,000 outstanding repairs notices for the city's 78,000 dwellings.

The unemployment figures ... are appalling in themselves. But one has to talk to the people day after day to understand just what hopelessness means. Young people expect to be unemployed by parents who expect them to be unemployed. We have to realize the hollowness of the phrase 'parental responsibility' when unemployed parents – many of them single – live cooped up with energetic kids with nothing to do, and nowhere to go. If parents have lost their sense of purpose, they cannot command their children's respect ...

The crime rate is high, educational attainment low ...

Relations between black and white in the area [Toxteth] seem tolerable. But there is undoubtedly a serious breakdown of confidence between a great part of the population in the area and the police ...

Following this section – part Disraeli novel, part Beveridge Report – Heseltine lists the pluses. (On her own copy – which is preserved in The National Archives – Mrs Thatcher numbers them one to seven, in her own hand.) They range through the sporting, the cultural, the architectural, the higher educational and the new Liverpool Urban Development Corporation. He rose to his peroration and the plea for a new urban duty of care:

Merseyside's economic and social problems are severe. So too are those of other conurbations ... It is in my judgement our inescapable duty to respond to the problems of the main urban areas with urgency and resource. I opened this report by referring frankly to the inescapable connection between the riots and the visit which I was asked to make. I cannot stress too strongly that my conclusion and proposals are not based on my fear of further riots. They are based on my belief that the conditions and prospects in the cities are not compatible with the traditions of social justice and national even-handedness on which our Party prides itself.[56]

Finally came the policy recommendations for Liverpool specifically and for the inner cities generally. Here lay the challenge to the government's existing approach and to Mrs Thatcher, who had declared in the opening sentence of the Conservatives' first spending White Paper two years earlier, 'Public expenditure is at the heart of Britain's present economic difficulties.'[57] The key recommendation arising from Heseltine's three weeks on the streets of Liverpool was that a nationwide regeneration plan should be crafted with '[t]he existence of a ministerial presence in each conurbation [that] should enable a co-ordinated and area-based industrial and employment policy to be pursued, using both existing <u>and additional</u>* resources ... [For] I believe that now is the time to make a substantial commitments of extra resources to Merseyside and other hard-pressed conurbations.'[58]

The Treasury, those 'congenital snag-hunters', as the first post-war Chancellor of the Exchequer, Hugh Dalton, is said to have called them,[59] were deeply sceptical and powerfully resistant to the Heseltine manifesto. On 4 September, ahead of a meeting of an ad hoc ministerial group on 'IT TOOK A RIOT' later that month, Chancellor Howe wrote a letter to Mrs Thatcher in which he picked up on an option laid out, but rejected, in a CPRS report on Merseyside published two months earlier: 'Should our aim be to stabilize the inner cities – as Michael and the CPRS have suggested for Liverpool – or is this to pump water uphill? Should we go rather for "managed decline"?'[60]

The ministerial group was stacked against Heseltine. There would be no large-scale inner urban initiative. But he was permitted to continue what Geoffrey Howe called 'his "godfather" role for Merseyside',[61] and he energetically pursued what might be called One-Nation-in-a-single-department – Environment – in the hope that he 'would come back to [his] colleagues and say "Look, it works. Now let's do it on the scale that the crisis demands."'[62] He was still pressing for this when Mrs Thatcher sent him to the Ministry of Defence in January 1983.

* The double underlining is Mrs Thatcher's.

There is long-term historical value to be mined from 'IT TOOK A RIOT' as it captures Merseyside at a moment when the Gini coefficient was beginning to move strongly in the direction of greater inequality (0.27 in 1971, 0.26 in 1981, 0.34 in 1991[63]), with all the disquiet that movement generates and social-economic stress it brings.

There are many factors – local, regional, national and global – that go into the making of the sixth giant: Inequality. In national terms, a state that routinely spends about 40 per cent of its GDP on public purposes is very different from one which absorbs 25 per cent or less. That said, tax changes within a 40 per cent nation can make an important difference in Gini terms, and cutting taxes was a priority for her governments from the start. In June 1979 Geoffrey Howe's first budget lowered the basic rate of income tax from 33 per cent to 30 per cent and the highest rate from 83 per cent to 60 per cent; value added tax was raised from 8 per cent to 15 per cent to fund this – a substantial shift from progressive direct taxation to indirect. In 1988 Nigel Lawson, Howe's successor, cut the basic rate to 25 per cent and the top rate to 40 per cent.

With widening inequality in the UK more of the benefits of increased wealth went to the richer and considerably less to the poorer; health and other outcomes followed the same path. This is one theme of Richard Wilkinson and Kate Pickett's book *The Spirit Level: Why Equality is Better for Everyone*.[64] It is well established that in most developed countries, the higher someone's social class and income, the better their health and social outcomes are likely to be. For example in the UK 'although life expectancy increased for all social groups between the periods 1972–6 and 2002–05, health inequalities—gaps in life expectancies between social groups—have persisted'[65].

By 2009 the UK was also performing very poorly in comparison with similar European countries on mortality among the under-fives as well as showing significantly worse outcomes for those suffering social deprivation.[66] The USA, with a consistently higher Gini coefficient, has from the mid-1980s a higher infant mortality rate[67] and lower life expectancy than the UK.[68]

Tax changes were placed in a bigger bundle – which also contained a weakening of the bargaining power of trade unions, the privatization of nationalized industries, the continuing de-industrialization of the

British economy, the abolition of wage councils and the rise of part-time working. This is a significant part of the explanation of why 'by 1992 a quarter of the population had an income under half the average, against only 10 per cent in 1979'.[69] One big and growing element was the spectrum of inequality magnified by *international* factors captured in the portmanteau word 'globalization'.

Globalization has proven to be a particularly wrathful and relentless obstacle on the road to social justice. In a discussion on BBC Radio 4's *Rethinks* series in June 2020, Andrew McAfee, co-founder and co-director of the MIT Initiative on the Digital Economy, said, 'Inequality is a race between technology and education. Technology tends to increase inequality and education tends to lessen the inequality because it provides skills to people.'[70] McAfee was drawing, he said, on the works of Jan Tinbergen, the Dutch economist and joint first ever winner of the Nobel Prize for Economics in 1969, who made the critical connection between rapidly developing technology and increasing inequality in the mid-1970s when the winds of globalization began to blow.[71]

As the tax changes flowed through the 1980s UK economy, the rise of the so-called 'tiger' low-wage economies in the Far East and Asia drew manufacturing jobs away from the old industrial areas. Globalization also created a world market, with its high salaries for senior figures in finance, commerce, IT and oil and gas producing income differentials that brought enormous resentment and a widespread sense of injustice.

None of this appeared to worry a Gini-proof Mrs Thatcher, the greatest celebrant of free-market capitalism ever to occupy No. 10. The political impossibility of privatizing the NHS having prevailed, finding a new method of injecting market principles into the central institution of the welfare state became a cause dear to her in what turned out to be the twilight years of her premiership. The idea of the 'internal market' with its split between 'purchaser and provider' was brought to British shores by Professor Alain Enthoven, a specialist in health provision management at Stanford University in California.[72] A home-grown suggestion from Ian McColl, Professor of Surgery at Guy's Hospital, for the recreation of independent hospitals marched in step with this.

The combined result was *Working for Patients*, a White Paper that was 'given the most lavish launch ever for a government initiative'[73] on 31 January 1989, when Kenneth Clarke, the ever-genial health minister, was carried by boat from Westminster down the Thames to a studio in Limehouse to beam the message to medical staff in cities across the land.

Nick Timmins was present:

> There were essentially three ideas: the internal market with its purchaser/provider split, with health authorities doing the purchasing and hospitals, both public and private, doing the providing. But onto this was grafted self-governing hospitals (later to be known as NHS Trusts as part of the massaging of language that was to occur), and a second set of purchasers in the form of GP budget-holders (later to become fund-holders in an attempt to avoid connotations of budgets running out).[74]

This led to a huge and protracted row between Clarke and the doctors' union, the British Medical Association, who ran a brilliant poster campaign against him. My favourite was:

WHAT DO YOU CALL A MAN WHO IGNORES MEDICAL ADVICE? MR CLARKE

He nonetheless prevailed and, in many ways, his attempt to mix the 'social' and the 'market' set the pattern for the governments to come after Mrs Thatcher had entered her political Valhalla.

What of education – Tinbergen's antidote to the inequalities carried by the winds of globalization? Here, too, the late 1980s saw a significant change with Ken Baker's Education Act 1988. When she appointed him in 1986, Baker expected Mrs Thatcher, as a former education secretary herself, to give him

> [a] list of things to do. Not at all; she said to me, 'The problem in education at the moment is the teachers' strike. It's been going on for eighteen months – this is something that must be resolved, settled. And on all the other issues, I want you to think about them and come back to me in six weeks' time and tell me what you think you want to do.'

Baker told me thirty years later that he was 'a bit flabbergasted' because

> I knew what I wanted to do. I wanted to get more technical schools. I wanted to get computers into schools in a much bigger way. I wanted to make some schools independent of local authorities and I wanted a national curriculum. I took them back to her and she said she liked what she saw . . . [and] . . . We had things like National Curriculum, we had tests, we had league tables, we had City Technology Colleges independent of local authorities, we had grant maintained schools . . . [75]

Ken Baker is still the great evangelist of technical education and has spent his seventies and eighties in partnership with industry seeding University Technical Colleges across the land.

One part of our 2016 conversation still has great relevance for discussions about After Covid Britain:

> HENNESSY: One of the great spinal cords in your career, Ken, is the passion for technical education. Now why is it that we didn't get it right? It's there in the 1944 Education Act which was Rab Butler's great moment. Sir David Eccles, Minister of Education in '55 really wanted it, as did his Prime Minister Anthony Eden. And yet it didn't happen. Now what is it about our country that is resistant to this concept of technical education, which many people would say is absolutely critical and always was to our industrial and economic future?
>
> BAKER: Snobbery is the answer.
>
> HENNESSY: Simple as that?
>
> BAKER: There were 300 technical schools in existence in 1945. But they were closed over the next five or six years because everybody wanted to go to the school on the hill . . . and they didn't want to go down to the school in the town with shabby premises, dirty jobs, greasy rags [and] it's still desperately needed.[76]

It is. It was to Mrs Thatcher's great credit that she let Ken Baker run it as his big theme as education secretary.

As long as anybody is interested in Margaret Thatcher's duty of care, there is a line from an interview with *Woman's Own* magazine in 1987 that will flash up on the dashboard of memory: 'There is no such thing as society.' To her lasting (and justified) irritation, few people allowed her to finish her paragraph, which concluded: 'There are individual men and women, and there are families. And no government can do anything except through people, and people must look after themselves first. It's our duty to look after ourselves and then to look after our neighbour.'[77]

In her memoir, she explained at some length the wider thoughts behind her words: 'The error to which I was objecting was the confusion of society with the state as the helper of first resort . . . society for me was not an excuse, it was a source of obligation.'[78]

Point taken. But 'no such thing as society' wasn't the most glorious rallying cry for a nation. And it's hard to imagine any of her post-war predecessors in No. 10 thinking that, let alone saying it.

From the outset of her governments, Mrs Thatcher saw the levels of public spending she inherited in 1979 as fundamental to the UK's economic problems. How effective was she in rolling back welfare budgets?

The picture is mixed. As a proportion of GDP there were some significant reductions (housing and education), but the biggest absorbers of public money (health and social security) remained noticeably resistant to her appetite for cuts (see Table 3).

This was her unfinished business. She left in November 1990 as restlessly as she had arrived in May 1979. She had so much more to do but the majority of her Cabinet wished for another pair of hands to do it – and for a quieter life.

Table 3: UK public expenditure as a percentage of GDP, 1978/9 vs 1990/91.

Department	1978/9	1990/91
Housing	2.6%	0.9%
Education	5.4%	4.8%
Health	4.6%	5.0%
Social security	9.9%	10.6%

5

Social Market

My own life history was different from that of most of my predecessors at Number 10. My Conservatism came from what I saw, what I felt, and what I did as well as what I read. It shaped what I wanted to do in office. When I was young my family had depended on public services. I have never forgotten – and never will – what the National Health Service meant to my parents, or the security it gave despite all the harsh blows life dealt them.

John Major, 1999[1]

I've always argued for free markets with a social conscience . . . the last decade or two capitalism has been working not as it should do. It made us very, very much richer for about twenty years up till the financial crash of 2008 but the rewards were being distributed ever more unevenly and too large a section of the population were being left behind.

Kenneth Clarke reflecting on Covid and after,
22 June 2020[2]

TB [Tony Blair] said he was rested, had had a great time and was really up for the battles ahead. He had read Nick Timmins's book on the welfare state and it had clearly made an impression on him. We had blundered our way through the pre-Christmas period but we still lacked a clear route map for the issue as a whole.

Alastair Campbell, 5 January 1998[3]

*We should never lose sight of the ambition to make this coun-
try a far fairer and far more equal society.*

Gordon Brown, 8 May 2000[4]

*They [reforms] were needed [in 2010] not just to fix our
broken economy, but to mend our broken society. Thirteen
years of Labour had left us with a school system that, despite
the beginnings of worthwhile reform, encouraged mediocrity.
We had a welfare system that discouraged work [and] a
health system that was struggling under the weight of new
demands and bureaucracy.*

David Cameron, recalling May 2010 in 2019[5]

All incoming prime ministers since 1979 seem to have felt on day one
as if a huge, insatiably demanding behemoth was lurking waiting for
them in the shadows of Downing Street, when they arrived fresh from
receiving the Queen's commission to form a government – invisible to
the pack of journalists and photographers, but there nonetheless. And
this behemoth, the very instrument intended to see off the Beveridge
giants, carried its own distinctive label: THE WELFARE STATE.

John Major prepared his touchstone remarks for his assumption of
office in the car between Buckingham Palace and Downing Street.
Mrs Thatcher had wanted him rather than Douglas Hurd and above
all Michael Heseltine to succeed her. But had she seen them, she would
have been appalled by the words he scribbled down on a scrap of
paper setting out '[s]ome of the things that I believed. My hopes of
creating a nation at ease with itself. I wanted to put behind us the Poll
Tax riots [in Trafalgar Square 31 March 1990], the exclusion of so
many minority groups and those left outside the race to prosperity
that we had seen in the 1980s . . .'[6]

This captured his personal sense of duty of care – his way of building 'a nation at ease with itself', as he said on the steps of No. 10 in
what Thatcherites saw instantly as a reproach to their deposed
champion.[7]

It's interesting that Major didn't craft a few extra words about

Europe. For it was Europe as well as the poll tax – with which Thatcher had been seeking to replace local authority rates – plus her relentless style as 'empress' of Downing Street* that brought her down. This set a pattern for Europe-as-Conservative-premier-slayer. Within two years it seriously and permanently weakened his own premiership on so-called 'Black Wednesday' in 1992; brought down David Cameron in 2016 and slew Theresa May in 2019.

For Geoffrey Howe had been able to take no more when, in the House of Commons on 1 November 1990, Margaret Thatcher set her face against Britain ever joining a single currency and any idea that a federal EU should emerge. 'No, no, no,' she said in her finest primary schoolteacher style, quite softly, each 'no' quieter than the last. Howe resigned and Heseltine mounted the leadership challenge that would see John Major into the premiership. 'Who would have thought it?'[8] he is reported to have said opening his first Cabinet meeting. Chris Patten told his favourite lobby correspondent that ministers felt like the 'Prisoners' Chorus' in Beethoven's *Fidelio*, emerging from the dungeons blinking into the sunshine and singing of freedom.[9]

I've long suspected that perhaps the greatest regret John Major had was his inability to do more about the aspirations he wrote down on that little piece of paper on the car journey from the Palace to No. 10 on 28 November 1990. Many years later, I had a chance to ask him about it:

> HENNESSY: I've always had the impression ... that if you could do it again ... [t]here are certain things you would have done if you'd followed your instincts ... One of which would have been to put a lot more funding into the NHS ... Do you have some regrets that you weren't even more John Major, the inner John Major, than you actually turned out to be [during] '92– '97?
>
> MAJOR: Well, it wasn't just political ambitions. It was money ... the terrible economic recession we had at the beginning of the 1990s: we spent the best part of five to six

---

* Major's description – he called his memoir's chapter on her demise 'An Empress Falls'.

years putting that right . . . in terms of social reforms I would like to have made . . . we didn't have the money.

HENNESSY: What would they have been?

MAJOR: . . . Firstly, education. Not having had much of it, I'm very much in favour of other people getting it, and widening it . . . I would have liked to have upgraded the education profession . . . I would have looked to the provision of more homes, largely small units in the inner cities . . . And of course I would have wanted to make reforms to the health system. Now I believe, with the money that we had built up in the economy by '97 that we too, had we won the election, would have put a lot more money into the health service, and looked at reforms of the health service. So I shall live with regret to my dying day that I did not have the wherewithal, and was not in a political position, to go down the route of these reforms which were the sort of things I wished to do from the first moment I dreamed of going into politics.[10]

Major's ministers relished his early collegiate Cabinet Room style. Several of them appreciated, as William Waldegrave put it, that the new PM 'sensed that the electorate now wanted to find a way of humanizing the irreversible Thatcherite revolution' (though, Waldegrave continued, he 'never found the language' in which to convey this fully).[11]

After his Downing Street years, however, he did find those words in one of the most vivid passages in his memoirs, the section dealing with the thinking behind his Citizen's Charter idea, which he had cooked up as Chief Secretary to the Treasury before the premiership gave him his big chance to implement it:

In addition to improving the quality of public service, I wanted to raise the standing of those hundreds of thousands of people who work selflessly in all branches of them . . .

On the other hand, life experience had not left me naively starry-eyed about the public services. As a young man without money or privilege behind me, I had also come up against the dark side of the coin. Telephones answered grudgingly or not at all. Booths closed while customers were kept waiting . . . Remote council offices where, after a long bus journey, there was no one available to see you who really knew about the issue ... This was the weekly reality for millions of people in Britain up to the end of the 1980s ... They deserved a personal, prompt and quality service.

The conservative view of the political right in the 1980s was that this could only be done by privatization. In some instances that was the right medicine ... [but] to rest our fortunes entirely on privatization seemed to me to be too ideological, too lacking in vision or ambition. The services that could not and should not be privatized – chiefly schools and hospitals – were important to millions of daily lives.[12]

Here lay instincts utterly removed from most of the radical options in the 1982 CPRS paper, though he was a privatizing PM. Railways, perhaps the most controversial of all the denationalizations, were placed in the private sector on his watch.

What he called 'the Tory Right's attitude problem'[13] caused John Major, a genuinely sensitive man, much grief during his six-and-a-half year premiership (not least over Europe) and they patronized him about his devotion to the Citizen's Charter. The 1991 White Paper that founded the charter turned out to be like the mind and instincts of its begetter – a bringer of steady, unspectacular, incremental improvement. By the time the Blair tide swept Major out of Downing Street in May 1997, no fewer than forty-two individual charters had sprinkled 'performance indicators' and league tables across the whole range of public services plus a serious injection of 'customer care' into the delivery of said services, with providers competing for 'Charter Marks'.[14]

The 'market' slice of John Major's version of the 'social market' was outlined in *Competing for Quality*, a second 1991 White Paper, which made 'market testing' a running principle of government whereby 'departments and Executive Agencies will in future set targets for testing new areas of activity in the market to see if alternative sources give better service and value for money'.[15]

It was John Major's misfortune that such measures – for him so central to his mission – bored many people at the time with their earnestness and have since been overshadowed by the European Question. This holed his premiership below the waterline on 16 September

1992, Black Wednesday, when the pound sterling, hammered by the currency markets, left the European Exchange Rate Mechanism, igniting a searing civil war within the Conservative Party and worsening his relationship with his predecessor.[16] 'He is not the Thatcherite you think he is,' warned Michael Forsyth when she told him to vote for Major.[17] It seemed to shock her when she discovered this for herself. In March 1991, only four months after her departure, her dam burst. As Major wrote in his memoir, 'she publicly attacked what she saw as my "tendency to undermine" what she had done in office. I was, she said, giving more power to government.'[18]

Even on his big theme of improved public services Major is mostly remembered as the PM who denationalized the railways. Also forgotten is the similarity between his version of social market policies and the Christian Democratic political tradition of western Europe – though here he drew the line at the extra workers' rights proposed in the EC's 'Social Chapter' of the Maastricht Treaty. He secured a British opt-out in December 1991, arguing that the 'proposals for a Social Chapter would reverse our domestic reforms to the labour market and push up unemployment'.[19] This successful negotiation (Major was a naturally gifted negotiator) helped him to a surprise twenty-one-seat victory in the April 1992 general election and, for a short while, defanged his party's and his Cabinet's Eurosceptics – but only until the humiliation of sterling's collapse on Black Wednesday and Germany's refusal to help avert it.

The Conservative right never forgave him for not being Margaret. She grew more strident in her disdain for him to the point where she thought her legacy would be safer in the hands of Tony Blair, who had become Labour leader following John Smith's untimely death in May 1994. Thatcher's authorized biographer, Charles Moore, captures the way her private views seeped out: 'She became fond of saying to private inquirers, "The trouble is that we converted our opponents." She said that Blair was "a patriot" and that "He'll protect my legacy", by which she meant chiefly her trade union reforms, her privatizations and her commitment to free markets.'[20]

Major himself told Moore that she had said 'People would be perfectly safe with Tony Blair.'[21]

In May 1997, the country thought so too. Blair entered No 10 with

Table 4: UK annual economic growth, 1991-7.

1991	1992	1992	1994	1995	1996	1997
-1.4%	+0.1%	+2.3%	+3.6%	+2.2%	+2.3%	+3.6%

the force of a 179-seat majority in the House of Commons behind him, as well as inheriting a respectable trend of economic growth from the Major administration after the recession of the early 1990s (see Table 4).

At this point Idleness was over twice as bad as it had been in 1945–51 (unemployment rate 6.5 per cent[22] vs <3 per cent*). The rate had followed the condition of the economy; it had peaked in 1982 at 13 per cent, dropping to 5.8 per cent in 1990 before rising sharply to 10.3 per cent in 1993 and then dropping again.[23] The school leaving age had been raised to sixteen in 1972, so in practice Ignorance was tackled and most now stayed until after the GCE exams should have been taken. During the Second World War only 14 per cent were awarded any grade on the school certificate, whereas in 1991 65 per cent got at least 1 GCSE at the equivalent grade; however over 9 per cent of boys and over 6 per cent of girls still left with no graded GCSE result.[24] In terms of Want, child benefit had replaced family allowance and tax allowances in 1979 and was now paid to the mother for all children. This particularly benefited families where little tax was paid as they now received more. But households in relative poverty (less than 60 per cent of median income) were 19 per cent higher than in 1961 (13 per cent).[25] While most houses now had a WC and a bath-room,[26] there were still 4 per cent declared unfit for human habitation in 1996 (mostly in the rental sector), and a decline from 12 per cent in 1967.[27] Squalor also loomed with homelessness, which had risen in England† from 51,000 households in 1978 to 143,000 in 1992.[28] It continued to rise and in 2005 there were 267,000 accepted as home-less.[29] And finally, Disease. While more and more people were being treated and many health indicators were improved because of the revolution in the quality, scope and effectiveness of treatments, the

* The figures for unemployment are an average over the year.
† This does not include rough sleepers unless they have applied for housing.

NHS's ability to deliver a good service remained dependent on the size of its budget from the government. When Labour came to power in 1997, total numbers waiting for hospital treatment stood at 1.3 million, the highest since the start of the NHS,[30] and those on the waiting list for more than a year had risen to 50,000 in 1999.[31]

As a result British politics, its welfare state and its duty of care were his for the remaking – or almost. His chief political competitor now lived next door and sat opposite him at the Cabinet table. Gordon Brown, Chancellor of the Exchequer, for long the senior figure of the two, had plans to turn the Treasury into a ministry of welfare and social policy.

In a spectacular failure of political management, Blair brought in Frank Field to undertake a root-and-branch review of the welfare system – a new Beveridge, no less – without making him Secretary of State for Social Security. Field was one of the freest independent spirits ever to sit on the Commons benches in the post-war years. He was also deeply immersed in duties of care having made his name as a young man as director of the highly respected Child Poverty Action Group. Making up the welfare quartet was Harriet Harman, who was appointed Secretary of State for Social Security with Field as her minister of state. It was a fissile mixture, 'because' as she told me 'Tony Blair – I didn't know at the time – wanted to appoint Frank Field as Secretary of State for Social Security and send a huge message that there was going to be a transformation of social security. But Gordon had not wanted Frank Field to be Secretary of State, not least because Frank Field believed in universality rather than ... means testing.'[32] The great caesura that came to be known as the TB/GBies was evident from the start.

It was bound to end badly. Alastair Campbell, Blair's press secretary, is the great chronicler of the emotional cartography of the Blair premiership. In his diary entry for 26 February 1998 he captures the moment when the welfare scrap really got to Blair: 'TB and I left for Paddington and the train to Reading [for a welfare reform consultation]. In the car, as ever, he went over his various current angsts ... He was alarmed about Harriet. He thought Frank Field's White Paper was crap. He felt they were both proving to be useless.'[33]

The five giants looked on while Labour's welfare factions slugged it out between No. 10, No. 11 and the two ministers in the Department of Social Security.

Blair's great worry about Field's proposals was cost. A private source told Nick Timmins of Blair's reaction when the estimate came in from Field's own department: 'Only ten billion, Frank?'[34] The germ of Field's thinking was a new bargain for the nation, a new common bonding between the 'haves' and the 'have nots'. I recall a conversation with Frank at the time. He felt this might be the last time it was possible to persuade the better off to buy into the idea of such a measure of redistribution based on the principle of 'compulsory universalism', as Nick Timmins described it.[35]

Field's key idea was a new kind of social insurance for old age. The middle class would be required by law to build up a second pension in the private or the mutual sectors, which they would pay for themselves. The government would stump up for the lower paid and the poor. Field reckoned this new duty of care would only add £3 billion a year to the welfare bill rather than the £10 billion official figure that so shocked Blair.[36]

Brown prevailed – the mightiest (and chippiest) Chancellor of the Exchequer of modern times. Both Field and Harman left the government in the July 1998 reshuffle (she returned; he did not). In the judgement of John Rentoul, Blair's biographer, 'It set back welfare reform by two years.'[37]

When I rang Frank during the Covid summer to confirm my recollection of our conversation in 1997 (which he did), I suggested it was universalism's last throw. He agreed, but offered the intriguing thought that putting social care right post-pandemic might revive universalism if the country could be persuaded they were paying a social insurance contribution rather than a tax.[38]

Alistair Darling, Harriet Harman's replacement, a shrewd, steady, effective and collegiate operator in all the ministerial jobs he held, shared Brown's approach to welfare. He had been Chief Secretary to the Treasury before moving to social security, and in his first speech as Secretary of State for Work and Pensions he declared that 'state spending should be concentrated where it is needed most'.[39]

Gordon Brown's big idea was 'Welfare to Work'. He was a bone-bred redistributionist and his (successful) tactic was to do this without frightening the money markets. The ace Brown-watcher, Bill Keegan, described it as a mixture of tax concessions [through the 1999 Working Families Tax Credit] or extra payments to the poor and minimizing concessions to the upper income groups ... sometimes referred to ... as 'redistribution by stealth', but it was more a policy of alleviation of poverty combined with promotion of incentives to work. The upper echelons of income earners continued to enjoy low marginal tax rates *and* a world in which very higher salaries were much publicized but little questioned.[40]

Table 5: UK annual growth in GDP, 1997–2001.

1997	1998	1999	2000	2001
3.6%	3.4%	3.1%	3.1%	2.6%

With steady annual growth in GDP (see Table 5), such a policy of redistribution without pain was successful in its own terms, but the curse of Gini still fell across the land: there was little change in the overall measurement on inequality of income between 1997 and 2001. Nigel Lawson even went so far as to tease New Labour for continuing 'the good work of Thatcherism'.[41]*

Tony Blair's big idea was the abolition of child poverty within a generation (i.e. twenty years), a pledge he made, appropriately enough, in his Beveridge Lecture at Toynbee Hall in East London on 18 March 1999. Blair himself described what one might see as his personal New Beveridge as a 'historic aim'.[42] Here there was unanimity of purpose with his Chancellor: 'In Brown's hands that aim was turned into halving child poverty by 2010 and abolishing it by 2020, the measure being that no child should live in a family on less than 60% of the median income.'[43]

The Toynbee Hall child poverty pledge was a truly noble aspiration for a generation and one fundamental to any duty of care. At the half-way point in the plan, which roughly coincided with the terminus of the Blair/Brown years in 2010, child poverty had been reduced by a quarter, not a half, thanks partly to an extra £18 billion spending on families with children by 2010.[44] The Sure Start scheme also sought to target aid

---

* Peter Mandelson, regarded at the time as the high priest of New Labour, famously remarked in 1998: 'We are intensely relaxed about people getting filthy rich, so long as they pay their taxes.'

to the poorest pre-school children in 250 Sure Start centres in the most deprived areas of the country.[45]*

The engine room of wealth creation, annual economic growth, had continued to increase after 2001, but the years of the Brown premiership, 2007–10, were to be scarred by the consequences of the Great Financial Crash of 2008. From 2011 until Covid, the Cameron–May years never recovered the buoyancy of 1993–2007 (see Tables 6 to 8).

To this macroeconomic picture, add substantial change to the structure of benefits (as we shall see shortly) and the prospect of meeting the grand ambition of abolishing child poverty grew bleaker. As the target date of 2020 passed, the number of children living in relative poverty after housing costs in the financial year 2019/20 (substantially before the imposition of Covid lockdown) was 4.28 million, a rise of 410,000 since 2009–10.[46] However the proportion of children in poverty stayed remarkably constant over the ten years: 29.4 per cent in 2009/10 and 2018/19 rising to 30.7 per cent in 2019/20.[47]

Table 6: UK annual economic growth, 2002–7.

2002	2003	2004	2005	2006	2007
1.9%	2.8%	1.8%	2.4%	2.1%	1.6%

Table 7: UK annual economic growth, 2008–10.

2008	2009	2010
−1.1%	−4.9%	+1.1%

Table 8: UK annual economic growth, 2011–18.

2011	2012	2013	2014	2015	2016	2017	2018
0.7%	0.8%	1.5%	1.8%	1.6%	1.1%	1.3%	0.8%

Before looking at the slimmed-down benefits system of the 2010s, what does a wider audit of the Blair–Brown years show? After two years of spending restraint in 1997–9 there was an injection of NHS funding

* However the places were an open offer to provide a social mix in order not to stigmatise the poorest.

of the kind Major wished he himself had made; a growing involvement of the private sector using the private finance initiative (PFI) projects pioneered by the Conservatives; a substantive improvement in existing hospitals and schools and the construction of new ones; and a huge reduction in hospital waiting times – in short, a market social democracy in action.

PFIs were intended to attract considerable quantities of private money for the pursuit of public purposes. Private sector companies would compete for contracts to design, build and operate schools, hospitals, prisons, defence installations and roads for thirty years, all without increasing the formal public borrowing figures in the national accounts. The social democratic defence of this would be that it helped diminish the gap between 'private affluence and public squalor' – a divide that had preoccupied centre-left politicians (including Gordon Brown[48]) ever since they absorbed J. K. Galbraith's 1958 classic, *The Affluent Society*.[49]

I was shaped by that brilliantly written book too. But PFIs have always worried me in terms of intergenerational justice. Here we were, the best provided-for generation ever, effectively saying to our children and grandchildren that PFI will give a great boost to our facilities, but you will pick up that tab over the next three decades paying off our deferred debt.

It was a strategy of a kind and the results were impressive. By the time Labour left office in 2010, 115 hospitals had either been built or rebuilt by PFI schemes in England costing £11.5 billion with a total lifetime repayment of nearly £80 billion. Other PFIs across the public sector cost £55 billion with a total repayment of over £300 billion.[50] All in all, it was a remarkable piece of political economy – nothing less than a remix of the mixed economy, and secured for the Chancellor and later PM the soubriquet 'Brown the Builder', showing his duty of care through bricks and mortar. But it was truly mortgaging the future.

In terms of grand, all-embracing strategy, however, what struck me increasingly was the continued non-appearance of an approach of real Beveridgian breadth. In my *Distilling the Frenzy: Writing the History of One's Own Times* I analysed the regular post-war defence/strategic reviews, and as I write, Whitehall is experiencing its thirteenth or fourteenth since 1945 (depending on how you define and count them) but we haven't mounted a single national welfare strategic exercise since

Beveridge reported in 1942. The tireless Frank Field noticed what I had written about defence reviews and with Andrew Forsey produced a welfare one in 2018 under the consciously Beveridgian title of *Not for Patching: A Strategic Welfare Review*.[51] By 2016, around a quarter of the country's income (and almost two-thirds of its public spending) was devoted to the welfare state* in the continuing attempt to slay the 'giants'.[52]

The time we really needed a welfare review was when Blair arrived in No. 10. It could be argued that Brown, in his 1998 comprehensive spending review, did this as the centralizing Chancellor inside the 'Ministry of Welfare' he built within the Treasury's walls – a kind of stealth Beveridge.

To reassure the electorate, both had pledged in 1997 to stick to the Conservatives' spending plans for two years.[53] In April 1999 the true Gordon began to show himself. The big beneficiaries were health (4.7 per cent annual rise in real terms over four years) and education (over 4 per cent real-term rise over the same period). Social security found its place in Brown's spending boost too (£13 billion extra in cash terms over three years[54]). Add to this the introduction of the first ever statutory minimum wage of £3.60 an hour on 1 April 1999, plus the steady growth rates and falling unemployment, and the whole amounted to a more generously funded and extended duty of care. It was Brown's most truly creative period in either of the top offices. From the perspective of Covid Britain, it does seem a genuinely gold-flecked age.

Table 9: UK defence spending as a percentage of GDP, 1986/7–1996/7.

1986/7	1987/8	1988/9	1989/90	1990/1	1991/2	1992/3	1993/4	1994/5	1995/6	1996/7
4.6%	4.3%	3.9%	3.9%	3.9%	4.1%	3.8%	3.5%	3.2%	2.9%	2.8%

One aspect of the post-war consensus that saw a significant change in the duty of care in the 1990s and 2000s was defence spending, with the fall of the Berlin Wall in 1989 and the failure of the coup against Mikhail Gorbachev in 1991. The Cold War diminished rather than ended because the deep Cold War remained in the submarine world and the East–West intelligence tussle surged once more in the late

---

* This includes spending on health, welfare, pensions, tax credits, personal social services and housing.

2010s. Spending naturally reflected the pre-Putin easement as the figures for defence as a proportion of GDP show (see Table 9).[55] Between 1997/8 and 2007/8 the defence spending remained between 2.4 and 2.5 per cent of GDP.

As one forty-year global threat sank down the league table of anxiety, another, long in the making and also set for the long term, continued to rise in the public's consciousness – the seventh Giant of climate change. There were – and are – always climate change sceptics, but by the time the Climate Change Act 2008 was pieced together, there was a high level of consensus about this increasingly menacing threat to the country and the world.

In my judgement, the 2008 law ranks as what I would call a 'foundation' statute comparable to the National Health Service Act 1946 – the test being that the country is a fundamentally different place before and after it. The Climate Change Act led the world in laying down legally binding targets for greenhouse gas emissions (down by at least 80 per cent by 2050) and CO_2 emissions (by at least 26 per cent by 2020 against a 1990 baseline).

In 2005, the year before David Miliband was sent by Tony Blair to the Department of the Environment, Food and Rural Affairs to pilot the legislation through, David Cameron devoted his first trip as Leader of the Conservative Party to driving a team of huskies over the shrinking ice-caps of Svalbard in the Norwegian Arctic: 'Global warming was real, and it was happening before our very eyes,'[56] he later wrote.

The UK was also leading the world in another part of climate action. Gordon Brown, on whose prime ministerial watch the 2008 Act became law, had when Chancellor commissioned his Chief Economic Adviser, Nick Stern (seconded from the London School of Economics) to inquire into the economic opportunities and risks of climate change. Written in a vivid style worthy of Beveridge and Keynes, the 700 pages of *The Economics of Climate Change* achieved considerable national and international reach when published in 2006:

Using the results from formal economic models, the Review estimates that if we don't act, the overall costs and risks of climate change will be the equivalent of losing 5% of global GDP each year, now and forever. If a wide range of risks and impacts is taken into account, the estimates of damage could rise to 20% of GDP or more. In contrast, the costs of action – reducing greenhouse gas emissions to avoid the worst impacts of climate change – can be limited to around 1% of global GDP each year . . . The costs of stabilizing the climate are significant but manageable; delay would be much more dangerous and much more costly.[57]

It is to the great credit of Blair and Brown that climate change became part of the calculus of government-in-the-round, not just the environment ministry. The NHS, for example, after the passage of the 2008 Act, recognized itself as 'the largest public sector emitter of carbon emissions' and undertook its own policies for sustainability.[58]

But brewing in the sub-prime mortgage world of the US, the wrathful gods of finance were getting a hold in a storm that would sweep across countries and continents, in the monetary equivalent of a pandemic. It was for the crash of 2008 and its immediate aftermath that Brown's premiership – the pinnacle for which he had been priming himself since his adolescence – will be remembered. The best of his formidable gifts were devoted to persuading the G20 to move in concert to prop up the global economy when the sub-prime mortgage problems of the United States suddenly sent a pulse of intense uncertainty through the entire financial world. Coping with it would inevitably bring cuts to the Beveridge elements of the duty of care. As Nick Timmins put it in his summary of the welfare state in the Blair/Brown years, 'the architects' plans were far from perfect. Some of the building had been shoddy. But reconstruction it had clearly been. The question [in 2010] was how much of this refurbished edifice would withstand the earthquake of the financial crisis.'[59]

The Conservatives returned to office in May 2010 in coalition with the Liberal Democrats, who had not been represented at the Cabinet table since Churchill's wartime government. The master policy was deficit reduction through an austerity programme which included one substantial welfare reform – the fusing of six in-work and out-of-work benefits into a single payment to be known as Universal Credit.*

This streamlining had been worked up in opposition by the former

---

* The six were: income support; the means-tested versions of both jobseekers' allowance; employment and support allowance; housing benefit; child tax credit; working tax credit.

Conservative Party leader Iain Duncan Smith, through his Centre for Social Justice. Many years later he told me he intended his review to be a new Beveridge. When I asked him why he hadn't done one he said, 'I believe that we did while I was at the Centre for Social Justice ... we looked at what I call the five modern pathways ... family breakdown, debt, failed education, worklessness and addictions.'[60] His problem as Secretary of State for Work and Pensions was the huge hole the 2008 financial crisis had dug in the growth-path of the British economy and the Treasury's relentless pursuit of spending cuts in an attempt to repair the public finances via Chancellor George Osborne's austerity programme.

David Cameron supported what he called 'the simple but profound idea' of Universal Credit in the cause of both streamlining the benefits and the removal of disincentives to work. 'But it was,' he recalled, 'inevitably, very complicated to implement. It was also hard to get Iain to consent to the idea of saving money as well as implementing his reforms. In the end, we won him round. The Emergency Budget [of 2010] cut £11 billion from the welfare budget.'[61]

Complication and cost bedevilled the introduction of Universal Credit. Eventually, Duncan Smith left the Cabinet over it, in March 2016, just before Cameron himself resigned after losing the EU referendum, arguing that the Treasury was balancing the books on the backs of the poor. With his Liberal Democrat allies gone from the Cabinet after the Conservatives won a majority in their own right in May 2015, he had found himself outgunned.

The problem with floating Universal Credit onto a sea of austerity was that it was certain to cost more if one of its key purposes was to be met, i.e. to support for the first time people doing 'mini jobs' of only a few hours a week. Previously there had been no real in-work support for lone parents until they were doing sixteen hours.[62]

One element of the post-2010 reforms aroused particular detestation – the so-called 'bedroom tax'. It was part of the £11 billion of cuts in welfare and withdrew housing benefit from any extra rooms deemed surplus to a family's requirements.[63] This could involve cuts of 25 per cent in a family's benefit and tenants had to pay up or move – which was especially difficult for those in council or housing association homes, as David Cameron later acknowledged.[64]

Another change with real personal impacts was the dramatic cuts in the legal and justice system – legal aid, in particular, which was part of the UK's post-1945 duty of care in the shape of the Legal Aid Act 1949. The Legal Aid, Sentencing and Punishment of Offenders Act 2012 (LASPO) changed the scope of civil and family legal aid. Whereas previously a matter qualified for legal aid funding unless it was specifically excluded by the Access to Justice Act 1999, LASPO reversed this position. 'With legal aid available in fewer areas of law, the volumes of publicly funded cases dropped, and expenditure fell by approximately £90 million in civil cases and £160 million in family cases.'[65] These changes seriously reduced access to the law for those with slim or near non-existent means; the Covid experience later added still greater difficulties (as the House of Lords Constitution Committee, of which I was a member, reported in 2021).[66] Another dose of inequality has been injected into society by reducing the scope of state assistance to the citizen-in-court. Access to justice is a constitutional matter of utmost importance in a country that claims to operate on the cardinal principle of the rule of law.[67]

Devolution – another form of constitutional change accruing within the UK since the late 1990s – added to inequality, too, with social provision beginning to vary significantly between the constituent parts of the kingdom. For example, the Scottish Executive flatly refused to introduce a bedroom tax.[68] Scotland also decline to introduce student fees for higher education. Free higher education for all who qualified for it was abandoned in principle when the Blair government introduced a university degree-course tuition fee of £1,000 a year (raised to £6,000 in 2006 and to a maximum of £9,000 by the Cameron Coalition) alongside a system of student loans.[69]

The biggest Anglo-Scottish fissure in the duty of care opened up in social care for the elderly. Scotland accepted the majority view of the 1999 report of the Royal Commission on Long-Term Care that all should receive free personal care in old age but the Westminster government did not.[70] It remains a disparity made all the more pressing by the experience of the care sector during the Covid crisis and the continuing difference in funding within the Union.

The fragility of the United Kingdom, and the tensions that fragility generates, have run through British politics like an ever-widening fault line in the twenty-first century, made all the more vexing and unsettling by the European Question's increasing entanglement with the Scottish one.

I have meagre gifts when it comes to forecasting, but this was fore-seeable. Unusually for me, I kept a daily diary during the Scottish referendum campaign in 2014 (which I published as *The Kingdom to Come* in 2015). In it I laid out a prediction I dearly hoped would not come true. Much of it, I fear, has. This was the sequence. In the summer of 2014, before the result, while visiting family in the exquisite Orkney Islands, I wrote:

> I am prone, on my rare moments of gloom, to agree with a wise friend of mine who spent his life inside the Secret Intelligence Service, attempting to thwart the Queen's adversaries overseas. He has long believed that the people we find hardest to defend against are ourselves. And some of our internal arguments on the road to the referendum of 2014 have turned into 'domestics' that threaten not just the peace of our everyday lives but our very existence as a United Kingdom at home and as a thoroughly outward-looking nation abroad. Said 'domestics' go under the label of the 'Scottish Question' and 'Britain in Europe'. One thing is sure: the shared experience of the Questions will not leave political relationships as they were nor the nature of the United Kingdom unchanged. The 2014 referendum will score a line across the history of these islands, even if it doesn't cut sufficiently deep to sever.[71]

Then came my post-referendum result forecast:

- 30–40 SNP members elected to the Westminster Parliament in May 2015.
- SNP win another outright majority in the Scottish Parliament in the Holyrood elections of May 2016, with another referendum as the party's top election pledge.
- At some point between 2016 and 2020 the UK as a whole votes in a referendum to leave the European Union while the vote in Scotland is strongly to stay in.

In my judgement that would mean a second independence referendum in the 2020s which could well go the way of separation.[72]

This is what has happened (so far):

September 2014 Scottish Referendum
  – No 55.3%; Yes 44.7%
May 2015 UK general election: of 59 Scottish seats
  – SNP 56; Labour 1; Conservatives 1; Lib Dems 1
May 2016 Holyrood elections, number of seats
  – SNP 63 seats (2 short of an overall majority) Conservatives
    31; Labour 24; Scottish Greens 6; Lib Dems 5
June 2016 EU Referendum
Percentage of the vote (Leave:Remain)
  – UK: 51.9%:48.1%
  – England: 53.4%:46.6%
  – Scotland: 38.0%:62.0%
May 2017 UK general election of 59 Scottish seats
  – SNP 35; Conservatives 13; Labour 7; Lib Dems 4
December 2019 UK general election of 59 Scottish seats
  – SNP 48; Conservatives 6; Lib Dems 4; Labour 1

In July 2019, the day Boris Johnson won the leadership of the Conservative and Unionist Party, I said to a Scottish Conservative friend of mine at Westminster, 'You do realize that your party, the Unionist Party, has just ensured Scotland will separate?' Immediately I felt bad about my overheated remark because my Conservative friend is acknowledged to be the most courteous man not just in the House of Lords but very probably the entire British Isles (as a Scottish Office minister he would leap out of his official car to open the door for his female driver).

A year later, on 23 July 2020, a few hours after Boris Johnson had landed in Orkney, I wrote in my diary:

I can feel the very political tectonics not just of Scotland but the entire kingdom shifting – and in the wrong direction. I fear the scenario I described six years ago is grinding its way to fulfilment. Against the backdrop of Stromness harbour, he [Johnson] declares, 'The Union is a fantastically strong institution.'[73] I wish it were. I was one of those who thought that the substantial devolution of powers to a new Scottish Executive and Parliament in 1999 would head off independence at the pass, or, more precisely at Berwick, Carter Bar and Gretna Green. My

great friend Tam Dalyell, the most gloriously independent-minded politician I have ever known, tried to persuade me otherwise. I fear that
inside this decade, Tam will have been proved right and I shall be din-
ing on humble pie (though sadly not with Tam who died in 2017).

There has always been a problem with the Union of Scotland and
England since its creation in 1707, an element perhaps of it being a
union of convenience rather than love. Humour, one of the great
lubricants of politics, can sometimes tell a quite profound story. Devolution has produced very few jokes but there is one that I cherish. I
owe it to my Scottish friend Lord Robertson of Port Ellen. According
to George, God was in a particularly benign mood on the day he
made that bit of earth we came to know as Scotland. He gave the
feisty, witty, clever, disputatious Scottish people a beautifully varied
landscape, great mountains, huge lochs, arable land and pasture of
the highest quality; climate a bit wet, midges a tad too ferocious, but
nevertheless, islands of charm, storms and fascination.

'Forgive me, Almighty,' said a member of His Advisory Council on
Making the Earth. 'Aren't you being a touch overgenerous to these
"Scots", as you call them?'

'Mebbe', replied God. 'But you wait to see who I am going to give
them as neighbours.'

The 'neighbour problem' has always been with us, partly given the
size of the English population and economy compared with Scotland's. Yet, until recently, Scottish politics was dominated by *national*
UK parties. Very few people in England noticed its entering a new
political phase in the late 1950s when the numbers of Conservative
and Unionist (the name Scots Conservatives still used) MPs in Scotland began their slow decline. In the 1955 general election Scotland
returned a majority of Conservative and Unionist MPs for the final
time. In the 1959 general election the Conservative majority rose
from sixty to a hundred, while in Scotland it declined from thirty-six
to thirty-one. As Peter Clarke noted, 'The 1959 general election was a
little noticed turning point in the decline of Unionism. For it left them
for the first time since 1950 with fewer Scottish seats than Labour.'[74]

Labour appeared to be solidifying its dominance until a vivid por-
tent of what was to come shook Scottish and UK politics when the

remarkable and energetic Scottish National Party (SNP) candidate, Mrs Winifred Ewing, won the Hamilton by-election in 1967 in one of Labour's great industrial barbicans in the west of Scotland. In the 2015 general election every one of these redoubts fell to the SNP – a shocking spectacle of political extinction but one long in the making, especially after the Catholic Scots lost their fear that a Scottish Parliament would be an Edinburgh version of Belfast's Protestant-dominated old Stormont.

Another threat to the Union in the early 1960s came from the doughty geologists of BP at work in the rough waters of the North Sea, who confirmed the presence in considerable quantities of that highly political commodity, oil – most abundantly in the Forties Field, 110 miles east of the Moray Firth. This was at a time when the technology of the oil rig had developed sufficiently to siphon it out and land it in the great vats of the Shetland Isles and down the east coast of Scotland. 'It's Scotland's Oil' swiftly became the most natural of rallying cries for those who wished to build an independent political nation with the financial bounty from the black gold. 'My kingdom for a rig!' the Queen might have exclaimed (but didn't).

Intellectually, too, there was a ferment underway. The break-up of the United Kingdom for some may not just seem desirable, but feasible – even likely – as well. I suspect Tom Nairn's 1977 study, *The Break Up of Britain* (in which he foresaw a 'stunted, caricaturial' Scotland breaking free to a political and cultural freedom in a 'post-imperial British Isles'[75]) was not the most popular reading during winter nights for the men on the rigs (the riggers were all male, initially), but it stimulated – or alarmed – minds, including the Queen's, as was made carefully but plainly evident in her Silver Jubilee address to both Houses of Parliament in Westminster Hall on 4 May 1977.[76] Within just under four decades, the independence question was put to the test in a referendum in 2014, when the kingdom just about held.

On 31 May 2016, almost exactly two years later, and just a few weeks before the EU referendum, I was in Orkney for the commemoration of the Battle of Jutland, marking a hundred years since Jellicoe had taken his Dreadnoughts, the Grand Fleet, this country's great deterrent, out of Scapa Flow through the Sound of Hoxa and into the North Sea for the long-awaited showdown, one of the very greatest in

European history, with the Kaiser's High Seas Fleet. Churchill said of Jellicoe that he was the only man who could lose the war in a single afternoon.[77] Had he lost the battle a hundred miles off the Danish coast, Germany would have broken the Royal Navy's blockade between Scotland and Norway, which cut Germany off from world markets. The Royal Navy's losses were searing, but it maintained its mastery of the northern waters until the end in November 1918 when the High Seas Fleet sailed to Scotland to surrender and languish interned in the waters of Scapa Flow.

In 2016 the Royal Navy asked me to be David Cameron's historical adviser as he crossed the great natural harbour of Scapa Flow after the Anglo-German service in the exquisite rose-pink St Magnus Cathedral in Kirkwall to the beautifully kept war graves cemetery on the island of Hoy. Our craft proved fleeter than the vessels carrying the Princess Royal, the president of Germany and the Commonwealth high commissioners, so we passed ahead of them down the line of British and German warships, decks rammed with saluting sailors and whistling bosuns, and reached Lyness harbour first. The PM waited for his Range Rover to pick him up as I watched from a nearby minibus. There he stood, silhouetted against the waters, with the warships as his backdrop, a solitary figure pacing the Lyness jetty seemingly deep in thought and eating a bag of crisps in what turned out to be the twilight of his premiership.

Seventeen days later, the EU referendum having produced a Leave vote to both Cameron's and my surprise, he stood in front of No. 10 in the bright morning sunshine and announced his intention to resign. For Cameron, he went from head of government at Scapa Flow to political oblivion in a matter of weeks. And so began for the rest of us the strange and bewildering life of Brexit Britain as the curse of the European Question fell, scowling and disruptive, not just on Tory prime ministers but on every square inch of our still tenuously united kingdom.

Before the condition of the economy would be changed by Covid (March 2020) and Brexit (January 2021), it is worth reflecting on how the slaying of the five giants was progressing. There had been a long period of austerity since 2010. Michael Marmot and his team at University College London produced a searing report on how little had changed for the better for the most deprived since then in 'Health

Equity in England: The Marmot Review 10 Years On'. Some of their findings regarding the five giants in England give a flavour of this.

WANT

According to the report:

> While more people are in work now than in 2010, average weekly wages have not recovered to the levels of 2010. Data from the Office for National Statistics (ONS) show that average weekly earnings at 2015 prices were £502 in September 2019, only £5 higher than in 2008. The Resolution Foundation describes that [between 2008 and 2018] ... there has been a reduction in average real weekly earnings [−1%] as well as a large reduction in benefits available for working age people and children.

DISEASE

Life expectancy and infant mortality had both been improving over the years as in the rest of the world although not quite as well in the lower social classes. But as Marmot says,

> For part of the decade 2010–2020 [pre-Covid-19] life expectancy actually fell in the most deprived communities outside London for women and in some regions for men. For men and women everywhere the time spent in poor health is increasing. For the lowest decile, infant mortality has increased in some of these years.

IGNORANCE

In education 'clear and persistent socioeconomic inequalities in educational attainment that were present in 2010 remain'. Although Manchester and London had reduced the disparity between the least and most deprived areas with specific support from the government, 'Funding has decreased by eight per cent per pupil with particularly steep declines in funding for sixth form (post-16) and further education.

Youth services have been cut since 2010 and violent youth crime has increased greatly over the period.'

IDLENESS

While unemployment had fallen, considerably more were in insecure employment; the numbers on zero-hours contracts rose from less than 200,000 in 2010 to about 800,000 in 2018.

SQUALOR

The total number of households in temporary accommodation increased by 74 per cent between 2010 and 2018 and the number of children living in temporary accommodation increased by 69 per cent ... Housing conditions have improved [since 2010, but] in 2017/18 around 1.9 million private renters reported an issue with condensation, damp or mould in their home.

Though undoubtedly the five giants have taken a serious hammering since 1945 and the conditions of life have improved massively since the end of the Second World War, it is also the case that far too many people in the United Kingdom are suffering from a variety of deprivations that they need not be as citizens of the sixth largest economy in the world.[78]

6

The Brexit Effect

The British have a better understanding than the continentals of institutions. Continentals tend to believe that problems are solved by men ... the British feel the necessity of parliamentary action: they feel it in their bones ... The British are reputed to be difficult partners and so they are when they negotiate on their own account, in their own way. But they are loyal colleagues when they sit with you on the same side of the table. Then, you can count on them to make things work.

                                                                    Jean Monnet, 1976[1]

British membership of the Community will not stick. Lacking the essential foundation in opinion, it is built on sand ... The continental nations have no direct experience of their own to tell them what the sovereignty of Parliament means to the British people; but the evidence of history should be sufficient to show the dangers of tampering with it ... The course of British politics and the force of public sentiment will constrain any British government to oppose the transfer of political decision which is implicit in all the objectives of the Community.

                                    Enoch Powell, address to a press luncheon, Brussels, 28 September 1972[2]

One of the great questions facing Britain in my adult lifetime is which of these extraordinary thinkers – the first the foremost imagining mind of the European idea, the second the most national sovereignty-steeped British politician of his day – would turn out to be the closest to our unfolding political reality after the UK's accession to the EEC in 1973. From a shared belief in the UK's parliamentary institutions – and not just how we do our politics but also how we conceive of ourselves as a nation – their expectations of Britain's European years were vividly different.

Both were right in thinking Parliament would be the cockpit where the strikingly fissile matter of Britain and Europe would be fought over with a peculiar mixture of high passion and deep tedium. If it were a political symphony, the final movement would be far from the 'Ode to Joy' of Beethoven's Ninth, the anthem of the European Union. Its souring, dissonant atonality wore us out and left our exhausted politics in poor shape for the moment when British history arrived at the caesura between Before Covid and After Covid.

Why was this so? This is not the place in which to replay the day-to-day, almost hour-by-hour Battle of Brexit. But a brief summary of why it proved so harmful to both the human and institutional life of the country is necessary and, I hope, illuminating, because its searing and unsettling effects helped to diminish our sense of the duty of care. It carved great chunks out of our national solidarity.

In my judgement, there were six capital 'Q' questions in play simultaneously that tore at the country in a malign combination of forces.

- The European Question itself, to be or not to be a member of an integrating community of European nations and its institutions, the greatest single tormentor of post-war British history.
- The related Britain's Place in the World Question.
- The Structure of British Politics Question.
- The British Institutions Question (the capacity of Parliament's ability to take the strain and to resolve all the other questions).
- The Condition of Britain Question and the inequality, human and geographical, that fuelled it.
- The very Union of the UK Question. In peacetime, no political issue has come so heavily freighted as this.

The result of the June 2016 referendum threw all these questions into stark relief and increased the destabilizing and unpredictable interplay between them. The resulting frenzy felled two prime ministers and brought into being under Boris Johnson the most narrowly formed Cabinet of modern times built around a single shared requirement – the willingness, if necessary, to accept a no-deal, hard Brexit.

This was not the ideal basis for peopling a government that within three months of Johnson's huge victory in the December 2019 general election (an overall majority of eighty seats) would be faced with a peacetime national emergency without precedent. The virus that gathered force within only a couple of months ignored boundaries and cared not for customs unions, single markets, free-trade areas or the political jousting on the House of Commons benches. To reverse the famous words of Winston Churchill in 1940, when he assumed the premiership, all their lives had been anything but a preparation for this hour and this trial.* From early March 2020, Covid dominated the political weather and added its huge, volatile and unstable weight to the existing questions that had left us exhausted, dripping with recrimination and perpetually at each other's throats.

THE EUROPEAN QUESTION

In its July 2020 report on Russian penetration, the UK Intelligence and Security Committee of Parliament examined, inconclusively, the likelihood of Moscow's interference with the 2016 European Referendum.[3] It talked of the desire of the Russian state to effect a 'general poisoning of the political narrative in the West by fomenting political extremism and "wedge issues"'.[4] Wedge issues, the report explained,

> are highly divisive subjects which bifurcate a country's population often (but not always) into socially liberal and socially conservative camps and which often to at least some degree transcend traditional political party boundaries. Examples of wedge issues include abortion and gun control in the US and Brexit in the UK.[5]

---

* Of 10 May 1940, the day he became prime minister, Churchill later wrote: 'I felt as if I was walking with destiny, and that all my past life had been but of preparation for this hour and this trial.' Winston S. Churchill, *The Second World War*, vol. 1: *The Gathering Storm* (Cassell, 1948), p. 601.

Wedge issues like Brexit are, by their very nature, highly impervious to consensual impulses. Bridge issues, as I would call them, such as support for the NHS at a time of national crisis, are, by contrast, natural consensus-builders.

As we have seen, Britain in Europe has been a 'wedger' from the outset, never a 'bridger'. Why is this? We have to start with the minds out of which came the prototype – the 1950 design for a European Coal and Steel Community. Its architects were clever, Catholic, left-wing French bureaucrats of whom Monnet was cathedral-builder-in-chief. Many Brits (though not I) have trouble with at least three of the five characteristics of the constructors. If the idea had emerged from the silkily sceptical and worldly wise post-war British minds in the Foreign Office, the Treasury and the Board of Trade, it would have been a much less grandiose affair, far less intrusive and interventionist.

Picture how it might have been – the very loosest of free-trade arrangements – with a small secretariat housed in a high-unemployment area which needed the jobs and despatching a handful of letters a year to the member states asking, 'Would you mind awfully doing a bit more on free trade, here, and, perhaps, there – but only if you've got time?' No fusillade of directives. No fuss. No overarching philosophy – grandiose and tedious at the same time – and certainly no proselytizing for an ever closer union.

It's been a constant irritation to the people of the UK that this new Europe was definitely not a British design – a classic example of the not-invented-here syndrome. But there is much more than that to the Britain-in-Europe Question in many British minds. It carries a passion way beyond such structural and procedural resentments.

For it has to do with sovereignty and identity – who we are, where we are and what we have lived and experienced as imprinted and hoarded in the memory section of the brain. Above all, in the late 1940s and early 1950s (and since) we have seen ourselves as the people of 1940–41 who stood sovereign, defiant and alone with the Empire and Commonwealth while Europe succumbed to tyranny between the fall of France and Hitler's invasion of the Soviet Union. These feelings and factors are not containable within the traditional left/right structure of UK party politics when they come in batallions.

The terrain where sovereignty and memory meet was beyond party.

Its fields were relentlessly tilled by Enoch Powell above all. It was on a visit to Russia in 1989, talking to a group of bemedalled veterans of the Great Patriotic War, that he declared, 'What an important thing memory is, collective memory. It's really collective memory that makes a nation, its memory of what its past was, what it has done, what it has suffered and what it has endured.'[6]

It was Lord Kilmuir, a veteran pro-European and the Lord Chancellor in Macmillan's Cabinet (until he was purged in the 1962 'Night of the Long Knives' reshuffle), who tried to persuade his colleagues that the sovereignty question must be faced full-on if the British people were to be persuaded that the country should join the EEC. He told the Cabinet in April 1961, as Macmillan eased them towards agreeing that the UK would apply, that:

> [political] association within the Six* might ultimately involve a significant surrender of national sovereignty. Adherence to the Treaty of Rome would limit the Supremacy of Parliament, which would be required to accept decisions taken by the Council of the Community. It would restrict the right of the Executive to make treaties. It would also involve a final right of appeal from our courts to the Supreme Court of the Community. A major presentation would be needed to persuade the British public to accept these encroachments on national sovereignty.[7]

Kilmuir went unheeded. There was no 'major presentation' on the reality of sovereignty loss. As a result, each shift towards a more closely integrated Europe seemed to come as a shock to the public who were not among the, I suspect, tiny number of the Queen's subjects familiar with the cold print of the Treaty of Rome. Because of this sleight of hand, resentment gradually brewed among a considerable proportion of the population who simply didn't like being told what to do (as they saw it) by foreigners (as they saw them).

Referring to the years when the UK finally legislated for membership in 1971–2 (entry taking place on 1 January 1973), the former Cabinet Secretary, Richard Wilson (Lord Wilson of Dinton), shrewdly

---

* West Germany, France, Italy, the Netherlands, Belgium and Luxembourg – the original founder members and signatories of the 1957 Treaty of Rome

observed, 'We Brits always go into our big decisions as if under anaesthetic, only waking up many years later and wondering "Did we really mean to do that?"'[8] The same might be said of constitutional change *within* the UK (as distinct from ceding powers upwards in the EU case) in the form of devolution to Scotland in particular in 1997–8.

Looking back, there was never a period during our membership that the bulk of the country felt any real warmth towards the European idea. Compared to notions of the Union, which for many nourished a sense of Britishness they felt in their bones, the EU left people cold. Feelings, when they did heat up, were kindled by externally derived irritation which translated into the UK's being a near-permanent awkward squad in the meeting rooms and negotiating suites of Europe for most of the period of our membership (Monnet was putting the most constructive spin on this that he could in 1976). Tedium laced with resentment make a sourly life-diminishing combination. 'Why couldn't *they* be more like *us*?' was a widespread feeling.

Perhaps enthusiastically embracing Europe was expecting too much of a people and a country that had witnessed in the first half of the century a remarkable slippage from turn-of-the-century maritime and imperial, Dreadnought-protected superpowerdom to shaky, empire-shedding fading great-powerdom. The self-image the country stored in its collective hippocampus was very far from that of a contented medium-sized power tucked up inside a huge regional group tranquilly accepting that memories of the glories of playing the world game were to be quietly stored away, brought out occasionally for a bit of fond recollection and polishing. This is why the question of Europe was tightly bound in to the other great much-debated rolling phenomenon of . . .

THE BRITAIN'S PLACE IN THE WORLD QUESTION

How we have tortured ourselves with this throughout my lifetime. Consider one revealing metric – the roll call of defence/strategy reviews from the age of Attlee and Bevin to the Johnson days:

1949 The Harwood Review (Labour; Attlee)

1951 The Chiefs of Staff Report on Defence Policy and Global Strategy (Conservative; Churchill)

1957 The Sandys Review (Conservative; Macmillan)

1964–6 Healey, Mark I (Labour; Wilson)

1968 Healey, Mark II (Labour; Wilson)

1974–5 The Mason Review (Labour; Wilson)

1981 The Nott Review (Conservative; Thatcher)

1990 Options for Change (Conservative; Thatcher)

1994 Front Line First (Conservative; Major)

1998 The Strategic Defence Review (Labour; Blair)

2002 The Strategic Defence Review 'New Chapter' (Labour; Blair)

2010 The Strategic Defence and Security Review (Coalition; Cameron/Clegg)

2015 The Strategic Defence and Security Review (Conservative; Cameron)

2018 Mobilizing, Modernizing and Transforming Defence (Conservative; May)

2020–21 The Integrated Review of Security, Defence, Development and Foreign Policy (Conservative; Johnson)

That is fifteen reviews in seventy-one years.

Some were more strategic than others. All were about money – the financial overstretch that comes when the bundle of aspirations for the projection of British power and influence outstrip the money to fund them, which they always do. An American journalist who knows us well, Stryker McGwire (formerly *Newsweek*'s Bureau Chief in London) described this perpetual shaper of British policy as our desire to be a 'pocket superpower'[9] – to keep a wide spectrum of capabilities, forever trimming them down a bit but never wishing to abandon a big one such as the UK nuclear weapons programme. In its way, this was an 'itch after the amputation' as on old SIS friend once suggested, as was the aspiration of the UK's global intelligence reach (thanks above all to the intelligence alliance with the US).

From the time Macmillan began to sculpt his Cabinet into a pro-Common Market shape in 1960, the question of Britain-in-Europe has been intertwined with the fading-great-power problem and crucial to its mitigation and reversal in two ways: as a booster of UK economic growth that would fund these global aspirations without strain, and as a new cricket pitch on which to score the boundaries that our statecraft could gracefully execute.

Geoffrey Howe put this most elegantly with his penchant for quoting Archimedes: 'Give me a place to stand and I shall move the world.'[10] For many, including Howe, Europe was to be that place – the new geopolitical force-multiplier for British influence not just in Europe but across the world. For others, it was quite the reverse. Britain's place in the world depended upon the sanctity of its sovereignty-infused home islands. Give me an archipelago on which to stand and I shall move the world.

When these rival notions clashed it was like the colliding of two great weather systems – a political equivalent of the ever-swirling Pentland Firth where the North Sea and the Atlantic meet and the weather can change four times a day between the northern tip of Scotland and the southern islands of Orkney. The result? An immense strain on . . .

THE STRUCTURE OF BRITISH PARTY POLITICS QUESTION

The duty of care did well by the left/right divide of UK politics after the coalition broke up in May 1945, though its suspension between 1940 and 1945 had done the nation very great service. Why? Because, in my judgement, happy and safe is the country wherein the nature of its political competition is between liberal capitalism and social democracy. The former is the best mechanism yet designed by mankind to foster economic growth and innovation; the latter, the best means so far devised to inject a measure of redistribution and permit a flowering of social justice.

This became the standard model (to borrow a concept from physics) of post-war British politics. The post-1945 settlement did well by it as the parties competed over who was the better protector and funder of the welfare state (though Mrs Thatcher would undoubtedly have preferred a different standard model). Sometimes the electorate voted for a serious dose of one rather than the other. Most of the time it seemed to prefer a fusion of the best bits of each. Parliament brokered its shape and handled its occasional showdowns. Whitehall turned it into policy and implemented it.

The standard model could be criticized as a political arrangement for offering 'a better yesterday', to use Ralf Dahrendorf's rather unkind description of the aspirations of the breakaway Social Democratic Party, the SDP.[11] But it worked, and it brought a high level of political stability. Europe, by contrast, aroused inflammation and stress. It busted up the major political parties from within rather than between (the Liberals/Liberal Democrats apart, given their consistently pro-European policies). And it generated more passion per square political foot than any other question. At its worst, it took on some of the characteristics of a war of religion, with its almost millenarian ferocity and use of apocalyptic language.

For some on the left the weevil of class politics also intruded. I have long remembered from the very earliest months of our EEC membership in 1973 Jack Jones, the formidable leader of the Transport and General Workers Union, telling Susan Barnes for a *Sunday Times* profile that 'so many of the strongest advocates for Europe were – how shall I put it? – the type who like high-class social life. Europe would be more *available* to them. They look at Europe through wine-spattered spectacles.'[12] Though he didn't name him, Jones plainly had Roy Jenkins in his mind. There was also a powerful and enduring conviction on the left that the EEC/EC/EU was a capitalists' club, adherence to whose rules would prevent the achievement of socialism in the UK.

The European Question also increasingly picked up the electricity the immigration debate brought to British politics, especially when enlargement of the EU drew in the former Soviet satellites in eastern Europe. Immigration, too, was a political question that defied any easy or neat left/right division. Paradoxically, it played strongly in those areas of the country most dependent on the inward manufacturing investment that the EEC/EC/EU membership encouraged.

As a result, a party political structure designed to cope with the early-twentieth-century capital/labour divide creaked and groaned under the strains brought by Europe, which fed directly into . . .

THE BRITISH INSTITUTIONS QUESTION

Parliament is the place where all the other questions have to be resolved. For there is a simple, if crucial deal, that underpins a Parliamentary democracy in an open society: 'Raised voices, yes; raised fists, no.'

This was the field on which Jean Monnet's and Enoch Powell's attentions were focussed in the 1970s – Parliament as *the* shock-absorber for what Chris Patten later called 'the great psychodrama' of British politics.[13] And the deal held: voices were raised throughout but fists did not fly. It was not always an edifying sight, but the House of Commons is where the great battles were fought and the crucial show-downs took place, apart, of course, from the Parliament-sanctioned referendums of 1975 and 2016. The merest glance at the Brexit timeline shows plainly the central locus of Parliament throughout.

Brexit timeline

7 May 2015: Conservative mandate In the general election, David Cameron wins a twelve-seat majority with a manifesto that includes the commitment to hold an in/out referendum on the UK's membership of the European Union.

23 June 2016: The referendum The referendum sees Leave campaigners win a narrow victory with 51.9% against and 48.1% for Remain. Cameron resigns immediately as prime minister.

13 July 2016: New PM Theresa May becomes prime minister.

17 January 2017: Lancaster House speech[14] May sets out the type of Brexit deal she will be pursuing when formal negotiations begin. The key points covered in the speech included:
- UK law
- The common travel area
- Immigration
- Rights for EU nationals
- Workers' rights

- Free trade
- Security

29 March 2017: Article 50. May triggers Article 50 of the EU's Lisbon Treaty, which starts the clock on the process of the UK leaving the EU.

8 June 2017: Snap election. Having surprised many by calling a general election, the PM loses her majority in Parliament. Northern Ireland's DUP – led by Arlene Foster – makes a deal with the Conservatives and its votes allow them to stay in power.

26 June 2017: Negotiations begin. Formal negotiations on withdrawal begin between the UK and the EU.

22 September 2017: Florence speech[15] In an effort to break a deadlock in the negotiations, the PM sets out the UK's position on how to move Brexit talks forward on the following key areas:

- Transition period
- Joint security
- A 'divorce bill'
- Leaving the single market
- Rights of EU citizens in the UK
- Northern Ireland border

13 December 2017: Westminster rebellion. Rebel Tory MPs side with the Opposition, forcing the government to guarantee a vote on the final Brexit deal when it has been struck with Brussels.

15 December 2017: Negotiations Phase 2. The EU agrees to move on to the second phase of negotiations after an agreement is reached on the Brexit divorce bill, the Irish border and EU citizens' rights.

2 March 2018: Mansion House speech. The PM gives a third speech outlining her plans for the next phase of negotiations.[16] Topics included:

- Free-trade agreement
- The five 'tests' for the negotiations
- Labour mobility
- Mutual recognition

- The Northern Ireland border
- That 'no deal' is better than a bad deal

19 March 2018: Negotiations progress. The UK and EU make decisive steps in negotiations. Agreements include dates for a transitional period after Brexit day, the status of EU citizens in the UK before and after that time and fishing policy. Issues still to be sorted out include the Northern Ireland border.

6 July 2018: Chequers statement. The government forms a final list of demands from the EU at a 'Cabinet Away Day' at Chequers attempting to reach a general consensus on the content of the Brexit legislation, and how the final round of negotiations will progress. It covered:

- The Brexit departure date
- The end of free movement of people
- Post-Brexit financial contributions
- A new customs regime
- A common rulebook for goods
- The status of EU law
- Preparation for a 'no deal Brexit'

12 July 2018: Brexit White Paper,[17] outlining the government's approach to managing the country's withdrawal from the EU is published.

15 November 2018: The clock runs out. Theresa May presents the deal to Parliament, where it founders.

25 November 2018: EU summit. EU leaders agree to the prime minister's Brexit deal.

14 January 2019: First vote. The government is defeated in a 'meaningful vote' on the withdrawal agreement.

12 March 2019: Second Vote. The government is defeated in a second 'meaningful vote' on the withdrawal agreement.

21 March 2019: First extension. The prime minister secures a short extension to Article 50 to delay Brexit until 12 April. The EU has said that agreement on a further extension of Article 50 to the end of May would be possible, but only if the UK approves a withdrawal agreement before 12 April.

10 April 2019: **Second extension**. The prime minister and EU leaders agree to a flexible extension of Article 50 until 31 October 2019. The UK has until this date to agree and pass a withdrawal deal.

23–26 May 2019: **European elections**. The UK participates in European elections, selecting seventy-three MEPs in twelve multimember regional constituencies.

24 May 2019: **Theresa May resigns**. Theresa May declares that she will step down as prime minister on 7 June 2019. The Conservative Party will select a new leader (and prime minister). The new government will take the lead in delivering Brexit.

24 July 2019: **New PM**. Boris Johnson succeeds Theresa May as prime minister.

17 October 2019: **EU summit**. The final scheduled summit of EU leaders before the 31 October deadline begins in Brussels. Boris Johnson announces that a revised deal has been struck.

19 October 2019: **Benn Act deadline**. In accordance with the terms of the Benn Act, the PM asks the EU for a further extension of its departure date, as a deal has not been approved by Parliament, and Parliament did not consent to the UK leaving without a deal.

22 October 2019: **MPs vote on the withdrawal agreement**. The Withdrawal Agreement Bill passes its second stage reading in the House of Commons, but fails to pass its programme motion, ensuring that the UK's departure on 31 October will be delayed, with the EU's agreement.

28 October 2019: **Third extension**. The European Union agrees to grant the UK up to three more months to finalize its departure. Brexit will take place on the first day of the month following the ratification of the Withdrawal Agreement, 'or on 1 February 2020, whichever is the earlier'.

1 December 2019: **First possible departure date**. According to the terms of the extension of Article 50, the UK can leave the EU on this date if the House of Commons and the European Parliament ratify the exit deal before this date.

12 December 2019: General election. A general election is held and a new eighty-seat overall majority Conservative government is formed.

20 December 2019: Withdrawal Agreement Bill. The EU Withdrawal Agreement Bill is introduced to Parliament, with MPs passing its second reading stage.

1 January 2020: Second possible departure date. According to the terms of the extension of Article 50, the UK can leave the EU on this date if the House of Commons and the European Parliament ratify the exit deal after 1 January 2020.

31 January 2020: Brexit. At 11 p.m. UK time, the United Kingdom leaves the European Union after forty-seven years and one month.*

Monnet was wrong. We did not, in the end, make things work. Enoch Powell was right: it did not 'stick'.

The House of Commons was seriously stress-tested by Brexit, not least because it coincided with the always activist speakership of John Bercow.† During the course of the post-referendum debates, he became an expansionist, if not imperial, Speaker, and to the rage of many Conservatives he changed procedure and precedent in a dramatic fashion.

Bercow's memoir, *Unspeakable*, burns white like magnesium in the pages that cover House of Commons proceedings following the withdrawal agreement that emerged from Mrs May's negotiations with the EU-27 on 25 November 2018. Writing of her government, Bercow claimed:

> . . . deliberately, bare-facedly, shamelessly – they pulled the debate for a full month, resuming only on 9 January [2019] and providing for all

---

* This very useful timeline was drawn up by the Institute and Faculty of Actuaries, with minor additions and amendments by the author.

† Before taking the Speaker's chair in 2009, Mr Bercow had sat as a Conservative MP for Buckingham, but his political views had shifted from the right, as his memoir makes plain, ending up as a 'left-of-centre Tory'. John Bercow, *Unspeakable: The Autobiography* (Weidenfeld and Nicolson, 2020), p. 151. In June 2021 he joined the Labour Party.

full five days' debate so that the vote would take place only on 15 January, exactly five weeks after it was supposed to occur.

On . . . 8 January, the government tabled its Business of the House motion prescribing a five-day debate. Having had an earlier such motion amended against their wishes, the government whips tried to avoid that by including in the motion 'forthwith' (such motions are not debated and have typically been deemed by the Speaker to be unamendable). However, this struck me as profoundly undesirable in this case, even hazardous . . . I sensed that it would not suit a majority of MPs who desperately wanted to decide on the PM's deal and then to explore alternatives if it was rejected.[18]

The scene was set for a constitutional showdown both in private in Speakers' House and in the Chamber:

Dominic Grieve [Conservative remainer and former attorney general] tabled an amendment on the evening of 8 January that would require the Prime Minister, if her deal was defeated the following week, to bring forward her new Brexit plans within three days rather than three weeks. Late that evening a senior [House of Commons] clerk called my office to seek my agreement that the amendment should not be published on the Order Paper the following day, as she thought it could not be put to a vote. The government's motion did indeed use the word 'forthwith' – clearly on Clerks' advice – and was therefore in her view unamendable. I disagreed and instructed that it should appear on the Order Paper the next day.

At our daily briefing on 9 January, looking down at his papers rather than at me, the Clerk of the House [Sir David Natzler] referred to the amendment but said that, of course, it could not be voted on because of the wording. Again I disagreed, and told them I was selecting it. Ashen-faced and as shaken as if he had just learned of an appalling tragedy, the Clerk looked up open-mouthed and stared at me in disbelief. No Speaker had ever made such a ruling, he said. It was against precedent.

We were, I said, in unprecedented times. The notion that a minority government* should be free to exert unfettered control as part of a

---

* Mrs May had lost the Conervatives' overall majority at the 2017 general election and was governing with the aid of the ten Democratic Union MPs from Northern Ireland on a 'confidence and supply' arrangement.

scandalous time-wasting plot was absurd. That such a plot was intended to blackmail the House to accept a deal it didn't want, or else
suffer the indescribable calamity of a cliff-edge [i.e. no-trade-deal]
Brexit was not merely ridiculous. It was disgusting and obscene.[19]

The Grieve amendment was eventually passed by 308 to 297 after
spectacular rows between John Bercow and the government chief
whip, Julian Smith ('You will not dictate what happens here,' he said,
'shaking with rage', according to Mr Bercow) and Andrea Leadsom,
leader of the House ('whose near-pathological hatred of me was well
known'[20]).

It was nasty and it was undignified. But this extraordinary episode
was but one example of a deeply recriminatory parliamentary weather
system. It was not dispelled until the last weeks of 2019, when Sir
Lindsay Hoyle succeeded John Bercow, bringing a very different style
to the chair, and Boris Johnson persuaded the House of Commons
to set aside the Fixed-Term Parliaments Act 2011 with the Early General Election Act 2019. This enabled him to request the Queen to
dissolve Parliament and, thereby, to trigger the general election, which
duly delivered a majority Conservative government in the House of
Commons.

It could be argued that, for all that it was coarse and undignified in
much of its Brexit-related behaviour, Parliament was doing its job and
simply reflected the ferocity and crudity of the wider national debate
that split families and tested friendships like no other political issue of
the post-war years.

In fact, the Euro virus ceased to rage with such ferocity once the
election result ensured British withdrawal from the EU would take
place on 31 January 2020. But it did not disappear. Parliament had
eventually, after extraordinary contortions, done its dispute-resolving
work. We *were* coming out. Parliament had rowed itself into exhaustion –
unsurprisingly, since some were witnessing the fulfilment of the primary
object of their political lives while others had spent theirs dedicated to
making Britain-in-Europe work. But the future trade agreement with
the EU we had left remained to be negotiated by the end of the year,
trouble lurking in nearly every potential clause. And now a huge pile
of unfinished business awaited, in the hugely demanding form of . . .

THE CONDITION OF BRITAIN
QUESTION

It was plain from the moment we saw the electoral map of Brexit that Leave areas very largely coincided with areas of relative deprivation where Beveridge's five giants still roamed unvanquished (see Figures 2 and 3). It was the same kind of shock-to-action that Michael Heseltine had attempted thirty-five years earlier, especially but by no means exclusively, in the urban areas. It was the latest version of what Victorian politicians called 'The Condition of England Question'.

The forgotten-Britain element struck home with the (initially) great beneficiary of David Cameron's political demise, Theresa May, and her historically minded special adviser Nicholas Timothy. On that bright summer morning of 13 July 2016, after she returned from accepting the Queen's commission to form a government, she stood in front of No. 10 and made the finest speech of her political life, concentrating on the needs of those very people whose sense of outsiderness had cried out through the Euro vote. It became known as her 'burning injustice' speech:

> . . . the burning injustice that, if you're born poor you will die on average nine years earlier than others. If you're black, you're treated more harshly by the criminal justice system than if you're white. If you're a white, working-class boy, you're less likely than anybody else in Britain to go to university. If you're at a state school, you're less likely to reach the top professions than if you're educated privately. If you're a woman, you will earn less than a man. If you suffer from mental health problems, there's not enough help to hand. If you're young, you'll find it harder than ever before to own your own home . . . [My] mission [is] to make Britain a country that works for everyone.[23]

It was a genuinely felt duty of care embodied in her first public words as prime minister. Brexit (the PM-slayer) and her throwing away her small but workable Commons majority in the May 2017 general election largely deprived her of her chance. And although with his pre-Covid 'levelling-up' agenda her successor, Boris Johnson, picked up his version of the torch of reform, Covid Britain has thrown these inequalities into even sharper relief.

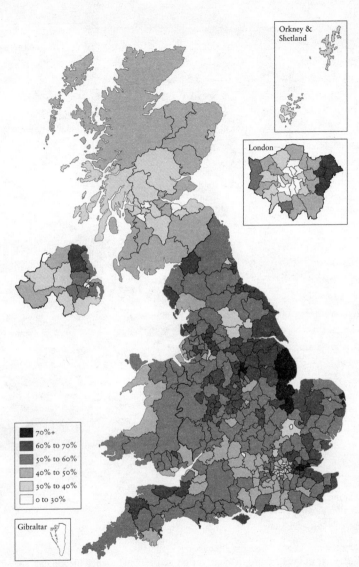

Figure 2: Voting to leave by counting area.[21]

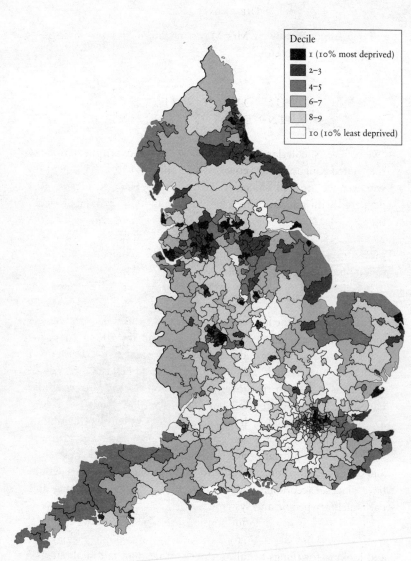

Figure 3: Index of multiple deprivation 2019: constituency rankings.[22]

Long forgotten now is Mrs May's placing in her very first paragraph on 13 July 2016 of . . .

THE UNION OF THE UNITED KINGDOM QUESTION

'We believe,' she declared, 'in a Union not just between the nations of the United Kingdom but between all of our citizens, every one of us, whoever we are and wherever we're from.'[24] Her premiership was peppered with references to 'our precious union'. Quite apart from the exponential, big picture track towards mid-2020s Scottish independence I had anticipated in *The Kingdom to Come*, the Leave vote threw up a swathe of practical problems that could not but place strain on the existing devolution settlement.

Put simply, there were no devolved parliaments or executives in existence in 1971–2 when powers were packed for shipment to Brussels. They came in the late 1990s. So when those powers – and hugely more – were repackaged for shipment back to the UK in 2020, the question arose, where would they stop? How many would finish up in Whitehall; how many in Edinburgh, Cardiff and Belfast?

There is a map in the government's *UK Internal Market* White Paper which captures this Balkanized homecoming vividly (see Figure 4). This map is littered with fissures and teeming with battlegrounds for those who seek Scottish independence. Even without Covid greedily, relentlessly absorbing the energies of Westminster and Whitehall and the devolved administrations, the unscramble from Europe would have placed exceptional and lengthy demands upon governing and parliamentary people and systems.

Coping with Brexit had not been one of our finer hours as a country. It had left us exhausted, touchy, scratchy, doused in recrimination and looking for things to fall out over rather than fall in about. We have been a nation seemingly on permanent grudge watch. In the last days of 'normality' before the virus arrived it would have been a slow business rebuilding a shared sense of purpose held together by the mortar of civility and the brickwork of tolerance.

Suddenly our energies and our priorities were wrenched away from

Northern Ireland transferred powers
- ✓ Economic development
- ✓ Agri-food and fisheries
- ✓ Environment and planning
- ✓ Health and social services
- ✓ Education and skills
- ✓ Employment law
- ✓ Some tax powers
- ✗ Fiscal and monetary policy
- ✗ Foreign policy and defence
- ✗ Constitution
- ✗ Elements of product standards (excluding agri-food products)

Scotland devolved powers
- ✓ Economic development
- ✓ Agri-food and fisheries
- ✓ Environment and planning
- ✓ Health and social services
- ✓ Education and skills
- ✓ Some tax powers
- ✗ Fiscal and monetary policy
- ✗ Foreign policy and defence
- ✗ Constitution
- ✗ Product standards (excluding agri-food products)

Scottish Government

Northern Ireland Executive

EU powers transferring to UK in a total of 160 policy areas which intersect with desolved competence

Welsh Government

UK Government – including new England-only powers

Wales devolved powers
- ✓ Economic development
- ✓ Agri-food and fisheries
- ✓ Environment and planning
- ✓ Health and social services
- ✓ Education and skills
- ✓ Welsh language
- ✓ Some tax powers
- ✗ Fiscal and monetary policy
- ✗ Foreign policy and defence
- ✗ Constitution
- ✗ Product standards (excluding agri-food products)

- ✓ Devolved/transferred to Welsh, Scottish and Northern Irish legislatures
- ✗ Reserved to the UK parliament (or excepted for Northern Ireland)

Figure 4: The UK's internal market after the transition period. Example areas of devolved competence and volume of new powers transferring to the devolved administrations.[25]

post-Brexit recovery and forcibly channelled into an entirely different kind of coping. A pathogen had struck which was heedless of national borders and utterly indifferent to geopolitics or the political economy of the terrain over which it bred and spread. Suddenly how petty seemed the matter of customs unions, single markets and free-trade agreements.

A true national emergency had taken hold. It was swiftly plain that life in After Covid Britain would be enduringly different from Before Covid Britain. Extra notions of a duty of care in multiple forms were added to those the country had lived by and debated about in the seventy-eight years since Sir William Beveridge signed off his report, as became apparent from almost the very first days of living in Covid Britain.

PART TWO

Covid Britain and After

7

Pathogen Britain and Its Lessons?

Nature cannot be fooled.
Richard Feynman, US theoretical physicist and Nobel Prize
winner, 1986[1]

It is a race we are still running as mutant variants threaten to
'escape' the vaccines and treatments we have developed to
bring the pandemic under control. And, if and when we do
cross the finishing line, sadly there will not be much time for
celebration. We will already be in training for the next one!
Professor Sarah Gilbert and Dr Catherine Green of the
Oxford AstraZeneca team, 20 November 2020[2]

. . . we must plan for the worst.
Sir Jeremy Farrar, Director of the Wellcome Trust[3]

I try to fathom
this devotion
They aren't my parents . . .
Why did all these strangers try so hard
to keep me alive?
It's a kindness I can hardly grasp.
The words tell me
that they wanted me to survive
I may never meet them again.
Michael Rosen on Surviving Covid after 47 days
intensive care at the Whittington Hospital,
North London[4]

It was a time like no other. Week after week it felt as if we were waiting for the 2020s to begin properly with a return to normality. For some, life could never be restored. For others, long-term sickness would blight their lives. Gradually, we all came to realize that a line had been scored across our shared history. There could be no going back to January 2020 – Covid would lurk and other pandemics would follow.

Britain's Covid experience in 2020–21 (see the 'Timeline of Lockdown Britain' at the end of the book) will be re-examined for decades to come, repeatedly trawled for explanations, plundered for lessons by those in authority who carry a duty of care – scientists recreating causes, courses and consequences, social scientists analysing the government's decision-making processes, political historians assessing the use of the huge quantity of powers Parliament lent to the state in the form of emergency legislation. Historians of science, too, will piece together the triumphant story of a lifesaving vaccine developed and produced faster than any other in medical and biological history.

The vaccination programme has been a remarkable success story in the duty of care. The 88 per cent with a first vaccine and 77 per cent with both at the end of August 2021 will continue to rise as healthy sixteen- and seventeen-year-olds start to be offered vaccines in England.

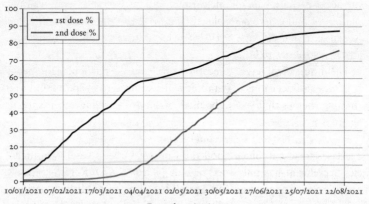

Figure 5: The cumulative percentage of those aged sixteen or over with a Covid vaccination in the UK.

Perhaps, above all, Covid Britain will rank in popular memory alongside the intense shared histories of the two world wars of the twentieth century – where were you and what did you do (or not do) in 2020–21? How did you cope with grief, loss, fear, being locked down? How did you feel? Films and novels will emerge from the pandemic as if it were a kind of historical growbag.

Every evening in 2020 we scanned the first drafts of its unfolding history on a dashboard of data – new cases, new deaths, the running total of mortalities, hospitalization rates, the R number; vaccine research, vaccine application, mutations of the virus. We became a nation of amateur epidemiologists. We began to understand something of the nature of 'zoonotic' viruses that can leap from one species to another.

The second draft of the British Covid story will begin in March 2022, at the same time as this book is published, when the public inquiry into Covid starts.* This inquiry needs to be shaped, propelled and steered by one overarching theme – the duty of care to the British people and how it was discharged by all those involved (ministers, officials, scientists, the NHS, Parliament, the private and public sectors and the press as well as that crucial if evanescent phenomenon, the Twittersphere). It needs to be one of *the* greatest, most incisive and authoritative reports of modern times.

As Professor Sarah Gilbert, Dr Catherine Green and Sir Jeremy Farrar declare, there will be a next time. And, as Farrar asserts, we must plan for it and where possible enshrine into law the kindness Michael Rosen experienced. Covid-19 is the laboratory bench for pandemic-stricken societies to come.

The inquiry will have to recapture and analyse particular moments, episodes and decisions in detail. It will also need to keep in mind four running themes that would be my key duty-of-care ingredients for its agenda.

First the preparedness prequel; the contingency planning and the exercises to test it. Since 2008 the Cabinet Office's Civil Contingencies Secretariat has published regular *National Risk Registers* (2008, 2010, 2012, 2013, 2015 and 2017)[5] based on unpublished, national risk assessments. In every edition 'pandemic influenza' has been top or

---

* Scotland's separate Public Inquiry will be started by the end of 2021.

joint top of the 'highest impact' list (but not necessarily of the highest likelihood). Public Health England ran Exercise Cygnus in 2016 based on the scenario of an influenza pandemic originating in the Middle East. It eventually published the Cygnus report after it had been leaked,[6] but we have no detail of subsequent decision taking on a) funding preparations or b) stockpiling personal protective equipment (PPE) for front-line staff. The latter should be part of the inquiry's wider treatment of the efficacy – or otherwise – of subsequent public procurements such as PPE and 'tracking and tracing' systems. Were ministers trained after Cygnus? To what extent did they take part in simulations or scenario planning?*

Questions for the 'prequel' section of the inquiry should include the adequacy of existing emergency legislation, particularly the Civil Contingencies Act 2004. In the event, it was not used. Instead, the government crafted a bespoke Coronavirus Bill.

Another question is whether the contingency planners and White-hall ministers fully took on board the fact that health policy is devolved to the 'four nations'. The Cygnus report showed that the devolved administrations were integral to the exercise. Fashioning a national UK strategy of a kind possible in pre-devolution days was, I suspect, more difficult in 2016–17 – which is why a sustained consensual approach was of such importance once the crisis began.

Surge capacity is also a critical factor in contingency planning. All parts of the UK's health and care-provision capacity began to face intense pressure when the pandemic struck, especially intensive-care capabilities in the hospitals. This was swiftly followed by the vulnerability of residents in care homes and the staff tending them – a position made more precarious still when hospitals started sending untested elderly patients back to their care homes in order to free up beds for the expected victims of Covid.

Once the 'highest impact' contingency had happened, the adequacy

---

* In early October 2021, in response to a freedom of information request Public Health England published *The Report on Exercise Alice: MERS Cov*, which took place on 15 February 2016 to test planning and resilience for a 'large scale outbreak' in the UK. Among other things, it stressed the 'crucial importance for frontline staff' of sufficient PPE. (Robert Booth, 'Coronavirus report in 2016 warned of need for training and more PPE', *Guardian*, 8 October 2021).

of the decision-taking machinery became and remained a central question – the second big theme for the public inquiry. Dominic Cummings, Johnson's Chief Downing Street adviser (July 2019 to November 2020) has kept this question high in public consciousness in his new role as Dom the Impaler in a riveting series of blogs, appearances before a House of Commons Select Committee and press interviews.

I try not to do rage, but I must confess I came very close to it in August 2021 when in an interview with Lynn Barber in *The Spectator*, Cummings recalled a conversation with Johnson in No. 10 in the summer of 2020: 'I said to him in July [2020], you're happier to live in chaos than to give me power to sort it out. And he laughed and said. "That's 100% right. I'm quite happy to live with the chaos because then everyone will stick to the king – which is me."'[7]

There is no virtue in chaos, even in the most tranquil of times. Creating or allowing deliberate chaos in a time of emergency is unforgiveable. My diary entry of 5 August 2021, I fear, lacked any trace of historical detachment:

> Another burst of impaling from Dom . . . If DC is to be believed (and No. 10 denied all of it), out of the chaotic mind of Johnson has come a new chaos theory of government devoid of any sense of duty to people and country, serving only his grotesque character and overwhelming passion to be number one, the centre of all attention.

I'm sure the inquiry will be far more temperate than I can manage. But when Johnson appears to give evidence, at which he will be under oath, I hope he will be asked about that alleged conversation.

As part of the decision-making strand of the inquiry, its members will need to capture the high policy sequences and the operational flows. They will need to assess whether or not the full Cabinet was involved in any meaningful way, my impression being that it was not.

The role, impact and provenance of scientific advice will be critical too, including the key advisory bodies such as Whitehall's Scientific Advisory Group for Emergencies (SAGE). This is the terrain upon which the most serious charges against the Johnson government have been made. Did the first and second lockdowns come too late? Would their application even a week earlier in each case have saved a substantial number of lives?[8] This question, I am sure, is where the inquiry will really put the state under the microscope, to use the prime minister's metaphor when announcing it on 12 May 2021.[9]

The inquiry will, I suspect, find it very difficult to recreate the ebbs and flows of discussion and debate between the key ministers and their special advisers as so much of the traffic was on apps beyond the reach of normal paper trails and state record keeping, as Dominic Cummings's serial recollections have shown.

What will be easier to reconstruct is the third running theme for the inquiry – the making of the Covid political economy. Standing next to Johnson at the 17 March 2020 press conference, the Chancellor of the Exchequer, Rishi Sunak, unveiled a set of measures which amounted to a new Covid duty of care as he said: 'We have never faced an economic fight like this in peacetime.'[10]

Over the next few days a great surge of state intervention was announced. 'This is not a time for ideology and orthodoxy,' Sunak declared. The government became the payer of 80 per cent of wages in a Covidvirus job retention scheme (up to a ceiling of £2,500 a month); Universal Credit was to be increased in April by £20 per week for a year (later extended to October 2021); VAT payments to HMRC for the coming quarter could be deferred; the Department of Transport suspended all rail franchises for six months and the railway companies were to receive small management fees in what struck me as a temporary renationalization.

I noted in my diary: 'This is Keynesian social democracy on steroids, a dramatic remix of the mixed economy/welfare state. A whole new political economy inside a week. It's the kind of programme a coalition government might have produced.'

So it was, but the politics of Covid will probably be beyond the inquiry's remit, though in my judgement, this theme is both crucial to the wider story of Britain and the duty of care. It is one of the great what-ifs of Covid Britain (the other being the timing of the lockdowns). I never believed in the possibility of a coalition in the formal sense of a reconstructed government with both Conservative and Labour ministers sitting together round the Cabinet table. But I was, for a short while, convinced that a high and sustained level of consensus between the parties was both possible and desirable. I'm sure the country would have welcomed it for as long as the pandemic blighted our islands.

Briefly, in the late spring of 2020, Johnson's personal experience of contracting the disease appeared to have changed him. On 29 March, looking pretty rough, he struck a strikingly consensual and un-Thatcherite note when he said in a video message: 'One thing I think the Covidvirus has already proved is that there really is such a thing as society.' The newly elected Labour leader, Sir Keir Starmer, reciprocated instantly, declaring that he would not engage in 'opposition for opposition's sake' and agreeing to meet the prime minister and his scientific advisers with a view to working together on this crisis. Just over an hour later Johnson tweeted, 'I have just spoken to Keir Starmer ... We agreed on the importance of all party leaders continuing to work constructively together through this national emergency.'

On Easter Sunday, 12 April, Johnson said of the NHS, 'I owe them my life'. On Easter Monday my shrewd friend Sir Nicholas Soames (Churchills have a feel for 'finest hours') told Jonny Diamond on BBC Radio 4's *World at One* that Johnson's words on the NHS showed he had 'moved up a notch' as PM from being a party politician to being a national leader. Having been 'on the cliff edge of life', Johnson would not wish 'to return to scrappy politics'.

But return he did. The consensus broke on the evening of 10 May 2020, when the prime minister broadcast to the nation. The press had been building up to it for days and a stream of non-attributable leaks had created the expectation of an announcement of a partial unlocking and the first steps back to work. This he duly did. But it was the manner of the build-up that caused the fracture.

The politics-as-usual leaking and spinning had angered Scotland's first minister, Nicola Sturgeon. She said she had learned the details of the PM's announcement from the Sunday newspapers rather than the government. Within minutes of Johnson's address ending, Keir Starmer said: 'We wanted clarity and consensus. We haven't got either.'

Trust is a close relation of consensus and the most precious of commodities in the relationship between government and the people. On 22 May a news story concerning the PM's closest aide broke that instantly crystallized into it's-one-rule-for-them-and-another-for-us.

The Cummings family's rural ride has also given Barnard Castle an immortal place in British political history. My daughter, Polly, summed up the whole affair: 'It has the strong feel of medieval court politics which usually ends up with someone's head on a pole.' And it caused an immediate evaporation in Johnson's and his party's standings in the opinion polls. On 2 June a YouGov poll indicated that faith in ministers as information providers had dropped from two-thirds in mid-April to less than half, but in scientists and national health organizations it was still around 80 per cent.[11]

I'm sure the public inquiry will leave these matters to the historians. But there is one hugely significant aspect of the emotional geography of Covid Britain that they will need to include among their running themes – the degree to which the British people went along with the mixture of laws and guidance that governed the way they lived, and kept their distance in the strange pandemic ecology which simultaneously atomized and collectivized them.

As Professor Chris Whitty, chief medical officer to the UK government, put it at the prime minister's press conference on 22 February 2021 (which laid out the 'road map' to 'Freedom Day'), the public had complied with the rules and guidance 'to an extraordinary degree'. It could have become unmanageable if they had not. There were moments – when the second lockdown came, for example – that I thought a measure of civil disturbance might have occurred triggering a copycat effect across our towns and cities. There were indeed anti-vax rallies and protests, but mercifully I was quite wrong and public trust and respect in scientists remained high.

The public demonstrated its care for others not just by rattling pots and pans for the NHS on successive Thursday nights but in countless acts of 'kindness to strangers', as the Queen put it in her 2020 Christmas broadcast.[12] In my home area in north-east London I was aware of the generosity of neighbours in offering to shop for others, volunteers who contacted the shielders (of whom I was one) or helped at larger vaccination sites and food banks.

The public made heroes and heroines of exemplary people too. At the older end of the age spectrum was the World War Two veteran Captain Tom Moore, who marked his personal centenary with one hundred excursions on his Zimmer frame to raise money for NHS charities. The public donated £33 million (£39 million including gift aid).[13] The Queen knighted him and a Spitfire overflew him in his Bedfordshire garden before he sadly succumbed to the virus.

At the younger end was twenty-three-year-old footballer Marcus Rashford, of Manchester United and England. He eventually persuaded the PM to extend free school meals for the poorest children during the 2020 school holidays.

In the middle, I would place Professor Sarah Gilbert and the entire Oxford team whose hard work introduced the vaccine in short time, which AstraZeneca initially produced on a non-profit basis. And Dame Kate Bingham, whose leadership of the Vaccine Task Force showed just how public procurements should be run.

The European football championships in 2021 introduced a dignified 'taking the knee' by the England team in a demonstration of solidarity against racism after the murder of George Floyd. Their remarkable manager, Gareth Southgate, went wide and deep with his thoughtful 'Dear England' letter of 8 June 2021 on the multiple notions of patriotism that unite us: 'It has been an extremely difficult year. Everyone in this country has been directly affected by isolation and loss. But we have also seen countless examples of heroism and sacrifice. It's given us all a new understanding of the fragility of life and what really matters.'[14]

Covid Britain brought forth, too, what in my judgement was the Queen's finest speech of her reign – her broadcast from Windsor Castle on the evening of 8 May 2020 to mark the seventy-fifth anniversary of VE day, the ending of the Second World War in Europe. Her props, like her words, made the linkage between 1940s Britain and what we were living through. She wore the brooch her father had given her for her eighteenth birthday in 1944. To her right on her desk was a photo of George VI in his admiral's uniform; to the left lay her ATS cap; behind, a photo of her with her parents and her sister with Churchill on the balcony of Buckingham Palace on VE night. The speech lasted but five minutes – apolitical but deeply consensual and very carefully crafted:

> Today it may seem hard that we cannot mark this special anniversary as we would wish.

Instead we remember from our homes and our doorsteps. But our streets are not empty; they are filled with the love and the care that we have for each other. And when I look at our country today, and see what we are willing to do to protect and support one another, I say with pride that we are still a nation those brave soldiers, sailors and airmen would recognize and admire . . .'[15]

It will be remembered, I think, as the Queen's 'our streets are not empty' speech. When she spoke that line, I must admit, I wept (not something I easily do).

I do not wish (or expect) the Covid inquiry team to be lachrymose amid their briefs and their files. But I do hope they catch the spirit and the intangibles, the human factors in our Covid experience, that they spare us and our leaders nothing and that they write their report in words that echo Beveridge and sing in a manner worthy of a great duty-of-care document. For, as Rudyard Kipling said of the Boer War, they have 'no end of a lesson'[16] to teach us and to prepare us for the next time 'nature cannot be fooled'.

If asked, which I do not expect to be, I would suggest the Covid inquirers call their report 'It Took a Virus', for that is what stimulated us collectively to sharpen and extend our sense of a duty of care for the vulnerable and those on the margins of society, hopefully for the foreseeable future. Though the government's intention, as I write, to stick to its plan for rescinding the £20-per-week Universal Credit in October 2021 is not encouraging.

Governments, as we have seen, perpetually have to face the dilemma of levels of welfare spending inside a shaky economy. Covid Britain saw a new version of this when ministers had to reach judgements between the conflicting needs of protecting the public and unlocking the economy. They will face many more tough choices in recovery Britain. But the generosity of spirit shown in abundance in Covid Britain should – and can be – turned into a spur and an inspiration to do better by our people. That is the key 'no end of a lesson' to be learned.

8

A New Consensus and a
New Beveridge?

No scientist is admired for failing in the attempt to solve prob-
lems that lie beyond his competence. The most he can hope for
is the kindly contempt earned by the Utopian politician. If
politics is the art of the possible, research is surely the art of
the soluble. Both are immensely practical-minded affairs.
Sir Peter Medawar, 1964[1]

Fear is a very bad adviser.
George Soros, 25 June 2020[2]

Blessings may break from stone, who knows how.
George Mackay Brown[3]

There was much to play for between the first and second lockdowns
as I watched both the natural and political seasons begin to change
from my window overlooking Scapa Flow, George Mackay Brown's
home waters, in September 2020. Could the art of the possible and
the art of the soluble be combined in such a way that in the early
2020s, our pathogen-scarred country might enter one of its most
worthwhile and productive phases? For all the mood swings caught in
the pages of my Covid-Britain diary, I remained convinced that it
could and utterly sure that it should. But for that to happen, Britain
would need both a new, more consensual politics and a shared programme made possible by that consensus, strengthening it in a cycle
of mutual reinforcement. It would also need a refreshed political language with which to convey the new possibilities.

TOWARDS A NEW POLITICS

It is easier to see British history falling into Before Covid and After Covid than it is to demarcate a new politics reflecting that shift, and not just because of the natural time lag between events and the political adjustments that may or may not follow.

That said, there was for a few weeks after the prime minister came out of hospital, more than a flickering of consensual possibility and Johnson's words reflected that, producing, as we have seen, little bursts of optimism not least because the leader of the Labour Party, Sir Keir Starmer, seemed a natural consensualist in approaching the health emergency – both in his temperament and in his use of political language. It did not last, to my great regret, for reasons I recorded as they unfolded. This was made all the more unfortunate by the plunge in trust occasioned by the Barnard Castle incident and its aftermath, and, later, the haemorrhaging of government authority as the emails containing examination results in 2019 were opened in England and Scotland.

Even in relatively normal times it is difficult for a government to regain trust and authority once it has been lost, whatever the majority it enjoys in the House of Commons. In extraordinary and relentlessly demanding circumstances it will prove even more demanding.

Yet there was still a 'never again' tang in the air – an appetite for co-operation, even a certain relishing of the (temporary) ending of bear-garden, rancour-fuelled exchanges that social distancing had brought to Prime Minister's Questions in the House of Commons. There was also a wish for our political class and our governing institutions to 'rise to the level of events'* we had already experienced and the uncertainties still to come.

The £20 uplift in Universal Credit was due to end on 6 October 2021, and as of mid-August there were no signs that it would be extended in spite of calls for it to continue, including from the six previous Conservative Secretaries of State for Work and Pensions. An IFS report in July 2021 noted that the extra £20 represented 'the first significant real-term increase in entitlements for out-of-work

---

* As Roy Jenkins used to put it.

claimants without children in half a century'. This lack of real increase has also 'left the safety net for those without children unusually thin by international standards, well below the average among developed countries'.

Fertilized by this Covid-accumulated experience, a new version of politics might yet flourish. Is this too much a reflection of a personal wish combined with a temperament at the Pollyanna end of the spectrum? Perhaps. But this is where Peter Medawar's 'the art of the soluble' plus 'the art of the possible' fuse into what is practical in terms of a shared programme for a hard-edged consensus as opposed to a soft one. Such a fusion could turn the politics of the 2020s into a productive phase of valuable shared achievement rather than an extension of the cult of recrimination into which the Brexit experience had plunged us as the pathogen first touched our shores.

Here, too, lies incentive for our politicians. The roulette wheel of politics gives most practitioners but a short time in office even if they achieve senior Cabinet rank. (There are exceptions: Rab Butler in the twentieth century; Jack Straw in the late twentieth and early twenty-first, whose memoir, revealingly, was called *Last Man Standing*.[4]) But, for most politicians, their period of influence is usually fleeting at best. If I were part of the 2020s political class I would wish, when retirement eventually comes, to be remembered as part of a generation that did good and necessary things, in tough and demanding times, for the enduring benefit of generations to come – as, I would argue, the wartime and post-1945 political class did with their version of a duty of care.

Is there a programme sitting waiting for that early 2020s generation – one that could carry *their* duty of care? I think there is. So here are my ingredients for a new Beveridge – an array of policies and initiatives to tackle injustice, inequality and economic and technical underperformance simultaneously. It is a programme that would run with the grain of our better past (especially those wartime and early post-war years of the 1940s and 1950s) and lead to a more equal, socially just nation funded by the levels of productivity that can come only from sustained scientific and technical prowess with a set of effective democratic and governing institutions to match. It would also, through its outcomes, provide a worthy memorial for those who lost their lives to Covid.

In my judgement there should be at the outset, five shared 'tasks', rather than 'giants', central to a new and productive consensus.

1. Social care
2. Social housing
3. Technical education
4. Preparing our economy and our society for artificial intelligence
5. Combating and mitigating climate change

I would add a sixth – refreshing the UK constitution – but the objective in that case is a) far from consensual and b) needs to await developments in Scotland so that we have an answer to the first-order question of the very configuration of the kingdom whose constitution we would reshape. It needs, I think, the illumination that a royal commission (that ancient and now rarely used instrument of state) can bring and could be created swiftly. Its purpose? A mind-clearing and possibility-testing body to think *ahead* of events as a prelude to action *after* the medium-term future of the Union is known. (I shall return to this theme in the next chapter.)

The 'five tasks' for the early 2020s all have an immediacy and urgency that cannot wait for a wider refashioning of the measurement and uses of wealth that might occur. If I were a politician, rather than a non-party crossbench member of the House of Lords, this would be my core manifesto for the 2020s.

Social care

I have placed social care at the top of the list for three reasons. First, when Covid tore through the nation's care homes, it shone an intense light on the pressing and persistent needs of both carers and cared for and their families. Second, fashioning a national care service would, at last, complete the *old* welfare settlement that sprang from the Beveridge Report and the shared experience of the Second World War. Third, because this could be a talismanic reform, a pacemaker and pessimism-breaker at the heart of a post-Covid consensus. Social care is that rare thing in UK politics: a policy almost universally regarded as reform whose time has come.

In November 2019, before the pandemic, the health think tank the King's Fund identified eight key deficiencies in the provision of social care in England and Wales:

1. Means-testing: it's not like the NHS.
2. Catastrophic costs: selling homes to pay for care.
3. Unmet need: people going without the care and support they need.
4. Quality of care: fifteen-minute care visits and neglect.
5. Workforce pay and conditions: underpaid, overworked staff.
6. Market fragility: care home companies going out of business.
7. Disjointed care: delayed transfers of care and lack of integration with health.
8. The postcode lottery: unwarranted variation in access and performance.[5]

In August 2020 the King's Fund revisited its octet of concerns in the unforgiving light of Covid and lockdown one. They found that 'deficiencies' 1 and 2 had 'barely been mentioned' over the past few months.

Instead the public focus has rightly been first, on *quality of care*, as Covid-19 wrought a terrible death toll and, in many places, fundamentally changed the way care was being delivered. Second there has also been some . . . focus on *unmet need*, as Covid-19 both created more need and made it more difficult to meet existing need. A third key area . . . has been the difference in the ways local care systems have dealt with the pandemic and the potential for the existing *postcode lottery* . . .

The report noted the welcome recognition the crisis had brought to the care workforce before concluding that disjointed care was very apparent, 'most obviously in the ongoing dispute about discharge from hospital during the early stages of the pandemic'.[6]

The systematic inadequacies of social care provision had been horribly exposed. The country should never have been in this position in 2020. For it had looked for a time as if social care would be *the* great welfare improvement of the Blair years. At Labour's 1996 party conference he stressed the wrong of the elderly having to sell their homes to fund their care. In 1997 and in 2001 the country gave him huge parliamentary majorities. The field of reform was Tony Blair's to conquer and in 1998 he established a royal commission on long-term care chaired by Sir Stewart Sutherland, philosopher and accomplished university administrator, to map its contours. In March 1999 its report, *With Respect to Old Age*, was published.[7]

But the path of reform did not run swiftly or easily. The Sutherland Commission was split, with two of its members wanting more means-testing than the majority. The new, post-devolution Labour/Liberal Democrat Scottish administration ran with it, but the Blair government did not. Twenty years later the House of Lords Economic Affairs Committee, in a biting report titled *Social Care Funding: Time to End a National Scandal*, drew on a House of Commons briefing paper to capture the depressing litany of vicissitudes that had befallen the social care question over the years since the Sutherland Report. This was its outline:

- 1999: A government-appointed (Sutherland) royal commission published proposals for reform. These included a more generous means-test and free personal and nursing care. The proposals were accepted in part by the then Labour government (free personal and nursing care was introduced subsequently by the Scottish government, citing the royal commission's recommendations).
- 2009: A Green Paper by the Labour government proposed a National Care Service, and a subsequent White Paper proposed a two-year cap on social care charges initially, followed by free social care after 2015.
- 2011: The coalition government established the Commission on the Funding of Care and Support (the 'Dilnot Commission'). This commission proposed a cap on lifetime social care charges and a more generous means-test.
- 2014: The coalition government legislated to implement the Dilnot Commission's proposals with cross-party support, but the newly elected (post-2015) Conservative government in July postponed their introduction from April 2016, citing funding pressures and a lack of preparedness by local authorities. In 2017 the implementation of the proposals was postponed indefinitely.

- 2017: The Conservative government committed to publishing a Green Paper on social care in the March 2017 Budget, a commitment reiterated in the Conservative Party manifesto for the 2017 general election, which also included a proposal to introduce a floor on the costs an individual could incur. The Green Paper has been delayed numerous times: the proposed date for publication was April 2019 but the secretary of state blamed 'Brexit and the need for bandwidth' for the missed deadline.[8]

The ingredients of a cross-party consensus were there but crude electoral politics prevented them from being fashioned into the agreement needed. As the Institute for Government (IfG) put it in their evidence to the Lords Economic Affairs Committee:

Proposals including a government discussion paper in 2010 on how to fund free social care were quickly dubbed a 'death tax' by the Conservative opposition and dogged the Labour Party throughout that year's election. During the 2017 election campaign the shoe was on the other foot. The Conservatives' social care manifesto commitment quickly became known as the 'dementia tax' and is widely seen as contributing to the Government losing its majority ... Painful precedents such as these mean that political parties are reluctant to discuss how to raise money to fund health and social care.[9]

The Lords committee report was duly and justifiably scathing about the harmful effects of the raw politics of care in the 2010s:

Cross-party co-operation will be necessary if progress is to be made on reforms to social care funding. It will be easier to achieve if reforms make the system easier to understand. Evidence shows that people who have not had direct exposure to the social care system do not appreciate the extent to which people are responsible for paying [for] their own care, and that the system is too complex. This inhibits discussion around reform. As proved by the 'death tax' and 'dementia tax' refrains in recent election campaigns.[10]

The IfG was right to stress cost as part of the problem. A comprehensive national care system would represent a substantial and permanent new financial obligation for both state and taxpayer. As

Nick Timmins stressed, one reason for the lost two decades was that the question of reform 'looked irresolvable for as long as the electorate continued to vote in governments determined to control public spending, recessions aside, at around 40 per cent or so of GDP'.[11]

The Lords Economic Affairs Committee tackled this head-on:

> The Government should introduce a basic entitlement to publicly funded personal care for individuals with substantial and critical levels of needs. Accommodation costs and the costs of other help and support should still be incurred by the individual. The Health Foundation and the King's Fund estimated this would cost £7 billion if introduced in 2020/21.[12]

The Lords report, one of the most significant the House has produced in recent times, had particular bite because of the committee's membership. Its chairman, Michael Forsyth (Lord Forsyth of Drumlean), is a small-state, low-tax, free-market man to his fingertips and its members included two former Chancellors of the Exchequer (Norman Lamont and Alistair Darling) and two former permanent secretaries to the Treasury (Terry Burns and Andrew Turnbull).

Since they reported in July 2019, Covid has changed so many of the political, economic and social dials, but the ten 'principles' they laid out for the reform of social care are even more valid:

> Any long term funding solution for adult social care should:
>
> - Put more money into the system through a combination of public and personal funding;
> - Be simple and easy to understand for those accessing public funding;
> - Ensure local authorities can afford to provide care to all those whose needs meet the legal eligibility criteria, which must be interpreted fairly and consistently across local authorities;
> - Quantify and address serious unmet needs;
> - Ensure the level of unpaid carers in the system does not suffer a steep decline and is sustainable;
> - Better protect individuals from catastrophic costs;
> - Reduce the disparity between entitlement to help in the National Health Service and the adult social care system, ensuring that entitlement is based on the level of need, not the diagnosis;

- Allow local authorities to pay care providers a rate that covers the costs of providing care, without the need for cross-subsidy from self-funders;
- Distribute adult social care funding more fairly across local authorities;
- Invest in the social care workforce and ensure a more joined up approach to workforce planning with the National Health Service.[13]

Putting social care right – in effect placing a national care service where it belongs alongside the National Health Service – is fundamental to any post-Covid duty of care. This, above all, we owe to those who have died in the care homes and to their families. And the Johnson government recognized it in its White Paper *Integration and Innovation: Working Together to Improve Health and Social Care for All*, designed 'to tackle the health inequalities exposed by Covid-19', which it published in February 2021.

The White Paper and the Health and Care Bill it sketched out was about organization, *not* the key matter of funding adult social care (that was to await further 'proposals this year'). But it described the integrated care systems that would bring together local authorities and the NHS as arising from the 'experience of the pandemic [which] has made the case for integrated care even stronger'. Once again, a settlement for the funding of social care seems to be within touching distance – but we have been there many times before and in June 2021 a planned meeting between PM, Chancellor and health secretary to agree a funding method (either a rise in general taxation, or a special or hypothecated care tax, or addition to national insurance) was postponed until the autumn. The announcement finally came on 7 September.

Its essential ingredients were:

- To raise £36.3 billion over 3 years to fund the NHS catch-up (£28.8bn) and social care in England (£5.3 bn) and Scotland, Wales and Northern Ireland (£2.2 bn).
- To fund it by increases of 1.25% in national insurance contributions and tax on dividends, and from 2023, national insurance to be paid by working pensioners.

- From 2023 a cap of £86,000 would be placed on individual contributions to personal care at local council rates, but no equivalent cap on hotel costs in care and nursing homes.

This was immediately controversial as the Johnson government had made no attempt to build that cross-party consensus which the House of Lords Select Committee had rightly judged to be essential to the shaping and durability of the policy. It also generated a spirit of internal tension within the Conservative Party not only because of the extra public spending involved but also because, as the Chancellor Rishi Sunak explained, it represented 'a permanent new role for the government'.

The Labour Party withheld support for the proposed settlement claiming the burden of extra taxation fell excessively on the working population and insufficiently on the rich. When the House of Commons divided on the proposed rises in taxation on 8 September, the Government won by 319 to 248.

The greatest immediate concern was that funding the pressing Covid demands on the NHS would crowd out the public money needed for social care. The Institute for Fiscal studies warned that 'an ever-growing NHS budget could swallow up this week's tax rise' - an anxiety strengthened by Johnson's refusal to set targets for clearing the NHS backlog in a BBC interview on 8 September.[14]

To the Prime Minister's credit, however, he tackled head-on the criticism that the new arrangements broke two of his party's 2019 general election manifesto pledges: that neither National Insurance contributions nor general taxation levels would rise. 'A global pandemic was in 'nobody's manifesto', he said.

In this and in many other ways, Covid Britain has changed the rules of politics. The pity was that it was not consensually done – because, on social care, in my judgement, this time consensus really was there for the taking.

Social housing

Ever since Mrs Thatcher's government introduced the 'right to buy' for council tenants in 1980, the UK provision of social housing has been locked in a vortex of decline. In 1981 30 per cent of houses were socially rented; by 2016 the stock of social housing had fallen to 17 per cent – a huge shift.

There were attempts to reverse the trend. For example, a

> commitment to replace a portion of the properties sold under the [right to buy] scheme was introduced in 2011, although the latest statistics [the Lords briefing paper was published in January 2019] suggest that these obligations are not being met. Over the same period, central government funding for building new homes for social rent was also reduced, replaced in part by funding for construction of homes for affordable rent, with rents up to 80 per cent of market rents.[15]

Harold Macmillan's post-war building programme is associated with council houses across the villages, towns and cities of the kingdom (the surge of increasingly harmful and unpopular high-rise blocks largely came later). In one of the biggest changes in the post-war years, the numbers living in council homes was down from 42 per cent of Britons in 1979, to just under 8 per cent in 2015,[16] as housing associations and private companies took over from most local authority providers. Surprisingly, housing seemed to lack a 'great champion' in the Cameron/Clegg coalition years. British politics was no longer producing Macmillans.

There were multiple factors at play. In the careful, politically neutral words of a House of Lords Research Briefing:

> It has been argued that ... housing trends have had implications for several housing-related issues. Statistics show that private renters spend a higher proportion of their income on rent than social renters. Although, in general, rents have risen mostly in proportion to income, renters in London, 25- to 34-year-olds and those on low incomes are facing increasing housing burdens. Real-term spending on housing benefit has also increased substantially over the past thirty years with some attributing this to the lack of investment in social housing. In addition, the homeless charity 'Crisis' has argued that insecure housing in the private sector has also led to increased rates of statutory homelessness, and that the lack of available social homes has posed additional challenges for local authorities when trying to house those to which it owes a duty of prevention or relief.[17]

Widening the lens beyond the social to the overall housing picture, by the time the coalition government ended in 2015, 'relative to its population, Britain had had western Europe's lowest rate of house-building for three decades'.[18] With a population nearing 66 million, 20 million more than the era of Macmillan's building drive as housing minister when the target of 300,000 new homes a year was reached and surpassed in 1953/4,[19] the annual figures were poor, even allowing for the fact that housing was now a devolved matter.

The 'right to buy' brought the palpable benefits of home ownership to council tenants who previously could not have contemplated it. The 1.75 million purchases under the policy created both individual family betterment and collective improvement to often run-down estates, blighted by long delays in repairs on the part of local authorities. But the failure to build more public sector housing to replace those moved into the private sector was a regrettable and avoidable consequence.

> Housing starts of all types in England – always too few [in Nick Timmins's judgement] – had risen from 140,000 in Labour's early years [after 1997] to a peak of just over 180,000 before they crashed to fewer than 80,000 in 2009. By 2016 they had crawled up to 140,000 again, when on the government's own estimate between 225,000 and 275,000 a year were needed.[20]

There has been a quickening sense of the fundamental place of shelter in any overall duty of care. Most significant of all in those terms was the tragedy of the 2017 Grenfell Tower fire in London's richest borough, Kensington and Chelsea, with its terrible death toll of seventy-two that highlighted the threat to life if safety standards are not given the paramountcy they deserve.

Richard Norton-Taylor, investigative journalist and playwright (his *Grenfell: Value Engineering – Scenes from the Inquiry* was based on the transcripts), saw the tragedy as 'symbolic of contemporary British Society . . . What is being exposed is how companies and local authorities passed the buck . . . incompetence, secrecy, cost-cutting, the consequences of government austerity policies, deregulation, the cost and unaccountable networks of people who knew each other.'[21]

Post-Grenfell audits indicated that another 250 blocks were clad in similarly dangerous material and some 2,000 blocks overall required remedial work, which made such apartments unsaleable until repairs were completed. In July 2021 the government finally set aside £5.1 billion for such post-Grenfell work, a third of what many experts believed to be needed. The money was announced on 5 July 2021 alongside the Buildings Safety Bill, which had been foreshadowed.

In 2017 the government undertook work with councils to produce more social housing.[22] In November 2020, the Johnson government published a 'Charter for Social Housing Residents' embedded in its *Social Housing* White Paper containing seven post-Grenfell pledges:

Safe in your home
Knowledge of how your landlord is performing
The prompt addressing of complaints
Respectful treatment
Regular meetings with landlord
Good neighbourhood
Support for first steps up the ladder to ownership

– all supported by a toughened legal regime for the Regulators of Social Housing, whose remit was henceforth to 'explicitly include safety'.[23]

Safe, good-quality shelter is always and everywhere a key piece of what Nye Bevan called 'the living tapestry of a mixed community'.[24] Bevan, who as Minister of Health 1945–50 was also responsible for housing and local government, was characteristically poetic about housing policy, not just as a meeter of needs but also as a healer of class divides. To that end he summoned those perambulators again.

> We don't want a country of East Ends and West Ends, with all the petty snobberies this involves. That was one of the evil legacies of the Victorian era . . . I hope that the old people will not be asked to live in colonies of their own – they do not want to look down out of their windows on an endless procession of the funerals of their friends; they also want to look down on processions of perambulators.[25]

Politicians can be divided into poets and plumbers (a distinction I owe to Trevor Smith, former Professor of Politics at Queen Mary). Bevan's genius – and Macmillan's, too, in his very different style – was a mix of both. Social housing policy is crying out again for a combination of the two, sustained as it could be by borrowing at the very favourably low long-term rates currently available in London's deep capital markets and propelled by a political consensus I hope is already in the making.

The government's initiative for rough sleepers, 'Everybody In', had moved at least 9,866 people into emergency housing, but there was thought to have been an upward trend in new rough sleepers during Covid-19 and considerable concern that it would rise again once hotels and other sites for temporary accommodation could no longer be used post-Covid.[26]

Technical education

A few days before picking up my pen to write this section, I noted in my diary that the North Yorkshire Moors Railway was having to turn to Russia for its coal because of the closure of the last mine in Northumberland – a symbolic end to the globe-transforming age of coal and steam begun by the British. One of the great and lingering mysteries of that age is why and how the nation that first blended craft skills, local mineral resources and the scientific wing of the Enlightenment has never, so far, managed to institutionalize and embed widespread and top-flight technical education, from day one at school to retirement and first pension payment. This has been bothering policymakers at least since 1868, when the Royal Commission on Endowed Schools declared:

> We are bound to add that our evidence appears to show that our industrial classes have not even that basis of sound general education at which alone technical education can rest . . . and unless we remedy this want we shall gradually but surely find that our superiority in wealth and perhaps in energy will not save us from decline.[27]

An extraordinary piece of prescience.

The yawning gap in our education and training provision is allied to the persistent failure to convert our science into industrial and commercial production – a central threnody since the Second World War in report after report, industrial strategy after industrial strategy.[28] Is it possible that a combination of Brexit and rebuilding the economy

1. Starting-gun for the post-war welfare state: Sir William Beveridge completing his landmark report in October 1942.

2. The giant-slayer: Beveridge's assault on Want, Ignorance, Disease, Squalor and Idleness caught the imagination of the press and the people.

3. The sermon on the shelter: Labour leader Clem Attlee helped down by his wife Violet, from an air-raid shelter in his Limehouse constituency on election day, 5 July 1945.

4. The economist as saviour: John Maynard Keynes, with his wife Lydia, disembarks in Southampton before rushing to the House of Lords to explain the loan he had negotiated in Washington in December 1945.

5. The uncomprehending, the anxious and the feline: Winston Churchill, Anthony Eden and Rab Butler in 1945 as the Conservative Party begins to absorb the political and policy lessons of its election defeat.

6. What it was all for: An East-End mum picks up her first family allowance in Stratford, London in August 1946.

7. An artist in the power of language: Nye Bevan, master-builder of the National Health Service, mobilises the Labour Party Conference, Margate, October 1950.

8. Tenements still to be felled: the Gorbals, Glasgow, 1956.

9. The patrician and the council house: Harold Macmillan, Minister of Housing and Local Government, inspects the fruits of his building programme in Manchester, April 1952.

10. The pursuit of equality: the London County Council opens its first comprehensive school, Kidbrooke, in Greenwich, 1954.

11. Searching for an elusive economic miracle: the Labour Front bench in 1966. Prime Minister Harold Wilson talks to his Chancellor, Jim Callaghan, who would himself become PM ten years later. Denis Healey is on Callaghan's left.

12. Idleness rises once more: the dole queue in Newtownbreda, Northern Ireland, 1974.

13. 'It Took A Riot': disturbances in Liverpool brought the leonine Environment Secretary, Michael Heseltine, to Toxteth, Merseyside, on a fact-finding mission in July 1981.

14. The sermon on the mound: Margaret Thatcher explains her version of a free-market duty of care to a less than ecstatic Church of Scotland, Edinburgh, May 1988.

15. A giant still to be slain: Tony Blair pledges to banish child poverty within a generation. Toynbee Hall, east London, March 1999.

A Welfare State for the 21st Century

16. The former 'Welfare' Chancellor now PM: Gordon Brown visits a Sure Start centre, in Manchester, September 2008.

17. European battles past and present: David Cameron, Joachim Gauck, the President of Germany and the Princess Royal on Hoy, Orkney, with Royal Navy and German Navy warships in Scapa Flow, commemorating the centenary of the Battle of Jutland on 31 May 2016, just weeks before the European Question ended his premiership.

18. 'A country that works for everyone': Theresa May, on her first day in No 10 pledges to tackle 'burning injustice', 13 July 2016.

19. The tragic symbol of a failed duty of care: seventy-two lives were lost when Grenfell Tower burned in Kensington, 14 June 2017.

20. 'Our streets are not empty': the Queen broadcasts on the 75th anniversary of VE Day flanked by a photograph of her father and her ATS cap.

21. The sound of gratitude: Tyneside claps for frontline Covid carers during the first lockdown, April 2020.

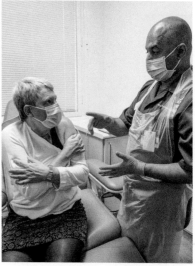

22. Queen of the Jabs: Kate Bingham, head of the Vaccine Taskforce, starts her Novavax trial at the Royal Free Hospital, London, October 2020.

post-Covid could enable the UK to fill the technical void at last? As we saw in Part One, there have been several attempts to complete this, the most conspicuous piece of unfinished business from the 1944 Education Act, not least by Kenneth Baker as Secretary of State for Education, with his fifteen City Technology Colleges.[29] Baker has been a keeper of the flame for technical education in the higher reaches of post-war British politics. And if the flame is to flare and prosper in post-Covid Britain his latest initiative, the forty-eight University Technical Colleges (UTCs) begun in 2010, could serve as the template for expansion. Their strength is the degree to which they shape their training to the needs of local and national employers. In some areas, the UTCs have experienced difficulties in filling all their places (maybe that social snobbery about technical education is still doing its malign work) and there is now a push on to redress the gender imbalance.[30]

The Covid days saw a considerable movement in technical education. In September 2020 the first intake of T-level students (a T level is the technical equivalent of an A level) started work. In January 2021 the Johnson government published a White Paper, *Skills for Jobs*, which sought to propel technical training to its deserved place in the educational sun.

Drawing on the longstanding experience of German chambers of commerce, it placed employers 'at the heart of the system' so that technical education and training boosted productivity and reduced the skills gaps through involvement in new 'Local Skills Improvement Plans'. Another promising innovation was the pledge of funding from 2025 through 'lifelong loan entitlements' 'to the equivalent of four years of post-18 education' with the intention of 'making it as easy to get a student finance loan for an approved Higher Technical Qualification as it is for a full-length degree'.[31] This reflected some of the thinking of the Augar Inquiry into Post-18 Education and Funding, which reported in 2019.[32]

Place the UTC as the institutional model, alongside the new T-level exams,[33] and the planned funding and institutional reforms become more possible than at any time since the 1944 Act. A consensus for such chasm-bridging could certainly be constructed, especially if its purpose is shared and fused with the fourth task, the imperatives of the coming age of Artificial Intelligence.

Artificial intelligence (AI)

Alan Turing adds a touch of magic to any activity, artefact or concept to which his name is applied, from Second World War code-breaking at Bletchley Park to the computer and artificial intelligence. Historians of science, for example, date the genesis of AI to a paper Turing published in *Mind* on 1 October 1950. It was called 'Computing Machinery and Intelligence'.[34] Turing's twenty-seven pages gave flight to the idea that from the early breakthroughs in digital computing, the machine equivalent of human neural networks might emerge: artificial intelligence.

After alternative waves of optimism and pessimism (so called 'AI winters'[35]) in the USA and the UK, the hour of AI seemed definitely to have come in the second decade of the twenty-first century with 'deep learning' neural networks.[36] Its immense power and width was captured (albeit prosaically) in the definition of AI used in the most recent industrial strategy (drawn up by the May government in 2017 and foolishly abandoned by the Johnson government in 2021): 'Technologies with the ability to perform tasks that would otherwise require human intelligence, such as visual perception, speech recognition, and language translation.'[37]

This was the definition used by a 181-page House of Lords Committee on AI which reported in 2018.[38] The key finding in that report, almost a master assumption, suffused its pages with a distinctly new-Beveridge feel:

> Artificial intelligence will change the way we all relate to the world around us. The questions AI raises challenge existing ideological questions which have defined politics in the UK. The economy and society are changing, and all parties must stand ready to embrace and direct that change. As a cross-party committee, we recognise that in order for the UK to meet its potential and lead the way for shaping the future for society, AI policy must be committed to for the long-term, agreed by consensus and informed by views on all sides.[39]

This 'views on all sides' point is crucial, as fitting out a society and an economy to both humanize and maximize the possibilities of AI requires a characteristic in desperately short supply in the political class – genuine humility.

There are less prosaic ways of thinking about AI than the government definition. As Sir Paul Nurse, geneticist, Nobel Prize winner and director of the Crick Institute, puts it in his *What is Life?*

> We have barely scratched the surface of understanding how the interactions between billions of individual neurons can combine to generate abstract thought, self-consciousness and our apparent free will ... Today's most powerful 'AI' computer programs are built to mimic, in a highly simplified form, the way life's neural networks handle information. These computer systems perform increasingly impressive datacrunching feats, but display nothing that even vaguely resembles abstract or imaginative thought, self-awareness or consciousness.[40]

The deepest of deep questions – 'what it really means to be', in Sir Paul's lapidary words – the AI-enabled transformations that *are* discernible command urgent attention not least in education both early and lifelong. One of the Lords' AI Committee's witnesses, Paul Clarke, Chief Technology Officer of Ocado, described what is needed as 'a pipeline of digital literacy that stretches all the way back to primary school'[41] to prepare for the possibilities and uncertainties of an AI economy and society. Theresa May's government established a National Retraining Scheme to further reskilling and Mrs May herself spoke at Davos in 2018 on the need to 'shape this change [AI] to ensure AI works for everyone'.[42]

There are two underlying questions and one key requirement for the coming AI Britain. First, will it lead to the productivity gains so widely predicted and once and for all fill the productivity gap that has blighted the UK economy since the end of the Second World War? Previous waves of the digital revolution have disappointed on this front, perhaps because new technologies tend to take longer to travel from lab to factory or office than policymakers and the public expect. As the celebrated American economist Robert Solow famously put it: 'You can see the computer age everywhere but [in] the productivity statistics.'[43] This wave, the AI one, promises to beat 'Solow's Paradox', as economists call it, because it will tear through the administrative and back-up functions of both public and private sectors in a manner not experienced when previous digital tides were sweeping aside swathes of white-collar jobs in a manner that the first waves of automation did in so many manufacturing firms.

Secondly, can the AI-to-come meet the Tinbergen test (see page 66)? Will the reskilling that results from it – redirecting the labour of those whose tasks are now performed by AI – cut against the growing inequalities that have accompanied the rise of knowledge economies? Can AI be both a transformer and a leveller? On this terrain so vital to the well-being of society, government as reskiller and retrainer must have a prominent place. The Covid experience already appears to have sped up the process of AI innovation and application. As Mark Carney, the former governor of the Bank of England, observed in December 2020, life under Covid not only stimulated the online economy but also pulled forward elements of the 'fourth industrial revolution . . . into this case and we really need to think about how we're going to do mass retraining and reskilling . . .'[44]

Finally, the great financial requirement. The huge 'black hole' Covid has left in the public finances means the UK needs a very substantial bounty from AI if the 'new Beveridge' social reforms are to be fundable (on 6 July 2021 the Office for Budgetary Responsibility warned Chancellor Rishi Sunak that the Treasury would have to find £10 billion extra a year for three years just to pay for the unfunded legacy costs for health (£7 billion), education (£1 billion) and transport (£2 billion).[45] In its way, it is the equivalent of Beveridge's insistence on full employment as the means of making his giant-slaying financially affordable.

And there is a another heavy resource-eater of truly giant proportions which is already here and which will be with us – all of us – until we draw our last breaths, what my lifelong friend John Browne, former CEO of BP, calls 'the grave reality of climate change'.[46]

Climate change

Whatever the debates about how much human activity has contributed to global warming, not for nothing did the atmospheric chemist and Nobel Laureate Paul Crutzen in 2000 describe the age in which we are living as 'the Anthropocene' – the planetary era that is being shaped by the activities of humankind.[47]

Combating and mitigating its effects is *the* first-order question facing the UK and all other countries – the ultimate duty of care and yet the most difficult to provide as achieving it requires multiple actions from household, industry and national infrastructure up to the global institutions and forums in which, ultimately, the world's greatest polluting nations and the developing ones will have to be persuaded to act in concert. The most the UK can hope to achieve on its own is to be one of the exemplary nations in reaching the great prize of carbon net zero. This will take a sustained, collective and consensual effort. It can also offer the world some extraordinarily accomplished scientists and technologists in the prodigious feats of engineering, physics and chemistry needed to decarbonize the world through, for example, carbon capture and storage and perhaps the ever elusive grail of nuclear fusion.

Our attitude to resources has utterly changed since the early postwar years with which this book began. Coal was then our indispensable black gold source of energy that had propelled our economic and industrial take-off. It also fuelled the UK's global and imperial reach and the sea power on which it rested, the great cry of government to the miners to dig for more. Ernie Bevin is said to have told the colliers, 'Give me another million tons of coal and I'll give you a new foreign policy.'[48] Now coal is the once-king of fossil fuels whom we must depose forever.

Coal and climate change are vividly on our minds and smoke belches out, usually now from a Chinese power station, in almost every television news bulletin that touches on the subject. It's far harder to grasp carbon emission in our everyday existence, which, I suspect, adds to the political difficulty of alerting the public to the problem in-the-round. One analyst who has accomplished this is Rob West, in an October 2019 paper titled 'Investing for an Energy Transition?'

> *Decarbonisation is challenging* because of the energy system's sheer size: 63,000 TWH of energy was consumed in 2018. For perspective, this is equivalent to a kitchen toaster running constantly, 24 hours per day, 365 days per year for each and every one of the world's 7.7bn inhabitants ...

The world relies upon this energy in ways that can often be difficult to perceive. The most energy-intensive process most of us will witness directly in our lives is an intercontinental flight, equivalent to around 3.6MWH of energy and 500kg of CO2 per person. Nevertheless flying is just 3% of global CO2.

The majority of our energy consumption is embedded in the products we consume and buildings in which we consume them.

Add up the numbers in Table 10, and these categories have covered virtually half the world's CO2 emissions, which will likely be invisible to most of us, as we go about our daily lives.[49]

Table 10: Estimated percentage of global CO2 emissions arising from various sectors.

Agriculture	13%
Steel	9%
Concrete	8%
Plastics	2%
Fertiliser	1%
Manufacturing above into products	10%
Shipping	5%
Total	**48%**

Source: Rob West, 'Investing for an Energy Transition', Thunder Said Energy, 13 October 2019.

Having spent three centuries using CO2 emitting energy to 'bend nature to our will',[50] we have but a few decades to bend that world towards sustainability and survival.

At the turn of 2020–21, there was an interesting and potentially hugely important confluence of thinking about how combating climate change could reshape the entire future of political economy, including its values and the way it is measured (to which I shall return in Chapter 9). The fundamental question was how to harness the extraordinary capacity of liberal capitalist economies to the cause of carbon reduction.

In 2020 Mark Carney, drawing on his long service as a central banker at the apex of the global financial system, declared bluntly: 'We've been trading off the planet against profit,' driven by 'a tragedy of the horizon ... with our horizon fixated on the current news, business and political cycles'.[51] The key, according to Carney, is developing

> a consensus for sustainability [whereby] we can unleash the dynamism of the private sector to put value in the service of values ... If society sets a clear goal, it will become profitable to be part of the solution and costly to remain part of the problem ... Building a sustainable future will be capital-intensive after a long period when there's been too little investment. It will be job-heavy when unemployment is soaring ... We need greater investment and innovation in critical technologies such as hydrogen, carbon capture and storage, and sustainable aviation fuels.

As for measuring economic performance: 'A financial system in which climate change is as much a determinant of a company's value as changes in credit worthiness or interest rates on technology' is what is needed.[52] Bill Gates made a very similar argument in *How to Avoid a Climate Disaster*: 'Markets, technology and policy are like three levers that we need to pull in order to wean ourselves from fossil fuels.'[53]

There was a strong similarity in Sir Partha Dasgupta's review *The Economics of Biodiversity*, commissioned by the Treasury and published in January 2021, in which the distinguished Cambridge economist, building on the Stern Report (see page 83), argued that: 'Introducing natural capital into national accounting systems would be a critical step towards making inclusive wealth our measure of progress.'[54] The description of a new 'well-being economy' in Sir Michael Marmot's December 2020 *Build Back Fairer* review linked both greater health equity and employment opportunity to a greening of the UK economy.[55]

Such transformations require a shift, too, in public perception and attitude. Could it be that a greater, more intense sense of nature fighting back against our hubristic manipulations is emerging out of the Covid experience of 'viruses that spill over into humans', as Professor Dame Sarah Gilbert, leader of the Oxford University vaccine team, puts it?[56] Will public opinion make a connection between natural habitats being destroyed and the emerging diseases unleashed in, for example, the creatures on sale in the wet markets of Asia and the Far East?

The Climate Assembly,* which reported to six parliamentary committees in September 2020, suggested it might be. Concentrating on pathways to meeting the UK's legislatively enshrined target of net zero emissions by 2050, one of their 'two most popular findings' was 'grasping the opportunity presented by COVID-19' in order 'to maintain the momentum in reducing emissions' (83 per cent of Assembly members).[57]

What also emerged strongly from their deliberations was the need for consensus. In a statement to mark the release of their report on 10 September 2020, the Assembly declared in a very Beveridgian spirit that it is 'imperative that there is strong and clear leadership from Government' that should 'forge a cross-party consensus that allows for certainty, long-term planning and a phased transition', adding, 'This is not the time nor the issue for scoring party political points.'[58]

Seeking consensus and avoiding political partisanship runs like a thread through my five Covid-and-after tasks. If a consensus around them did emerge, how could progress towards achieving them be measured? The playing out of some of these five tasks would be much harder to map than Beveridge's five giant-slayers. Social care, social housing and technical education would be relatively easy to measure in terms of laws passed, budgets allocated, numbers of beneficiaries, properties and/or institutional innovations. Tracking our success in readying ourselves to benefit from artificial intelligence or truly becoming carbon-neutral would be difficult but not impossible if international comparisons were used as the indicator.

One transformation, however, should it occur *would* be noticeable and gloriously refreshing – and entirely within our own power to achieve. For a regrettable feature of living in and observing pathogen Britain has been the coarsening of political conduct and political language that appeared once the Brexit Question inserted itself. How deeply scouring, how dreadfully predictable has been – and still

---

* The assembly members were 108 citizens representative of the UK population demographics.

is – the linguistics of Britain and Europe; how meagre the thinking, how stale the metaphors that are instantly on display, how strident the rancour. Unless we can put this aside, a political weather system driven by a jet stream of acrimony and recrimination will dominate our political climate to the huge detriment of life, society and politics in the 2020s and beyond on the road to 2045.

The great question of UK politics on that road is whether we can find the pessimism-breaking policies, the people, the purpose, the language and the optimism to shift that malign system and replace it with something much closer to who we are and, above all, who we can be.

9

The Road to 2045

All the members of human society stand in need of each other's assistance, and are likewise exposed to mutual injuries. Where necessary assistance is reciprocally afforded from love, from gratitude, from friendship and esteem, the society flourishes and is happy.

Adam Smith, The Theory of Moral Sentiments[1]

So to criticize inequality and to desire equality is not, as is sometimes suggested, to cherish the romantic illusion that men are all equal in character and intelligence. It is to hold that, while their natural endowments differ profoundly, it is the mark of a civilized society to aim at eliminating such inequalities as have their source, not in individual differences, but in its own organization, and that individual differences, which are the source of social energy, are more likely to ripen and find expression if social inequalities are, as far as practicable, diminished.

R. H. Tawney, Equality[2]

I cannot forget that I was crowned Queen of the United Kingdom of Great Britain and Northern Ireland. Perhaps this Jubilee is a time to remind ourselves of the benefits which Union has conferred, at home and in our international dealings, on the inhabitants of all parts of this United Kingdom.

HM Queen Elizabeth II, addressing both Houses of Parliament on the occasion of her Silver Jubilee, 4 May 1977[3]

It is difficult for a member of my generation to imagine the United Kingdom without Queen Elizabeth. As Lytton Strachey wrote of her last days in his celebrated life of Queen Victoria, 'The vast majority of her subjects had never known a time when Queen Victoria had not been reigning over them. She had become an indissoluble part of their whole scheme of things . . .'[4]

By 2045 we will have lost her, though I am confident we shall still have a monarch as head of state. But over what kind of kingdom will he preside? What will be its physical and even its mental geography? For, in the meantime, I can all too easily imagine a prime minister having to call on Elizabeth II or her successor to explain how the kingdom as they – we – had known it was lost.

The UK came very close to this on Thursday 18 September 2014, the day Scotland voted in its independence referendum. And, after a few discreet chats, I wrote out such a scenario in my diary entry for that day.

> I'm writing this about 9.45 a.m., on Thursday. Strange to think that by this time tomorrow my country could have a very different political, economic *and* emotional roof over all our heads. Imagine what will have to happen over the next few days if it's 'Yes':
>
> Friday [19th]
> Won't know the result until the Glasgow and Edinburgh returns come in towards the end between 5 and 6 a.m. Returning officers in the 32 districts can allow recounts. Suspect that when in doubt they will, which will delay matters.
>
> PM and HM Queen. Surely he [David Cameron] will want to go to Balmoral in person rather than phone from Downing Street. So swift flights from Northolt to Aberdeen to Balmoral and back. You can't tell the Sovereign you've lost her kingdom by telephone. Announcement that both Houses of Parliament will be recalled – probably for Monday.
>
> Treasury and Bank of England (which does have a contingency plan*) will be active from the moment the markets open.

* Whitehall departments had been forbidden to undertake any contingency planning by David Cameron.

Cabinet meets this afternoon.

We will be, as a wise insider friend puts it, in completely uncharted territory: 'The Cabinet Manual is silent on how to dismember the kingdom.'[5]

Just such an audience *can* be imagined between now and 2045; perhaps even between now and 2025. The Queen is known to cherish every particle of her kingdom as her Silver Jubilee address in Westminster Hall made plain in 1977. It would, for her, be the saddest of codas to her reign.

The Sunday before the referendum in Crathie Churchyard, after morning service, she had a brief but very carefully thought through exchange with a well-wisher who joked that they were not going to mention the referendum, to which she replied: 'You have an important vote on Thursday. Well, I hope people will think very carefully about the future.'[6]

It emerged later that Cameron had sought the Queen's help a week earlier when he had been at Balmoral. He did not reveal this in his 2019 memoir,[7] but he did so in the accompanying television series: 'I remember conversations I had with the Queen's private secretary, not asking for anything that would be in any way improper or unconstitutional, but just a raising of the eyebrow, even, you know, a quarter of an inch, we thought would make a difference.'[8] What was improper was Cameron's disclosing it, and thus embarrassing the Queen. Like all prime ministers, he knows that you don't blab on royal exchanges. (It's one of the fundamental precepts of the 'good chaps theory' of government.)

In my diary I described the Queen's 'Crathie moment' as 'Neutral – but nicely and very neatly done.'[9] My fear in the 2020s is that a future 'Crathie moment' won't have the effect it might have done in 2014 (it is impossible to know whether the Queen's mini-elegy in a Scottish churchyard actually moved voting intentions or not, but it was sufficiently well judged to do so).

The reason I begin this chapter with the Scottish Question is that, until it is next 'answered', it is impossible to speculate about the configuration let alone the political nature of the kingdom that we will be inhabiting in 2045. But there is much constitutional work to be done whatever happens. As the late Dr Andrew McDonald, the scholar and public servant who worked in a senior position at the Department of Constitutional Affairs as Constitution Director from 2003 to 2005 said, this is not the desiccated and abstruse subject of many a popular imagining: 'What can [constitutional] reformers hope to achieve? A symbol burnished and its meaning redefined. A nation's future is re-imagined. A national story retold. A shared understanding of what it is to be a citizen. A recognition of values held in common.'[10]

Constitutions are more than just laws and conventions. They live and breathe. They infuse relationships between state and citizen. They check excessive governing power. They are guarantors and replenishers of liberty. They are also vulnerable. As Linda Colley put it in her study of constitutions, *The Gun, The Ship and the Pen*, 'They are the frail, paper creations of fallible human beings. Wherever they exist, they only function well to the degree that politicians, the lawyers and the population concerned are able and willing to put sustained effort into thinking about them, revising them when necessary and making them work'.[11]

In the early 2020s, many of our constitutional arrangements cry out for review and refreshment. Yet the panoptic royal commission we need should wait until we see how the Scottish Question plays out. If separation comes, unravelling this deepest and most intimate of unions could make the unpicking of our forty-seven years within the European Community look easy. It will eat up government and parliamentary time, it will guzzle intellectual and emotional energy in copious quantities. It will take a decade to complete administratively and much longer than that to reconcile psychologically and emotionally.

It could lead also to a new politics. For example, if the centre left were to be in a position to compete for seats in the shrivelled, post-independence House of Commons, it would have to break the Edwardian, post-1906 pattern of Labour and the Liberals splitting the non-Conservative vote. This would need, too, some kind of proportional representation for general elections. It would be the most potent dissolver of familiar, traditional left–right structures. Failing such mould-breaking, the rump-UK could find itself in the unhealthy position of being governed by an endless succession of Conservative administrations, something that they themselves would not regard as good for democracy.

In the melt we would also need to place central-regional-local relations, plus devolution to Wales and Northern Ireland and decentralization generally. A new, post-Scottish separation settlement would require an examination of Parliament, the purpose and composition of the second chamber and its relationship with the House of Commons – a huge and difficult task in itself and tough to achieve with a House of Commons always unwilling to contemplate a House of Lords down the corridor made more powerful by virtue of being elected.

National security, too, would be a serious and tangled concern. For example, defence infrastructure, most importantly the Royal Naval Base on the Clyde at Faslane, where the Trident submarines and their missile warheads are housed, would be in play. Perhaps even our status as a permanent member of the UN Security Council would be up for review if the UK was reduced to England, Wales and Northern Ireland.

There is another aspect of the relationship between citizen and state that requires swift attention: the justice system. The dispensation of timely justice is not only a question of welfare (access; legal aid) but also a crucial ingredient of an open society – a place where citizen and state come face-to-face and respect for process and outcomes is of paramount importance. Covid has pushed the existing backlog of cases up to a breathtaking level. Here are the figures for late July 2020:

- Magistrate courts – 525,002 cases outstanding
- Crown courts – 43,676 cases outstanding
- Family public law – 14,230 cases outstanding
- Family private law – 51,199 cases outstanding
- Social security and child support – 76,596 cases outstanding
- Immigration and asylum – 19,902 cases outstanding
- Employment tribunal single claims – 38,419 cases outstanding
- Employment tribunal multiple claims – 5,729 cases outstanding[12]

In its report *Covid 19 and the Courts*, the House of Lords Constitution Committee, on which I sit, said of this backlog:

The swift administration of justice is a vital public service which underpins the rule of law. It is a familiar aphorism, often attributed to

Gladstone, that 'justice delayed is justice denied' . . . The Human cost of the backlog can be measured in part by defendants being held on remand in prison for longer, litigants and victims waiting longer for justice, and a greater likelihood of evidence being lost or forgotten during the lengthier waits for a hearing.[13]

The select committee was highly critical of the 'reduction in Government funding in the decade preceding the pandemic [which] left courts vulnerable going into the Covid crisis'.[14] As part of the coalition's austerity drive, the Ministry of Justice reduced funding for the Court and Tribunal Service by 21 per cent between 2010/11 and 2019/20.[15] Subsequently, the Ministry of Justice put in place a £250-million recovery programme that included fifty-four so-called 'Nightingale' courtrooms swiftly improvised in non-legal buildings to tackle the backlog.[16]

On the mechanics of government themselves, I'm not a great one for tinkering with the departmental boundaries at the best of times, and in tough periods it can be a truly undesirable displacement activity absorbing time and effort when there is none to spare. But I would make one urgent change – to early warning and assessment capabilities. For years I have wondered why Whitehall doesn't create an equivalent for the home front of the Joint Intelligence Committee and its supporting apparatus, the Joint Intelligence Organization. We never do for *ourselves* what we do, often in great detail, for other countries that concern us. An extended warning system would embrace potential shocks/dislocations to come from pandemics (as Sir Jeremy Farrar of the Wellcome Trust put it, we are now living in a world 'custom-built' for pandemics)[17] through climate change-related events and civil disorder to the break-up of the UK itself.

In the summer of 2020 I was in touch with an especially thoughtful retired member of the secret world. We were talking about the government's 'integrated review' of defence and security, which, I suspected, was not being led by assessment of intelligence and threats as much as its predecessor reviews had been. I asked my friend to have a stab at what a hostile power might produce on us by way of such assessment. Here is the result:

A foreign JIC looking at the UK might do so under headings related to **Vulnerabilities in War, e.g.**

- Would the UK Prime Minister launch the nuclear weapon or not?
- Would the UK's nuclear weapons actually work?
- Are there crippling gaps in their war fighting capability?
- How long would it take the UK to prepare to fight a war without allies?
- What would NATO, the Americans, and other possible allies do if we – the aggressor power – attacked? Anything apart from shout at us?
- What is the UK's state of preparedness for military action?
- Do the UK's armed forces have a realistic concept of casualties?

Critical infrastructure and gaps in resisting non-military pressure, e.g.

- What gaps are there in the UK's self-reliance in power generation? Food supply? etc.
- Can we close down the UK's IT? Which sectors could we cripple that way?

National cohesion and political will, e.g.

- What could we do to subvert the Union?
- What could we do to exploit ethnic and other differences?
- How is popular morale?
- Is the prevailing ideology widely shared or vulnerable?
- Are the political institutions trusted?
- Is the political leadership likely to be strongly supported in difficult circumstances?
- Does the UK population have the stomach for likely casualties in large scale armed conflict?

The UK's national security system

- Is our [i.e. the foreign country's] intelligence service's claim that the UK's Security Service's virtually exclusive concentration on counter terrorism has left us free to operate at will a safe judgement, or the result of a British trap that will blind us when they spring it?

- Has the UK improved its capacity to identify unconventional threats and make effective preparations against such contingencies? Our staff claim that their National Security Agency is good at drawing up lists of such threats (a pandemic was identified and placed high on the agency's list) but we need to know if action follows dependably (it did not in the case of the pandemic).

If I were prime minister, I would start my 'integrated review' by asking my officials, military and secret services to provide the answers to those questions with complete candour. Furthermore, I would apply a trio of tests to the review and its associated Defence White Paper: first, does it convince the country that, amidst all the economic consequences of Covid, it's still worth trying to be a serious military player in the world, especially as the public spending consequences of Covid Britain and after become ever more stark? Second, does it contain new thinking that would be of real use to our allies, NATO especially, in the post-Trump years? Finally, my secret service friend's question, do the two papers bring anxiety to the Queen's enemies (or potential enemies) in terms of the UK's effectiveness, individually and collectively, as an intelligent and capable adversary?

Moreover, I would go beyond the review period and combine all those questions in a defence-of-the-realm-in-the-round capability assessment as a matter of regular reporting to the National Security Council together with regular briefings for Parliament, its select committees and the public. I would also insist that the new warning system is built with a bias towards preventive action to combat the propensity to shelve.

Is there a picture to be painted of a new socio-political-economic settlement that could see us through to 2045 and beyond in the way the practical artistry of Beveridge and Keynes did for the early postwar years into which I was born and grew up?

Intriguingly, Keynes himself had drawn up the characteristics of the artist we need in an essay on Alfred Marshall that was written in 1924 and published in his celebrated *Essays in Biography* in 1933. The 'master-economist' Keynes wrote, assuming (as was the convention of the day) that such a figure would be a male,

. . . must possess a rare *combination* of gifts. He must reach a high standard in several different directions and must combine talents not often found together. He must be a mathematician, historian, statesman, philosopher – in some degree. He must understand symbols and speak in words. He must contemplate the particular in terms of the general, and touch abstract and concrete in the same flight of thought. He must study the present in the light of the past for the purposes of the future. No part of man's nature or his institutions must be entirely outside his regard. He must be purposeful and disinterested in a simultaneous mood; as aloof and incorruptible as an artist, yet sometimes as near the earth as a politician.[18]

As if that impossibly demanding job description was not already beyond the reach of any single mortal, we would need to add, in post-Covid circumstances, a Nobel Prize-winning level of scientific knowledge and the communication gifts of Sir David Attenborough. Clearly, this would need to be a genuine team enterprise.

All that said, there *is* the pattern of a new synthesis that is already just discernible – the outlines of a cartography for the road to 1945. It is there in Michael Marmot's health and inequality-shaped work on a new 'well-being economy', in the ongoing research of the Institute of Fiscal Studies' *Deaton Review of Inequalities*, in Partha Dasgupta's *The Economics of Biodiversity* review – all driven by the view, as Deaton puts it, 'that the inequalities we saw before the Covid crisis struck were not immutable'.[19] If we add to that Mark Carney's thinking on the harnessing of what Keynes called the 'animal spirits'[20] of capitalism to the cause of a zero-carbon economy and a revised notion of gross domestic product to embrace such values, a new concept of a social market economy seems a real possibility – whether or not we find an Adam Smith or a Maynard Keynes to give it voice – in a single volume comparable to the former's *The Wealth of Nations* or the latter's *General Theory of Employment, Interest and Money*.

In practical terms, how different might such a new social market economy look in comparison with the welfare arrangements in place in February 2020, the last month before Covid Britain? Particularly since the great financial crash of 2008–9, plentiful thought has been devoted to the pursuit of fairer, more egalitarian and more contented societies in such influential works as Richard Wilkinson and Kate Pickett's *The Spirit Level: Why Equality is Better for Everyone* (2009), in which they advance their central argument that the 'scale of income differences has a powerful effect on how we relate to each other ... that the scale of inequality provides a powerful policy lever on the psychological wellbeing of all of us'.[21]

If, as seems likely, our shared Covid experience proves to be what R. H. Tawney in his classic work *Equality* termed 'a source of social energy', it will breathe even more life into the existing, vigorous debates about such ideas as universal income or universal basic services as bringers of greater equality, social justice and perhaps even that most morally desirable sentiment 'serenity', of which Nye Bevan spoke. 'Serenity' is, for me, absolutely critical to well-being and one of the key – though largely unmeasurable – tests of equality.

The idea of universal basic income (UBI) is that 'the state would provide income for all citizens without any conditions attached, and regardless of other resources'.[22] It would not be generous; but it would be enough to live on. The idea has been around for at least forty years. Since 1982, the US State of Alaska has used a portion of its oil wealth to pay a 'dividend' to its citizens. Finland ran an experiment on it in 2017–18 which demonstrated an enhanced sense of mental well-being on the part of its recipients compared with that generated by the usual unemployment benefits.

UBI, unusually for a welfare policy, has attractions for both right and left. For the right it has a Gladstonian tang – that money is best left to 'fructify in the pockets of the people'.[23] They argue that UBI would do away with a large chunk of state bureaucracy and, in contrast to hypothecated payments, it would give its recipients consumer sovereignty. For the left, it would provide security for life without means-testing (it would flow to rich and poor alike), which would bring both material and psychological benefits.

Cost–benefit analysis bears down hard on UBI in the UK context, however. The House of Commons Library in October 2020 reckoned:

> A Basic Income of £100 a week for each person over the age of sixteen in the UK and £50 per week for each child would cost around £314bn a year. To put this in context, total spending on benefits, state pensions and

tax credits in the UK was forecast to be around £225bn in 2019–20. Payments at this level would nonetheless represent a significant reduction in support for many households currently claiming benefits.[24]

Though the UBI idea has attracted support in Liberal Democrat and Green Party circles, it is, I think, for those cost–benefit reasons unlikely to fly in post-Brexit Britain. In 2017 the all-party Commons Committee on Work and Pensions, then chaired by Frank Field, concluded that it was a 'distraction' from the task of improving the welfare system and urged the government 'not to expend any energy on it'.[25] They didn't and, I suspect, they won't.

A more likely runner is the rival concept of Universal Basic Services (UBS) developed by Anna Coote, Andrew Percy and a team at University College London since 2017.[26] The idea 'builds on the spirit of United States President Franklin Delano Roosevelt's New Deal and the post-war welfare states'.[27] It is based on the proposal that universal provision should be extended 'to areas such as housing, transport and childcare as well as to adult social care, and to access to digital information and communications'.[28] At its core, therefore, lie what the UCL team call the

collection of 7 free public services that enable every citizen to live a larger life by ensuring access to safety, opportunity and participation in

- Health Care
- Education
- Legal and Democracy
- Shelter
- Transport
- Information.[29]

The UCL team also float the prospect of combining UBS with a £20-per-week basic income supplement.[30] Not only would a UBS system extend the scope of the state as provider and carer, it would be costly too. Free communication services, they estimate, would need £15–20 billion a year,[31] about 1 per cent of GDP. Free local transport services would consume another £5–10 billion.[32] Place all these proposals together and they amount to a very significant extension of Barbara Castle and Brian Abel-Smith's idea of the 'social wage'.

UBS would need at least two factors to bring it within the realms of the possible: a centre/left government with a working majority and a buoyant economy on a sustained growth path. In the first weeks of 2021, both seemed far off. On 12 February, for example, the Office for National Statistics announced that in 2020 the UK economy had shrunk by 9.9 per cent, the largest fall in 300 years.*

Paying for Covid and the huge extra debt incurred will be a stress on the public purse for the bulk of the 2020s. In February 2021 I asked my friend Nick Macpherson, now Lord Macpherson of Earl's Court and Permanent Secretary to the Treasury in 2005–16, to draft a brief for me on how he saw the economic consequences of Covid. He kindly did so under the heading 'Some Thoughts of Where We Go From Here':[33]

Financial Cost of Covid – equivalent to a quarter of one of the twentieth century's world wars

For the UK, it is already clear that the cost will be substantially more than the global financial crisis [of 2008], though with the successful roll-out of the vaccine, it should fall well short of the cost of a World War.

In broad terms WWI cost 100% and WWII cost 110% of national income ... What about Covid? The Office of Budget Responsibility (OBR) projected in December [2020] that the national debt as a percentage of national income will rise a little over 20% this year [2021] compared to last ... Their estimates suggest that the cost of Covid will be about 25% of GDP ...

This financial year the British State is set to borrow £400 billion. That's a peacetime record. The economic recovery is likely to be rapid in 2021–22 but over the next two years the deficit will remain elevated. Revenues will take time to recover and spending on Covidvirus and its consequences will remain high. The national debt – a mere 27% of national income in 2001 – is set to rise to almost 110% by 2023.

Future public spending – structurally higher

---

* Since the 'Great Frost' of 1709, when it is estimated it contracted by 13.4 per cent two years after the Union with Scotland.

For three reasons:

1. Debt will be higher and this will need to be serviced. Fortunately interest rates even on a long term debt are at extraordinarily low levels. And much of the debt will be in the hands of the Bank of England.

2. The Covid crisis will lead to demands for greater capacity of the NHS and for care homes fit for the elderly, reinforcing demands which were already rising from demographic pressures.

3. More state activism in support of the economy – Covid has accelerated a trend which has been apparent since the Brexit referendum. In the short run, this is largely about supporting demand and incumbent firms, for the longer run it will be more about enhancing the capacity of the economy to grow.

Reducing the national debt – need to maintain confidence

Nobody expects the Government to follow the Gladstonian approach of running budget surpluses the better to reduce our national debt ... More likely, the Government will pursue the approach favoured by post-war governments. They will seek to stabilize the level of debt in relation to national income by seeking more rapid economic growth while slowly reducing the budget deficit to more manageable levels. The independence of the Bank of England means they are less likely to be aided by higher inflation ... as they were 1945–90.

A growth strategy – skills and productivity

The higher the growth rate in national income, the easier it becomes to square the circle of better demand for better public services at tolerable levels of taxation. All post-war governments have sought to increase the capacity of the British economy to grow. Arguably they have made very little difference ...

Since 2008, underlying growth has fallen to around 1% a year. Such little growth as there has been is largely attributable to a growing labour force. Productivity has hardly risen at all at just 0.3% a year over the last ten years. Nobody quite knows why. Possible explanations lie in the size of our financial sector, persistently low interest rates ... and chronic underinvestment ...

A growth strategy for the twenty-first century needs to prioritize:

4. Macroeconomic stability and free trade.
5. Public and private investment over consumption.
6. Houses, where there has been chronic undersupply for at least fifty years.
7. Skills . . . further education has been starved of resources.
8. Innovation . . . partnerships between universities and the private sector have been a rare industrial success story . . .

Getting and spending – a new social solidarity charge

National Insurance needs to be adapted to the modern age . . . A social solidarity charge could be introduced, at a rate of say 3 to 5%, on a temporary basis. And potentially . . . it could become permanent.

This is a substantial set of proposals from a seasoned technician-of-state, a repair-and-restoration prospectus plus a requirement, the other side of immediate recovery, for the UK to surpass those seven-and-a-half decades of post-1945 economic performance, which means that getting something along the lines of UBS will probably be beyond our reach.

As for the politics and welfare policies of recovery, the Labour leader, Keir Starmer, made what he trailed as his 'fork in the road' speech on 18 February 2021, with the Attlee government of 1945 as his inspiration. In his 'A New Chapter for Britain' speech he said he sensed 'a mood in the air which we don't often detect in Britain. It was there in 1945, after the sacrifice of war, and it's there again now. It's the determination that our collective sacrifice must lead to a better future.'[34] Five days earlier he described his intent similarly in *The Times*: 'Out of the rubble of the war you build a better future. Out of the sacrifice and solidarity of the last year or so, you build a better future.'[35]

Starmer said this was the moment for a 'call to arms – like the Beveridge Report was in the 1940s'. Michael Marmot, today's equivalent of William Beveridge, sets out in his most recent report the costs of inequality, stating that Covid 'got into the cracks and crevices of a society and forced them open with tragic consequences'. Starmer did not touch on the possibility of universal basic services but he did propose 'a new British Recovery Bond ... [which] ... could raise billions to invest in local communities, jobs and businesses ... investing in science, skills, technology and British manufacturing'.[36] It was a strong pitch to become the pacemaker for post-Covid British politics.

As the vaccine jabbed its beneficial, beneficent way across the kingdom, as the R number continued to fall (temporarily, alas) and the longing for family reunions and a degree of normality became ever more acute, and the question of what kind of recovery Britain awaited did indeed increasingly make the political weather, would the sense of shared purpose and kindness of strangers fade bit by bit? Would we sink back on the cushions of familiar ways and social comforts and tribal disagreements with a grateful sigh, as if experiencing the end of a bad dream?

The road to 2045 will be potholed with anxiety-inducing possibilities – not least the break-up of the UK – and will pass through a land of multiple uncertainties. But, if it is paired by something like the 'five tasks' of a 'new Beveridge', adhered to through thick and thin, the end might be a time of productive, common purpose and sustained betterment for the kingdom, united or otherwise.

There is a high road to be taken towards the centenary of the Second World War's ending – including a kingdom not sundered but flourishing. A mediocre or a low road, however, will be all too easy to tread if we settle for political business as usual, as we lived it before March 2020. A burst of Tawney's 'social energy' and a renewed sense of a duty of care will be crucial both to avoiding that and to our post-Brexit influence for good in the world. For a nation that no longer inspires itself will have absolutely no chance of inspiring others.

Epilogue: 'Wouldn't It be Nice?'

Only those institutions are loved which touch the imagin-
ation. Now that the chance has come to make a fresh start, we
ought to act on that truth, and think in terms, not of the least
that is essential, but of the most that we can achieve.

R. H. Tawney, 1917[1]

The great economic and social historian was writing about public
education in the years that would follow the ending of the Great War.
'A reconstruction of education,' he wrote, 'in a generous, humane and
liberal spirit would be the noblest memorial of all to those who have
fallen.'[2] His words fit 2020s Britain.

The institution on which we most depend for our physical and
mental well-being, the NHS, *is* loved. Its institutionalization of altruism really does touch our imaginations. Can we say the same of the
state as a whole? Far less so, indispensable though it is to a clean and
decent and functioning society. The management of Covid Britain by
central government has dealt it hard blows. In the period of reconstruction and recovery, a 'new Beveridge', and thereby a restoration of
trust and authority, is vital.

Fundamental to the Covid inquest will be how the state did or did
not discharge its duty of care to its people. Our shared pathogenic
experience has certainly sharpened our sense of this paramount, constant duty. Whether it has changed or deepened it permanently
remains to be seen.

I hope that we take the high road shown at the end of the previous
chapter. If we do it will involve that 'redistribution of esteem' as

described by the Harvard political philosopher Michael Sandel in *The Tyranny of Merit*:

> It is often assumed that the only alternative to equality of opportunity is a sterile, oppressive equality of results. But there is another alternative: a broad equality of condition that enables those who do not achieve great wealth or prestigious positions to live lives of decency and dignity – developing and exercising their abilities in work that wins social esteem, sharing in a widely diffused culture of learning and deliberating with their fellow citizens about public affairs.[3]

Summoning such a spirit from the depths of Covid would be a shining collective achievement for British society.

I am certain that out of the losses, the sorrows and the separations of Covid Britain, good things can come – that we can travel the road to 2045 with purpose, dignity and accomplishment. It can happen if we act determinedly enough. I think we will, and we know someone of the greatest eminence who does too.

Eavesdrop for a moment on the Queen's session on Zoom from Windsor on 25 February 2021 with the leaders of the vaccination programme. Here is her exchange with Derek Grieve, Head of the Scottish Government's Vaccination Division:

> DG: If I could bottle this community spirit and use it not just for the vaccination programme, but for other things, the job would be done.
> HMQ: Wouldn't it be nice?

It would – not only 'nice' but necessary too. We need a decade of real, shared accomplishment that can only come with a high level of consensus. It can happen. It is within our grasp. We have sovereignty over our duty of care – how we express it in language, deed and policy. It is a matter of shared purpose and sustained application. Above all it is a question of spirit that casts aside pessimism and invigorates 'recovery Britain' and the kingdom to come.

Timeline of Lockdown Britain

2020
PHASE 0: A NEW VIRUS

January   18   PM pledges government will act 'based on scientific advice'.

           22   First SAGE Meeting to discuss the Coronavirus (then named WN-CoV, now Covid-19) noted first in Wuhan, China.

PHASE 1: SHOCK, SWERVE AND SHUTDOWN

March   17   Prime Minister institutes daily press conference; Chancellor Rishi Sunak provides £350 billion to support industry and business.

           18   PM pledges government will act 'based on scientific advice'.

           20   Sunak announces further measures to support jobs.

PHASE 2: EARLY LOCKDOWN BRITAIN

           23   PM announces national lockdown with 'stay at home' instruction.

24 Matt Hancock, the health secretary, announces a Nightingale hospital for London at Docklands.

25 Over half a million sign up as NHS volunteers.

26 Sunak announces further measures to help the unemployed.

27 PM and Hancock have Covid; two more Nightingale hospitals to be built in Birmingham and Manchester.

30 Newspaper report on 2016 pandemic exercise (Cygnus), whose recommendations were not acted upon.

April

2 Hancock announces a 'five pillars' strategy.

3 Jonathan Van-Tam, deputy chief medical officer, sees a 'massive change in public behaviour'.

4 Keir Starmer elected as Leader of the Labour Party.

5 Queen broadcasts to the nation; prime minister admitted to hospital.

12 PM leaves hospital to recuperate at Chequers; issues a video in which he says, 'Our NHS is the beating heart of this country . . . it is powered by love'; later thought to be the day of peak deaths.

13 Anxiety increases about the level of deaths in care homes.

16 Cabinet decides lockdown must last for another three weeks.

17 Vaccine task force created.

21 PM says avoiding a second wave is his number one priority; care homes increasingly worried about the number of their residents coming back from hospitals with Covid.

23 Government recruits 18,000 officials for the new test-and-trace policy; first two voluntary subjects injected for Oxford vaccine study.

25 Total of hospital deaths passes 20,000.

30   PM says, 'we are past the peak of this disease' and pledges to seek the 'maximum possible consensus'.

May   1   Institute for Fiscal Studies issues a report suggesting BAME people are twice as likely to die from Covid.

3   PM reveals contingency plans were made for his death.

5   Starmer calls for a 'national consensus' on a back-to-work strategy.

6   PM says he 'bitterly regrets' the deaths in care homes.

PHASE 3: THE FRACTURING OF CONSENSUS AND THE DRAINAGE OF TRUST

10   PM lays out plan to ease lockdown; Scotland's first minister Nicola Sturgeon regrets lack of consultation; Starmer says, 'We wanted clarity and consensus. We haven't got either.'

11   Government publishes a forty-page 'road map'; PM says, 'our journey has reached most perilous moment'; we are encouraged to wear face masks.

13   Figures show that 40 per cent of Covid deaths have been in care homes; there are now 2.5 million people in the shielding category.

14   Office for Budget Responsibility predicts government borrowing will reach nearly £300 billion (15.2 per cent of national income; highest figure since 1944); Starmer says the consensus between the four nations of the UK must be brought back.

18 Professor Van-Tam says, 'we may have to learn to live with the virus in the long term'.

19 2.1 million people claimed unemployment benefit last month.

22 The *Guardian* and the *Daily Mirror* report PM's adviser Dominic Cummings drove to and from County Durham last month; did those journeys flout the government's rules?

23 Cummings says he will not resign; his and his family's visit to Barnard Castle reaches the Sunday newspapers.

24 PM says Cummings 'followed the instinct of any father . . . he behaved responsibly, legally and with integrity'; Starmer says, 'This was a test of the prime minister and he failed it.'

25 Cummings holds a press conference to explain his actions: 'I don't regret what I did.' He had 'not considered' resigning.

28 The *Daily Telegraph* reports that Durham police have concluded that Cummings did break lockdown rules on his Barnard Castle round trip but no further action will be taken; the country claps for the NHS and carers at 8 p.m. for the first time.

29 Sir Patrick Vallance, the government's chief scientific adviser, cautions on lockdown easing.

30 Professor Van-Tam warns of 'a very dangerous moment', adding, when asked about Cummings, that the rules 'apply to us all'.

PHASE 4: A TOUCH OF EASEMENT

June   1 Restrictions ease after ten weeks of lockdown.

2 Hancock says a second wave is likely to be 'patchy' and counter measures will be localized.

3   The R number is down to 0.7–0.9 but Vallance remains cautious; the Prince of Wales says, 'We have to put nature back at the centre of everything we do.'

4   PM hosts a vaccine summit; AstraZeneca is already manufacturing the Oxford vaccine.

6   Sir David King, a former chief scientific adviser, warns a second wave has already started as R moves above 1 in the north-west.

7   Hancock denies that failure to go into lockdown earlier cost lives.

10 Ex-SAGE member Professor Neil Ferguson tells Commons Health Committee that deaths could have been halved if lockdown had taken place a week earlier; PM announces 'support bubbles' whereby families can mix with one other; Starmer wants a task force to plan how to get everyone back to school.

12 British economy shrank 20.4 per cent in April (a fall nearly three times bigger than in the great financial crash of 2008–9).

13 Disturbances in fourteen towns and cities as the far right clashes with supporters of Black Lives Matter.

14 An *Observer* opinion poll indicates that confidence in the government's handling of the Covidvirus crisis is down to 30 per cent; PM is to set up a task force on inequalities.

15 Wearing of face masks becomes compulsory on all forms of public transport; ONS report that 35 per cent of the deeply shielded have experienced mental problems since lockdown began; footballer Marcus Rashford writes to the PM about extending free school meals across the summer holidays.

16 Government accedes to Rashford's request.

18 HMG abandons its 'world class' track and trace
    app; singer Vera Lynn dies aged 103; Bank of
    England injects another £10 billion as job
    prospects look worse than expected.

19 £1 billion for Covid catch-up in schools; government
    borrowed £103 billion in April/May (£55.2 billion
    in May, which is a record); R is holding at 0.7–0.9.

22 Able to mingle with up to six people; from
    1 August the English will be free of all restrictions.

23 Andrew Bailey, Governor of the Bank of England,
    says we were close to meltdown in some core
    financial markers in March, avoided by £20 billion
    of quantitative easing; PM tells the Commons, 'Our
    long national hibernation is coming to an end.'

24 Disturbances in Brixton.

25 Chief medical officer Chris Whitty warns of a
    second wave and says, 'the virus is still in general
    circulation'; 33.3°C at Heathrow (hottest so far
    this year); Liverpool win the English Premier
    League; scattered disturbances in London.

26 Sir Jeremy Farrar of the Wellcome Trust expects
    Covid cases to rise in the next few weeks and
    predicts a second wave in December.

30 PM speech in Dudley unveiling his interventionist
    post-Brexit social, educational and industrial
    strategy amounting to a 'New Deal'.

July   3 PM says we are about to take 'our biggest step yet
           on the road to recovery'; Whitty talks of balancing
           'the multiple risks'.

PHASE 5: THE GREAT UNLOCKING

5 At 5 p.m. there is a national clap to mark the
   seventy second birthday of the NHS.

6   PM criticizes 'too many of the care homes [which] didn't really follow the procedures'.

8   Sunak outlines a further £30 billion of state aid (including £10-per-head 'eat out to help out' discount for meals, Mondays to Wednesdays in August).

12   Opinion Poll in the *Observer*: Con 42 per cent, Lab 38; Lib Dem 6; on the question of trustworthiness Johnson −15; Starmer +18.

13   BBC report latest opinion poll on Scottish independence: 54 per cent in favour, 46 per cent against.

14   OBR forecast the greatest fall in GDP in 300 years; government sponsored report suggests a second wave might produce 120,000 Covid deaths between September and June if an R of 1.7 coincides with cold weather and a bad flu season.

15   Johnson promises an independent inquiry, but not until the pandemic is over.

16   Vallance says the UK's initial response to Covid was not good enough and warns that the virus could come back in different waves over a number of years as a vaccine would be unlikely to give permanent immunity.

17   Johnson unveils another 'road map', for a return to normality by Christmas; £3 billion extra allocated to the NHS to help see it through winter.

19   Johnson compares a second lockdown to the nuclear deterrent.

20   Oxford Group reports that their vaccine is safe and triggers an immune reaction.

23   PM in Orkney claiming, 'The Union is a fantastically strong institution.'

24   On the first anniversary of his becoming PM, Johnson admits the government 'could have done things differently' in the early days of Covid.

28 New restrictions in Oldham after more than one hundred cases in a week.

29 Henry Dimbleby Report on Children and Nutrition recommends a further 1.25 million should get free school meals.

30 Hancock talks of 'a second wave rolling across Europe'; large parts of north-west England and West Yorkshire must reimpose restrictions from midnight.

31 R has risen in England from 0.8 to 1.0; deep shielding ends for the elderly and the vulnerable; Whitty warns that 'England has probably reached the limit or near the limit of opening up'; Hancock gives Greater Manchester and parts of West Yorkshire three hours' notice of restrictions on the eve of Eid al Adha.

August 2 Government says there are no plans for a second national lockdown.

6 Bank of England keeps interest rates at 0.1 per cent, expects unemployment to rise to 2.5 million.

7 R has risen to 0.8–1.0 for the UK.

10 Sturgeon apologizes to Scottish students after a quarter of them have their marks downgraded by the algorithm.

11 U-turn in Scottish exams, no downgrades by algorithm; Russia claims first Covid vaccine ('Sputnik').

13 In England it emerges that 40 per cent of A levels were marked down from teachers' predicted grades.

14 Government says it will stick by 40 per cent downgrading.

18 Universities are deluged with applications as government now accepts 'mock' results will be recognized.

19 Pearson pull BTEC results on eve of release to bring them in line with A-level and GCSE results.

20 Opinion polls put support for Scottish independence at an all-time high: 55 per cent for vs 45 per cent against.

21 Restrictions from midnight in Oldham, Blackburn and Pendle as cases spike; Treasury announces UK debt has reached £2 trillion for the first time ever, which is the equivalent of a whole year's GDP output.

22 Sir Mark Walport of UK Research and Innovation says Covid will be present 'for ever in some form or another'; R moves up to 0.9–1.1 in the UK.

24 PM says it's time for all pupils to return to school in September and that risks are 'very very low'.

28 Restrictions are to be lifted in parts of the north-west and West Yorkshire.

29 YouGov poll indicates PM's net favourability rating has dropped to −15; Starmer's is at +8.

30 University and College Union warns of a surge in cases when students return next month.

31 With one night left to go, Sunak's £10 vouchers have subsidized 64 million meals.

PHASE 6: THE SHADOW STARTS TO FALL ONCE MORE

September 1 Marcus Rashford creates a Child Food Quality Task Force; Hancock says the 'best case' is that there will be a vaccine by the end of the year.

3 Sunak tells Conservative backbenchers taxes will have to rise.

5 SAGE warns new outbreaks are highly likely as students return to university.

6   Late evening, the *Financial Times* breaks the story that the government will introduce legislation overturning part of the Brexit 'divorce deal', most notably the protocol on Northern Ireland.

7   Johnson says if there is no deal by 15 October the UK will walk away from the EU negotiations.

8   Brandon Lewis, Northern Ireland Secretary, says in the House of Commons that the proposed Internal Market Bill 'does break international law in a specific and limited way'.

9   Johnson unveils 'Operation Moonshot' (3 million tests a day by the end of the year) and shifts the return to normality from Christmas 2020 to Easter 2021; John Major says, 'we will have lost something beyond price' if we don't keep our international promises.

11 R has risen to 1.0–1.2.

12 Mark Walport warns, 'we are on the edge of losing control of the virus'.

13 The 'Rule of Six' comes into force at midnight.

17 From midnight nearly 2 million people in England will be under new restrictions; an extra £500 million allocated to care homes for the winter.

18 R is now 1.1–1.4, Lancashire and Merseyside will be under restrictions from 22 September.

19 PM admits that the UK is now seeing a second wave.

20 Whitty and Vallance warn that a second wave could overwhelm the NHS; Vallance says we will have to learn to live with Covid.

21 Professor Neil Ferguson says we 'got quite close to being overwhelmed' by the first wave; Starmer claims Johnson is 'just not up to the job' of being prime minister; PM acknowledges that 'the virus has started to spread again in an exponential way'.

23   Autumn budget cancelled, it will now take place in the spring.

24   Sunak unveils Job Support Scheme to replace furlough at the end of October, and recognizes that the economy is facing 'a permanent adjustment'.

25   R rises to 1.2–1.5 in the UK; shortly, one quarter of the population will be subject to some kind of local lockdown.

26   Hundreds of students in Glasgow have been told to self-isolate after twenty-seven test positive.

27   Nearly 3,000 students now in lockdown; *Observer* opinion polls put Labour on 42 per cent, Conservatives down to 39 (best PM question has Starmer on 36 per cent to Johnson's 32).

28   From tonight refusal to self-isolate could incur fines of up to £10,000; forty universities have now reported Covid cases.

30   Vallance says the pandemic is not under control; PM calls for forbearance and common sense.

October   1   City Region of Liverpool, Warrington, Hartlepool and Middlesbrough are to go into local lockdown.

2   R rises to 1.3–1.6 in the UK; Royal Society warns that even if a vaccine is effective it's unlikely that we will be able to return completely to normal.

4   PM says, 'it's going to be bumpy to Christmas and perhaps beyond'.

5   Sunak tells the 'virtual' Conservative party conference that for those seeking work 'the overwhelming might of the British state will be placed at your service'.

6   PM turns to Beveridge Report for inspiration; eighty universities have now reported 5,000 cases between them.

7   The Academy of Medical Colleges warns that the NHS could be overwhelmed this winter.

9   Sunak extends Job Support Scheme but reduces it
    from 80 per cent of earnings to 66 per cent; R
    slightly down to 1.2–1.5.

PHASE 7: SECOND-WAVE BRITAIN

12 PM unveils the government's new three-tier alert
    system; Starmer says Johnson is 'several steps
    behind'; three Nightingale hospitals are being
    readied in Manchester, Sunderland and Harrogate.

13 Divide widens between the main political parties as
    Starmer calls for a two- to three-week 'circuit
    break'; Governor of the Bank of England warns of
    deep, long-term economic scarring.

14 Welsh government bans travel into the country
    from Tier 2 and Tier 3 areas in England; IPSOS/
    STV poll indicates 58 per cent in favour of Scottish
    independence, highest ever.

15 London goes into Tier 2 (7 million people) along
    with Essex, Barrow, Chesterfield, York and
    Erewash.

16 R worsens slightly to 1.3–1.5; Northern Ireland is
    going into a four-week 'circuit breaker'; Greater
    Manchester is holding out against Tier 3.

18 Sir Graham Brady, chairman of the Conservative
    Party's 1922 Committee and MP for Altrincham
    and Sale, supports Andy Burnham, Mayor of
    Greater Manchester.

21 Republic of Ireland locks down for six weeks;
    Mark Sedwill, former Cabinet Secretary, says
    Cummings's Barnard Castle journey was a mistake.

22 Scotland's clinical director urges people to prepare
    for a 'digital Christmas'.

23 Wales enters a seventeen-day 'firebreak' lockdown; R down slightly to 1.2–1.4; Marcus Rashford criticizes some Conservative MPs as 'insensitive' on food for children; Sir David King says England needs a lockdown now.

24 Rashford calls for calm and an end to the abuse of those who have criticized him.

26 PM won't budge but says, 'we don't want to see children going hungry this winter'; Warrington, Nottingham and parts of Nottinghamshire go into Tier 3.

27 Oxford vaccine team report a strong immune response across all ages; Hancock says a vaccine may be ready in the first half of next year; fifty-five Conservative MPs in the Northern Research Group call upon PM to produce a 'clear road map' on how to exit Tier 3.

28 SAGE warns second wave could be worse than the first with 25,000 in hospital beds by the end of November; Resolution Foundation reports 20 per cent of young people unemployed.

29 Housing secretary Robert Jenrick says government has no plans for a second lockdown; R is 1.56 in England; West Yorkshire goes into Tier 3; IMF estimates the UK economy will shrink by 10.4 per cent this year and grow by 5 per cent next year.

30 A November SAGE report revises 'reasonable worst case' for second wave could lead to 85,000 deaths – they ask for a national lockdown; PM and a small group of ministers meet to consider new data and decide on a second lockdown (this is swiftly leaked).

31 Following a virtual Cabinet meeting, PM announces a second lockdown to run, if the House of Commons approves, from 5 November to 2 December in England, which will revert to a three-tier system thereafter; Vallance says the key is to get R below 1.0 in four weeks; Job Support Scheme payment is to be extended to 2 December.

November 1 Cabinet Office minister Michael Gove says lockdown could go on beyond 2 December if R is not below 1.0; Sturgeon urges an end to all inessential travel between Scotland and England.

2 PM tells the Commons the country faces a 'medical and moral disaster' if no action is taken; COMRES poll shows 72 per cent in favour of second lockdown, 15 per cent disagree; five-tier strategy starts in Scotland.

3 2,000 troops are to help ready Liverpool to be the first area of mass testing; Whitty tells Commons Science and Technology Committee there was a 'realistic possibility' of lifting restrictions on 2 December, but a new system would need to be in place here to keep cases down.

4 NHS England moves to its highest alert level; Commons backs new lockdown regulations, 516–38; GPs told to be ready to distribute vaccine before Christmas.

5 Day 1 of lockdown-2 begins with R at 1.1–1.3; support at 80 per cent of wages to be extended to the end of March 2021; Bank of England pumps a further £150 billion into the economy as its governor warns that the economy will not recover until 2022; PM talks of a 'very real chance of safe and effective vaccines' and 'light at the end of the tunnel'.

6   Liverpool starts ten days of military-assisted mass testing; UK Statistics Authority criticizes HMG for lack of transparency over likely second-wave deaths 'reasonable worst case scenario'.

7   Johnson rings Rashford to pledge funding for meals for poorer children over Christmas.

9   BioNtech/Pfizer announces a vaccine that is 90 per cent effective; PM warns, 'we cannot let our enthusiasm run away with itself'.

10 Hancock says delivering the new vaccine will be a vast logistical task which could start on 1 December.

11 UK Covid deaths pass 50,000.

12 33,470 new cases (highest since the pandemic began); economic growth 15.5 per cent July to September (but falls to 1.5 per cent in September); Cummings announces he will be gone by Christmas.

13 PM asks Cummings to leave No. 10 with immediate effect; R falls slightly to 1.0–1.3.

15 Johnson goes into self-isolation for two weeks.

16 Moderna, a US company, announces that their new vaccine is 95 per cent effective; PM tells a group of backbenchers, 'Devolution has been a disaster north of the border.'

17 The four nations are co-ordinating plans for an easing of restrictions over Christmas.

18 BioNtech says their vaccine is 94 per cent effective for the over sixty-fives.

20 PM refuses to accept the findings of the independent adviser on the *Ministerial Code* that Priti Patel bullied her staff; R down to 1.0–1.1.

22 Sunak says there will be an extra £3 billion for the NHS in England.

23 Oxford/AstraZeneca announce that their vaccine is 70 per cent effective across all ages, that it will cost US$3 a dose and can be kept in normal fridges with 4 million doses ready by the end of 2020 and a further 40 million by Easter 2021; Johnson and Sturgeon urge caution about Christmas.

24 The four nations agree a five-day, three-household bubble can be formed for 23–27 December.

25 Sunak's autumn spending statement and OBR forecasts put numbers on the 'economic scarring' of Covid; cuts in overseas aid; pay pause for public sector workers except for doctors, nurses and the lowest paid.

26 IFS identifies a £40-billion hole in the public finances; PM announces post-lockdown tier system for England (55 million people will be in tiers 2 or 3) and warns of a third lockdown after Christmas if control is lost.

27 R down to 0.9–1.0 across UK; Johnson says UK will 'prosper mightily' whatever the outcome of the Brexit talks.

28 Gove says without tiering English hospitals could be overwhelmed; Sturgeon tells SNP conference, 'Scotland is on the cusp of history.'

30 New Covid infections have fallen by one third in England since the end of October.

December 1 PM wins Commons approval for tiering in England 291–78 (with Labour abstaining and 55 Conservatives voting against).

PHASE 8: THE CRUELLEST WINTER

2 Second lockdown in England ends at 12.01 a.m.; Pfizer BioNTech vaccine wins regulatory approval.

3   The first Pfizer vaccine arrives from Belgium; Word
     seeps out from the Brexit talks that the EU are
     adding late complications on the level playing field/
     governance question.

4   R is now 0.8–1.0 across the UK; news breaks early
     evening that Brexit talks have been paused owing
     to the serious divergences and that EU Commission
     president Ursula von der Leyen and Johnson will
     talk tomorrow.

5   An hour of telephone conversation produces a joint
     statement acknowledging 'significant differences'
     remain; negotiations to resume in Brussels
     tomorrow; Johnson and von der Leyen will talk
     again on Monday evening (7th)

6   Irish PM says talks are on a 'knife edge'.

7   After talking on the phone, Johnson and von der
     Leyen issue a joint statement saying, 'the conditions
     for finding an agreement are not there'.

8   At 6.31 a.m. Mrs Maggie Keenan receives the
     first anti-Covid jab in the University Hospital
     Coventry; government withdraws the
     international lawbreaking clauses in the Internal
     Market Bill.

9   After the Johnson/von der Leyen dinner No.
     10 says, 'very large gaps remain', but they do
     agree there will be a final decision by Sunday
     night.

10   Cabinet agrees with Johnson that the deal on offer
     'is not right for the UK'; German Chancellor
     Angela Merkel and the French President Emmanuel
     Macron refuse to receive Johnson in Berlin and
     Paris.

11   Johnson says a hard Brexit would be 'wonderful'
     for the UK; news breaks that the Royal Navy will
     be deployed to protect UK waters.

12 Tobias Ellwood, Chairman of the Commons Defence Committee, says talk of gunboats is 'undignified and irresponsible'; it is confirmed that Merkel and Macron won't see Johnson.

13 Johnson and von der Leyen agree 'to go the extra mile'; he says, 'there is clarity and simplicity in a WTO outcome'.

14 What Hancock calls 'a fast moving, mutant version of Covid is at work in the south-east; London and parts of Essex and Herts are to go into Tier 3 at 12.01 a.m. Wednesday; von der Leyen says there is 'movement' in the talks; No. 10 says no significant progress.

16 Von der Leyen tells the European Parliament 'a narrow path' has opened up towards a deal; the four home nations tighten Christmas plans.

17 In two days' time, two-thirds of the English population will be in Tier 3; Gove says chance of a deal now lower than 50/50; after a 7 p.m. call to von der Leyen, Johnson says position is 'severe' and EU will need to change its demands.

18 R has risen to 1.1–1.2 this week across the UK; fears that the new mutation of the virus is both spreading fast and difficult to trace; EU negotiator Michel Barnier says negotiations are at their 'moment of truth' and in their 'final hours'.

19 PM announcing a new Tier 4 and puts London and the south-east in it from midnight; the new variant spreads 70 per cent faster, and Vallance says it has taken off ('a horrible moment'); Sturgeon bans all travel into and out of Scotland; first minister of Wales Mark Drakeford puts the whole of Wales into Tier 4.

20 Hancock says the new variant (VUI 2020) 'is out of control'; biggest ever number of daily infections (35,928); Sturgeon says next mutation makes it 'imperative' that Brexit transition period is extended.

21 Transport secretary Grant Shapps rules out extending Brexit transition; negotiations underway with France to end its 48-hour ban on travel from the UK; 900 lorries stuck on the M20; over half a million people have now had the jab.

22 Another record level of infections (36,804); Barnier talks of 'final push in the negotiations'; over 3,000 lorries stuck in Kent; France agrees to reopen borders if drivers are tested.

23 Late evening word emerges from Brussels that a deal is there; at 744, more daily deaths than any single day since May; Hancock announces that a third variant has arrived from South Africa.

24 Deal agreed covering £637 billion of goods after fish compromise is struck; von der Leyen says, 'parting is such sweet sorrow'; Starmer says Labour will vote for the deal when Parliament meets on 30 December; Sturgeon says Brexit is taking place against Scotland's wish and the deal would never compensate for it.

25 The Queens's Christmas broadcast stresses her people's quiet 'indomitable spirit' and how we will 'continue to be inspired by the kindness of strangers'.

26 Gove calls for an end to the 'rancorous' and 'ugly' politics of Brexit.

28 Record number of new Covid cases and Covid sufferers in hospital.

29 Another record number of new Covid cases.

30 Oxford/AstraZeneca vaccine receives regulator's approval; primary-school children back at school next week, secondary-school pupils the week after; two-thirds of the English population are in Tier 4; MPs approve EU deal by 521–73; Lords vote down LibDems' fatal amendment by 466–101; Sturgeon calls it a 'democratic, economic, and social calamity'.

31 New cases reach another record; at 11 p.m. the UK transition period ends and with it forty-eight years of shared life inside the EEC/EC/EU; Sturgeon tweets, 'Scotland will be back Europe. Keep the light on.'

2021
PHASE 9: LOCKDOWN THREE

January 1 A study by Imperial College London shows that the speed of the new variant adds between 0.4 and 0.7 to R.

2 Another record for new cases.

3 Johnson warns of tighter restrictions to come over the next few weeks; he says Scotland should wait until the mid-2050s for a second independence referendum.

4 Eighty-two-year-old Brian Pinker receives the first AstraZeneca jab at the Churchill hospital in Oxford; at 8 p.m. Johnson announces another lockdown and says the government 'instructs' us to stay at home from the early hours of Wednesday morning; Sturgeon says mainland Scotland and Skye will lock down from midnight.

5 Last week 1 in 50 had Covid across the UK (1 in 30 in London); Sunak announces £4.6 billion in further cash grants to retail and hospitality;

Gove says new restrictions could last until March; IFS/Nuffield report stresses once-in-a-generation chance to tackle inequalities.

6   Commons approves the new lockdown regulations 524–16.

8   Highest number of new cases (68,503) and daily deaths (1,325) since the pandemic began; R is 1.1–1.4 across the UK; Moderna vaccine approved by the UK regulator.

9   Over 3 million tested positive in the UK since the pandemic began.

10 Hancock appeals for strict compliance: 'Every time you flex the rules that could be fatal.'

11 Whitty says, 'the next weeks are going to be the worst'; Starmer urges us to rebuild as the Attlee government built our welfare state 'from the rubble' after 1945; Prince Charles launches his 'Terra Carta' on sustainability.

12 Analyst David Spiegelhalter says Covid figures will continue to rise for the next three weeks, then the vaccine should have a noticeable effect in February.

13 Record numbers of daily deaths reported (1,564); more people have now died in the second wave than in the first; growing anxiety about the new Brazilian variant.

14 Increasing worries about Brazilian/Manaus variant; HMG bans flights from Brazil and Portugal; Rashford writes to PM requesting urgent review of policy for feeding needy children.

15 R is 1.2–1.3, number of new cases 14 per cent lower than this day last week; amid worries about the new variants, PM announces closing of all air travel corridors from 4 a.m. on Monday.

17 Former NHS chief executive Simon Stevens says
    NHS has never been in 'a more precarious
    position' since its foundation in 1948; every thirty
    seconds a new Covid patient is being admitted to
    hospital in England.

18 Record number of Covid patients in UK hospitals;
    Commons votes (non-binding) 278–0 to extend
    £20 per week Universal Credit top-up beyond the
    end of March.

20 A record day for reported deaths (1,820) as impact
    of Christmas easement affects the figures; UK has
    the highest death toll in Europe; Vallance says it
    would be 'insanity' to unlock too soon.

21 An Imperial College study suggests the third
    lockdown is only partially working; Northern
    Ireland to stay in lockdown until early March; PM
    says it's 'too early to say' if more restrictions might
    be lifted in England; government publishes skills/
    technical education White Paper.

22 PM announces that new British variant is 30–40 per
    cent more contagious; R is now 0.8–1.0; record
    Government borrowing in December (£34 billion).

24 Hancock says there are seventy-seven known cases
    of the South African variant in the UK; SNP agree
    a 'road map' to an advisory referendum on
    independence.

25 A record number of Covid patients in hospital
    (38,000); asked to set a date for schools to return,
    the PM replies, 'People don't want to see another
    big surge in infections.'

26 Total UK deaths pass 100,000, fifth highest death toll
    in the world; in response to a question at the press
    conference the PM says, 'I am deeply sorry for every
    life that has been lost . . . I take full responsibility for
    everything that the government has done.'

27 English schools will remain closed at least until 8 March; the Home Secretary proposed that returning UK travellers from specific countries will be taken to government-approved hotels for a ten-day quarantine, which they will have to pay for.

28 Noravax vaccine is effective against both the new British and the South African variants; on a visit to Scotland Johnson decries 'endless talk' about independence and says it's 'completely irrelevant' to handling the crisis.

29 EU Commission forced to backtrack after announcing it would abrogate the Brexit deal and halt vaccine movements into the UK from the EU via the Irish Republic.

30 Gove seeks to 'reset' relations with EU after spat over vaccines and the NI/Republic border; Johnson writes to parents saying he is 'in awe' of their home schooling.

31 Record number of jabs yesterday (598,389), of whom two were Peter and Enid Hennessy.

February 1 'Enhanced testing' teams are to go into areas where the South African variant is showing itself.

2 Oxford study indicates that the AstraZeneca vaccine reduces transmission of the disease by 70 per cent; New variants discovered in Liverpool and Bristol; Captain Sir Tom Moore dies of Covid; Dasgupta *Review on Economics of Diversity* published by the Treasury.

3 UK jabs total passes 10 million; Whitty says peak of the second wave has passed but pressure on the NHS will only ease when all over-fifties have been inoculated.

4   Quarantine hotels for incoming travellers from 'red list' countries will be ready on 15 February; Bank of England expects the economy to shrink by 4.2 per cent in the first quarter.

5   AstraZeneca says its vaccine does work against the Kentish variant (later renamed 'Alpha'); R down to 0.7–1.0.

6   An outbreak of the South African variant in Worcestershire.

7   A study by the Oxford team suggests the AZ vaccine provides only 'limited protection' against the South African variant (later renamed 'Beta') but it will help reduce hospital admissions and deaths from it; a hundred cases of the South African variant have been uncovered in the UK.

8   Government seeks to reassure public about the South African variant; Sir John Bell (Oxford) predicts, 'We're going to be chasing the variants pretty continuously.'

9   Jail sentences of up to ten years for incoming passengers travelling from 'red list' countries causes a big row as government outlines new measures starting on 15 February to protect the UK from incoming variants; 4,600 rooms for quarantine, in government approved hotels, will be ready; ONS say the second wave peaked on 19 January.

10   Kent variant now the dominant strain in the UK; WHO says AZ can be used against all variants and for all age groups; Shapps says don't book a holiday at home or abroad this summer; Hancock says he is going to Cornwall.

11   NHS White Paper to give the government more strategic control, replace competitive tendering and better align the NHS and local authorities on social care.

12 R falls to 0.7–0.9; the UK economy shrank by 9.9 per cent in 2020, the biggest fall for 300 years; latest opinion poll on Scottish independence shows first fall in four months to 53 per cent in favour vs 47 per cent not.

13 PM says he hopes restrictions can begin to be eased next month, starting with the schools in England on 8 March.

14 Nine in ten of the over-seventies in the UK have been jabbed; Lowest daily number of new cases (10,972) since October.

15 PM says coming out of lockdown will be 'cautious but also irreversible'.

16 1.7 million added to the 'shielders' in England, bringing the total to 4 million.

18 An Imperial College study indicates that infections have dropped by two-thirds over the past month; Keir Starmer delivers his 'A New Chapter for Britain' speech laced with new Beveridgisms and proposing a British Recovery Bond.

19 Johnson tells the G7 the UK will donate surplus vaccine to developing countries; R is now 0.6–0.9.

22 PM outlines four tests and five key dates on the road to removing all legal restrictions on contacts on 21 June; government will be guided by 'data not dates'; PM says the 'vaccine has decisively shifted the odds in our favour ... we are travelling on a one-way road to freedom'.

23 Sturgeon lays out Scotland's road to 21 April. Gove to review the possibility of vaccine passports. Unemployment rises to 1.7m, the young especially hard hit.

24 Government announces £700m Covid catch-up
   programme for school pupils; schools in
   England will assess and grade their
   students' examinations this summer.
   People with learning difficulties will get
   vaccine priority.

25 HM Queen urges everyone to have 'the jab which
   doesn't hurt at all'. Rough sleeping in England fell
   by one third in 2020.

26 Jonathan Van-Tam says there are 'worrying signs'
   that some people are taking their foot of the brake
   too soon. 'Don't wreck this now', he added as 1 in
   5 local authorities reported a rise in cases last
   week.

28 The Brazilian variant, the P1, has reached the UK,
   6 cases (one not traced) in 2 clusters – Northwest
   Scotland and South Gloucestershire brought in by
   returning travellers.

March   1 Data from Public Health England indicates
   that the vaccines have reduced the chances of
   serious illness by 80%, 38% of the adult
   population have been jabbed at least
   once.

2 ONS reports that Covid deaths were down a
   quarter in the week ending 19 February.

3 Budget: Furlough extended until end of September,
   £20m for Universal Credit uplift to continue
   for 6 months, tax rises will start in 2022.
   The total COVID support package, this year
   and last, is £352 billion, 'It is going to be the
   work of many governments, over many decades,
   to pay it back.'

4 To near universal outrage, HMG recommends a
   1% pay rise for health service workers to their pay
   review body.

5   Covid deaths fall by 41% in a week, new cases lowest since September. YouGov indicates a Conservative revival pulling them 13 points ahead of Labour. The 6th Brazilian strain case was found self-quarantining in Croydon.

7   *Scotland on Sunday* poll indicated 52-48% in favour of the Union. *The Observer* poll suggests 72% think the government's health pay offer should be more generous.

8   School children return in England.

9   Whitty and Vallance warn against accelerating the end of lockdown.

10 PM hints at change of position on NHS pay. Common's Public Accounts Committee publishes critical report on efficacy of NHS Test and Trace.

11 One year to the day since the WHO declared a pandemic. Biobank UK begins Long Covid Study.

12 'R' now stands at 0.6 to 0.8

14 Sir Ian Diamond, Head of ONS, warns that a third wave this autumn is 'inevitable' but the vaccine is starting to provide protection.

15 Several European Countries suspend AZ inoculating because of a scattering of blood clot cases.

16 Government published its *Integrated Review of Security, Defence, Development and Foreign Policy.* EU regulator approves use of AZ. New variant appears in the Philippines.

17 NHS warns of a 'significant' reduction in vaccine supply next month. EU considering banning exports of AZ including to the UK because AZ had 'under-delivered' to its EU customers.

18 MRHA safety review says benefits of AZ outweigh the risks. Department of Health says shielders can stop shielding on 1 April.

19 Anxieties arise in UK as third wave gathers
force in continental Europe, 'R' is slightly up
on last week at 0.6 – 0.9. HMG borrowed
£19.1bn in February. (£17.4bn higher than in
February 2020).

20 Hancock announces that half the adult population
of the UK has had a least one jab. France and
Poland go into lockdown.

21 Another daily jab record. Public Health England
warn that face masks and social distancing may
last for years.

22 PM warns of third wave 'washing up on our shores
as well'. *Defence in a Competitive Age* White Paper
is presented to Parliament.

23 On the first anniversary of the first lockdown, the
Queen speaks of 'the grief and loss felt by so
many'. Chris Whitty says 'people have responded
magnificently'. PM says there will be a permanent
memorial to those we have lost but rules out an
immediate inquiry. Later he tells the 1922
committee 'capitalism and greed' produced the AZ
vaccine.

24 Johnson raises possibility of compulsory jab for all
care home staff.

25 Report on 'Long Covid' published. HMG wins H
of C vote to extend emergency legislation for 6
months by 484 to 76.

26 'R' is 0.7 – 0.9 up slightly from last week.
ONS reports infections have risen slightly in
schools.

27 Wales partially unlocks. HMG considering booster
jabs for the over 70s this autumn to combat new
variants.

29 A day of qualified easement in England (two
households, six people outside).

30   PM joins with twenty other nations to press for an International Pandemic Treaty; YouGov poll for IPPR study finds that a quarter of NHS staff are more likely to quit than at this time last year.

April   1   ONS estimates there are 1.1 million Long Covid sufferers.

2   Much talk of HMG introducing 'Covid passports' for pubs/theatres. 'R' for England last week was 0.8 to 1.0 (unchanged).

3   Second night of rioting in Belfast

4   Third night of rioting in Belfast though less serious than the previous two.

5   PM says stage 2 of 'road map' will start in England on 12 April and that nothing in the data suggests HMG needs to deviate from it. Modellers warn of third wave between June and September. Fears of a new variant getting into Britain.

6   Oxford University study indicates that 1 in 3 survivors of Covid who had had a confirmed diagnosis are diagnosed with a neurological or psychiatric condition within 6 months.

8   Police in NI use water cannon for first time in six years.

9   Just after noon, Buckingham Palace announces that Prince Philip had died peacefully at Windsor this morning.

13   Government meets its target of a jab for all over 50s who want it with 2 days to spare.

14   Government to consult on making vaccinations compulsory for care home staff.

15 SNP publish manifesto for 6 May election. Sturgeon says 'a simple majority' of pro-independence MSPs would provide a mandate for another referendum before the end of 2023 with two years of negotiations to follow if a majority wanted to leave the UK.

16 Anxieties about a new Indian variant which has produced 77 cases in the UK so far.

18 NHS Providers says it will take between 3 to 5 years for NHS to catch up on waiting lists.

19 Concern rises about Indian variant (105 cases so far). Work stepped up on booster jabs.

21 What will later be renamed from 'India' to 'Delta' is designated a 'Variant of Concern' by Public Health England.

22 Oxford Study suggests vaccines are effective at reducing the transmission of Covid. Biden opens 'Earth Day' Global Summit by warning this is the 'decisive decade'.

23 Dominic Cummings writes a 1000-word blog, after No 10 sources accuse him of leaking to the press, in which he says 'It is sad to see the PM and his office fall so far below the standards of competence and integrity the country deserves'. Johnson dismisses one particular claim with the words 'I don't give a monkey's'.

25 Sturgeon says that for the UK government to try to block a second referendum if Holyrood returns a majority of pro-referendum MSPs, 'would be asking a court to effectively overturn the result of a free and fair democratic election'.

May 6 Bank of England raises growth forecast for this year from 5% to 7.25%.

7   Conservatives win the Hartlepool by-election taking 51.7% of the votes cast to Labour's 26.7%. Professor Van Tam says the vaccines have already saved 10,000 British lives.

8   SNP are one seat sort of an overall majority in Holyrood. The return of eight Green MSPs means that there is a majority for a second referendum.

9   Sturgeon agrees to attend Johnson's Covid Recovery Summit, in a telephone conversation she tells him a second referendum is 'a matter of when not if'.

12 PM announces a statutory inquiry to start in spring 2022 to 'place the state's actions under the microscope'.

15 Surge testing for Indian variant in 15 areas.

17 Government indicates that the 21 June 'Freedom Day' may have to be reviewed. Cabinet Secretary Simon Case tells the Lords Constitution Committee that the days of 'devolve and forget' are over in Whitehall.

20 Number of Indian variant cases has increased by 160% over the past week.

21 'R' is between 0.9 and 1.1 across the UK.

26 Cummings tells a House of Commons Select Committee that as a decision-taker Johnson is like a shopping trolley 'smashing from one side of the aisle to another'.

30 Government considering compulsory vaccinations for health and social care workers.

June   1   Zero deaths reported for the first time since July 2020. Scotland's Medical Director, Professor Jason Leitch, says that Scotland is at the beginning of a third wave.

3   The first (virtual) 4-Nations Covid Recovery Summit. No concrete decisions but they agree to meet again.

4 New Covid cases (6,238) are the highest since 26 March 2021. Indian variant (now known as 'Delta') has become the dominant strain.

6 New cases have risen by 49% in a week

14 Johnson announces a 4-week delay 'Freedom Day' will now be 19 July. Whitty warns 'we will have to live with the virus – which will continue to cause severe infections and kill people for the rest of our lives'.

18 Conservatives lose the Chesham and Amersham by-election to the Lib-Dems who won an 8,000 majority

24 Gordon Brown says the Union is more perilous noq that at any point in his life time.

25 Photos of Hancock, in a passionate embrace with a non-executive director of the Department of Health in his office, are published in the Sun.

26 Hancock resigns. Replaced by Sajid Javid.

29 Highest number of new cases since January (22,865). Javid says there is no need for restrictions to persist beyond 19 July.

July

2 Kim Leadbetter (Jo Cox's sister) Holds Batley and Spen for Labour in the by-election by 323 votes.

5 The Queen awards the NHS the George Cross on its seventy-third birthday.

16 ONS report that 1 in 100 have Covid in the UK.

PHASE 10: 'FREEDOM DAY' AND AFTER

19 What Johnson calls 'Freedom Day', when nearly all restrictions are lifted. YouGov poll suggest 35% think the ending of restrictions is the right thing, while 55% do not. Johnson says 'Please, please be cautious'.

21   HMG says all over-fifties will have had their first
jab by the end of July; all six teaching unions want
schools to return in a planned way Government
raises pay offer to nurses to 3%. Care Quality
Commission reports 39,000 Covid related deaths
in care homes over the past 18 months.

23   Joseph Rowntree Foundation estimates 500,000
people will fall into poverty in October 2021 when
£20 a week supplement to Universal Credit ends.

29   Public Health England estimate that the vaccines
have prevented 60,000 deaths and 22m cases in
England.

August   4   All 16-17 year olds in England to be offered the
vaccine.

5   Johnson on a visit to Scotland says: 'Constitutional
change is about as far from the top of my agenda
as it is possible to be'.

15   Kabul falls to the Taliban.

24   Sturgeon says Scotland will establish a judge-led
Covid inquiry by the end of the year.

September   7   Johnson announces 1.25% rise in National
Insurance and share dividends to pay for NHS
catch-up and social care, to raise £36.3 billion over
3 years (£5.3bn for social care)

8   House of Commons votes 319 to 248 for National
Insurance rise.

14   Johnson announces 'winter plans' for the NHS. If
current position is inadequate to prevent the NHS
from being overwhelmed, Plan B would require
vaccine passports, compulsory masks and more
people working from home. Professor Van Tam
says vaccines have probably saved 112,000 lives
and 24m cases in the UK

Notes

INTRODUCTION: IT TOOK A VIRUS

1. Archie Bevan and Brian Murray (eds.), *The Collected Poems of George Mackay Brown* (John Murray, 2005), pp. 410–12. 'An Old Man in July' appears in GMB's *Northern Lights* collection.
2. *Social Insurance and Allied Services. Report by Sir William Beveridge*, Cmd. 6404 (HMSO, 1942), p. 6.
3. Email from Sir Richard Aikens, 2 July 2020.

CHAPTER 1: NYE'S PERAMBULATORS

1. *Social Insurance and Allied Services*, p. 6.
2. Quoted in Michael Foot, *Aneurin Bevan: A Biography*, vol. 2: *1945–1960* (Davis Poynter, 1973), p. 105.
3. Ibid.
4. Kenneth O. Morgan, *Labour People, Leaders and Lieutenants: Hardie to Kinnock* (Oxford University Press, 1987), p. 205.
5. Martin Gilbert, *Winston S. Churchill*, vol. 7: *Road to Victory, 1941–45* (Heinemann, 1986), p. 367.
6. Quoted in Peter Hennessy, *Distilling the Frenzy: Writing the History of One's Own Times* (Biteback, 2012), p. 10. (This is as Castle reported Bevan's remark to Rob Shepherd and me in the early 1990s when we were preparing a Widevision Productions/Channel 4 Television documentary on post-war Britain called *What Has Become of Us?*, transmitted on 18 December 1994.)
7. *Employment Policy*, Cmd. 6527 (HMSO, 1944).
8. This table can be found in Peter Hennessy, *Never Again: Britain 1945–51* (Cape, 1992), p. 99.

9. Quoted in Peter Hennessy and Caroline Anstey, 'From Clogs to Clogs? Britain's Relative Economic Decline Since 1851', Strathclyde/*Analysis* Paper no. 3 (Department of Government, Strathclyde University, 1991), p. 21.

10. *Let Us Face The Future* (Labour Party, 1945).

11. Michael Young, *The Rise of the Meritocracy* (Thames and Hudson, 1958).

12. Interviewed for *What Has Become of Us?*

13. Antony Jay (ed.), *The Oxford Dictionary of Political Quotations* (Oxford University Press, 1996), p. 41.

14. Hennessy, *Never Again*, p. 56.

15. House of Commons *Official Report*, 16 February 1943, vol. 386, col. 1678.

16. Hennessy, *Never Again*, p. 76.

17. Ibid.

18. Robert Skidelsky, *John Maynard Keynes: Fighting for Britain 1937–1946* (Macmillan, 2000), p. 380.

19. Keynes's paper is most easily consulted in Robert Skidelsky (ed.), *John Maynard Keynes: The Essential Keynes* (Penguin, 2015), pp. 444–5.

20. Keir Thorpe, '"The Missing Pillar": Economic Planning and the Machinery of Government During the Labour Administrations of 1945–51' (unpublished PhD thesis, University of London, 1999).

21. https://api.parliament.uk/historic-hansard/commons/1947/jul/07/economic-planning-board-functions-and, accessed 20 August 2021.

22. Peter Hennessy, *Having It So Good: Britain in the Fifties* (Allen Lane/Penguin Press, 2006), p. 74.

23. 'More Than Half Of British Homes Don't Have A Bathroom - Archives 1950', *Guardian*, 21 March 2018.

24. Nicholas Timmins, *The Five Giants: A Biography of the Welfare State*, new edn (William Collins, 2017), pp. 172–3.

25. www.ons.gov.uk/peoplepopulationandcommunity/housing/articles/censusunearthedexplore50yearsofchangefrom1961/2021-08-09, accessed 26 August 2021.

26. Timmins, *The Five Giants*, p. 182.

27. The National Archives (TNA), T 229/136, 'Marshall Proposals. Alternative Action in the Event of Breakdown'.

28. Alec Cairncross (ed.), *The Robert Hall Diaries, 1947–1955* (Unwin Hyman, 1989), p. 161, diary entry for 20 July 1951.

29. Timmins, *The Five Giants*, p. 145.

30. Peter Calvocoressi, *The British Experience, 1945–1975* (Bodley Head, 1978), pp. 35–6.

31. House of Commons *Official Report*, 5th ser., vol. 418, cols. 1900–1901 (1946).

CHAPTER 2: THE PURSUIT OF CONSENSUS

1. Martin Gilbert, *Winston S. Churchill*, vol. 8: *Never Despair, 1945–65* (Heinemann, 1988), pp. 275–6.
2. R. A. Butler, *The Art of the Possible: The Memoirs of Lord Butler* (Hamish Hamilton, 1971), p. 90.
3. Ibid., pp. 145–6.
4. Paul Addison, *Churchill on the Home Front 1900–1955* (Cape 1992), p. 433.
5. John Colville, *The Fringes of Power: Downing Street Diaries 1939–1955* (Hodder and Stoughton, 1985), p. 647.
6. Anthony Montague Browne, *Long Sunset: Memoirs of Winston Churchill's Last Private Secretary* (Cassell, 1995), p. 14.
7. Butler, *The Art of the Possible*, p. 145.
8. Reginald Maudling, *Memoirs* (Sidgwick and Jackson, 1978), pp. 45–6.
9. Hennessy, *Having It So Good*, pp. 199–211.
10. Jay (ed.), *The Oxford Dictionary of Political Quotations*, p. 46.
11. TNA, T 236/3240, 'Sterling Convertibility. OPERATION ROBOT'.
12. Philip M. Williams (ed.), *The Diary of Hugh Gaitskell, 1945–1956* (Cape, 1983), diary entry for 9 November 1954, pp. 315–16.
13. Butler, *The Art of the Possible*, p. 155.
14. Ibid., p. 160.
15. Robert Shepherd, *Iain Macleod: A Biography* (Hutchinson, 1994), pp. 61–9.
16. Ibid., pp. 74–7.
17. Hennessy, *Never Again*, p. 416.
18. Charles Webster, *Health Services Since the War* (HMSO, 1988), p. 145.
19. Timmins, *The Five Giants*, p. 205.
20. Ibid., p. 206.
21. As recounted to the author by Dr Heffer.
22. Harry Eckstein, *English Health Service* (Harvard University Press, 1959), p. 2.
23. Michael Dockrill, *British Defence Since 1945* (Blackwell, 1988), p. 57.
24. Peter Hennessy, *Cabinets and the Bomb* (The British Academy/Oxford University Press, 2007); House of Commons *Official Report*, 12 May 1948, 'Armed Forces (Modern Weapons)', col. 2117.
25. Peter Hennessy, *The Secret State: Preparing for the Worst 1945–2010* (Penguin 2015).
26. Norman Tebbit, BBC Radio 4, 23 July 2015, in Peter Hennessy and Robert Shepherd, *The Complete Reflections: Conversations with Politicians* (Haus, 2020), pp. 68–9.

27. As recalled by his Foreign Office private secretary, Sir Roderick Barclay, in Michael Charlton, *The Price of Victory* (BBC, 1983), p. 75.

28. Bernard Donoughue and G. W. Jones, *Herbert Morrison: Portrait of a Politician* (Weidenfeld, 1973), p. 981.

29. TNA, CAB 129/48 (C51) 32, '"United Europe" Note by the Prime Minister and Minister of Defence', 29 November 1951.

30. D. R. Thorpe, *Eden: The Life and Times of Anthony Eden First Earl of Avon, 1897–1977*, p. 368.

31. Conversation with Douglas Jay, who chaired the meeting at which Attlee spoke, 4 March 1983.

32. Charlton, *The Price of Victory*, p. 195.

33. *The Next Five Years* (Conservative Party, September 1959).

34. Timmins, *The Five Giants*, p. 254.

35. Brian Abel-Smith and Peter Townsend, 'The Poor and the Poorest', LSE Occasional Papers on Social Administration no. 17 (1965).

36. Timmins, *The Five Giants*, p. 255.

37. P. Flora, *State, Economy and Society*, vol. 1 (1983), pp. 345–6, 440–2. Cited Rodney Lowe. *The Welfare State in Britain since 1945*, 2nd edn (Macmillan, 1999), pp. 348–9.

CHAPTER 3: NO SATISFACTION

1. TNA, PRO, PREM 11/4520, 'Town and Country Planning', 'Cabinet, October 25th, Modernising Britain'.

2. Harold Wilson, *The New Britain: Labour's Plan Outlined by Harold Wilson: Selective Speeches 1964* (Penguin Special, 1964), p. 36.

3. Quoted in Martin Wiener, *English Culture and the Decline of the Industrial Spirit, 1850–1980* (Cambridge University Press, 1981), p. 162.

4. Barbara Castle, *The Castle Diaries 1974–76* (Weidenfeld and Nicolson, 1980), p. 223.

5. John Cornwall, *Modern Capitalism: Its Growth and Transformation* (St Martin's Press, 1977), p. 11; OECD, *Economic Survey* (November 1979); Angus Maddison, 'Long Run Dynamics of Productivity Growth', *Banca Nazionale del Lavoro Quarterly Review*, no. 128 (1979), p. 4.

6. Paul Collier, *The Future of Capitalism* (Penguin, 2019), p. 8.

7. Alec Cairncross, *The British Economy Since 1945* (Blackwell, 1992), p. 306.

8. Ibid., p. 285.

9. TNA, PREM 11/3930, 'Remarks Made by Prime Minister at Cabinet on 28 May 1962'.

10. *The National Plan*, Cmnd. 2764 (HMSO, September 1965).

11. Cairncross, *The British Economy Since 1945*, p. 155.
12. Ibid.
13. Quoted ibid., p. 15.
14. Ibid., p. 14.
15. Source: C. H. Feinstein, 'Economic growth since 1870: Britain's performance in international perspective', *Oxford Review of Economic Policy* (Spring 1988).
16. Email to the author from Robin Wilson, 22 November 2017.
17. Enoch Powell (ed. Richard Ritchie), *A Nation or No Nation? Six Years in British Politics* (Batsford, 1978), pp. 43–4.
18. Timmins, *The Five Giants*, pp. 209–10.
19. Committee on Higher Education, *Higher Education*, Cmnd. 2154 (HMSO, October 1963).
20. Peter Hennessy, *Winds of Change: Britain in the Early Sixties* (Penguin, 2020), pp. 452–5.
21. Peter Hennessy, *The Prime Minister: The Office and Its Holders Since 1945* (Penguin, 2001), p. 150.
22. Ben Pimlott, *Harold Wilson* (HarperCollins, 1992), p. 62.
23. Ibid., p. 76.
24. Ibid., p. 75.
25. Harold Wilson, *The Labour Government 1964–1970: A Personal Record* (Michael Joseph, 1971), p. 699.
26. Timmins, *The Five Giants*, p. 230.
27. Wilson, *The Labour Government 1964–1970*, pp. 481–5.
28. Ibid.
29. Timmins, *The Five Giants*, p. 266.
30. Ibid.
31. Ibid., pp. 195–6.
32. Edward Heath, *The Course of My Life* (Hodder, 1998), p. 31.
33. Harold Macmillan, *The Middle Way* (Macmillan, 1938).
34. Heath, *The Course of My Life*, p. 33.
35. Ibid., pp. 33–4.
36. Ibid., p. 302.
37. John Campbell, *Edward Heath* (Cape, 1993), p. 267.
38. Hennessy, *The Prime Minister*, p. 335.
39. Heath, *The Course of My Life*, p. 452.
40. Ibid., p. 453.
41. Ibid.
42. Timmins, *The Five Giants*, pp. 236–42.
43. Susan Crosland, *Tony Crosland* (Cape, 1982), p. 148.

44. Margaret Thatcher, *The Path to Power* (HarperCollins, 1995), p. 170.
45. Ibid., p. 169.
46. Ibid., p. 171.
47. Peter Hennessy, 'Mrs Thatcher Shimmers Through the Hustings', *The Times, Higher Education Supplement*, 22 February 1974.
48. Timmins, *The Five Giants*, p. 314.
49. Castle, *Diaries 1974–76*, p. 319, diary entry for 1 March 1975.
50. Joel Barnett, *Inside the Treasury* (André Deutsch, 1982), p. 182.
51. Timmins, *The Five Giants*, p. 347.
52. Kenneth O. Morgan, *Callaghan: A Life* (Oxford University Press, 1997), pp. 540–41.
53. Hennessy, *The Prime Minister*, p. 385.
54. Morgan, *Callaghan*, p. 551.
55. Hennessy, *The Prime Minister*, pp. 379–80.
56. Morgan, *Callaghan*, p. 699.
57. Anthony F. Heath, *Social Progress in Britain* (Oxford University Press, 2018), pp. 17–18.
58. Ibid., p. 18.
59. I had come to this conclusion before reading Anthony Heath but, I am relieved to say, when I did I found that we shared that view. Ibid., pp. 17–19.
60. Frank Fraser Darling, 'Where Does Responsibility Lie?' BBC Reith Lectures, 1969: 'Wilderness and Plenty', first broadcast on BBC Radio 4, 14 December 1969.
61. Speech by the Prince of Wales at the 'Countryside in 1970 Conference', Cardiff, 19 February 1970. www.princeofwales.gov.uk/speech/speech-hrh-prince-wales-countryside-1970-conference-steering-committee-wales-cardiff.
62. James Lovelock, *Gaia: A New Look at Life on Earth* (Oxford University Press, 1979).
63. Ibid., p. 1.
64. Charles Moore, *Margaret Thatcher: The Authorized Biography*, vol. 3: *Herself Alone* (Allen Lane, 2019), p. 412.
65. Ibid., pp. 417–18.
66. Ibid.

CHAPTER 4: SAFE IN HER HANDS?

1. Thatcher, *The Path to Power*, p. 600.
2. Nigel Lawson, BBC Radio 4, 20 July 2015, in Hennessy and Shepherd, *The Complete Reflections*, p. 226.
3. 'Let our children grow tall'. Quoted in Timmins, *The Five Giants*, p. 357.

4. Thatcher, *The Path to Power*, p. 118.

5. Ibid., pp. 118–19.

6. Ibid., pp. 119–20.

7. Ibid., pp. 120–21.

8. Ibid., p. 120.

9. Ibid., p. 69.

10. Ibid.

11. Conversation with Lord Willetts, 16 May 2020.

12. Quoted in Timmins, *The Five Giants*, p. 370.

13. Tebbit in Hennessy and Shepherd, *The Complete Reflections*, p. 80.

14. Ibid., pp. 73–4.

15. Timmins, *The Five Giants*, pp. 378–9.

16. Ibid., p. 379.

17. Private email to the author from Nicholas Timmins.

18. Timmins, *The Five Giants*, p. 496.

19. Department for Communities and Local Government, '50 years of the English Housing Survey', November 2017, p. 13, https://assets.publishing.service.gov.uk/government/uploads/system/uploads/attachment_data/file/658923/EHS_50th_Anniversary_Report.pdf, accessed 27 August 2021.

20. Nigel Lawson, *The View from No. 11: Memoirs of a Tory Radical* (Bantam, 1992), p. 613.

21. Timmins, *The Five Giants*, p. 370.

22. Jay (ed.), *The Oxford Dictionary of Political Quotations*, p. 161.

23. Quoted in Timmins, *The Five Giants*, p. 372 citing the *Independent*, 8 June 1987.

24. Jay (ed.), *The Oxford Dictionary of Political Quotations*, p. 161.

25. Timmins, *The Five Giants*, p. 372.

26. Ibid., p. 406.

27. Ibid., p. 373.

28. Lawson, *The View from Number 11*, p. 303.

29. Margaret Thatcher, *The Downing Street Years* (HarperCollins, 1993), p. 277.

30. Ibid.

31. TNA, CAB 129/215–6, 'Longer-Term Options', 'Memorandum by the Central Policy Review Staff', 6 September 1982.

32. Ibid.

33. Ibid.

34. Ibid.

35. Ibid.

36. Ibid.

37. *The Economist*, 18–24 September 1982.

38. Norman Fowler, *Ministers Decide: A Personal Memoir of the Thatcher Years* (Chapmans, 1991), p. 186.

39. Lord Hailsham, *A Sparrow's Flight: Memoirs* (HarperCollins, 1990), p. 211.

40. Conversation with Lord Howell of Guildford, 15 June 2020.

41. TNA, CAB 128/74–11, Cabinet Conclusions, 9 September 1982.

42. Hugo Young, *One of Us: A Biography of Margaret Thatcher* (Macmillan, 1989), p. 301.

43. Timmins, *The Five Giants*, p. 397.

44. Ibid., p. 391.

45. Ibid., p. 371.

46. Ibid., p. 398.

47. Ibid., pp. 400–401.

48. Ibid., p. 401.

49. John Major, *The Autobiography* (HarperCollins, 1999), pp. xvii–xviii.

50. J. Denman and P. McDonald, 'Unemployment Statistics from 1881 to the Present Day', *Labour Market Trends Vol. 104* (HMSO, January 1996), p. 6.

51. Timmins, *The Five Giants*, p. 396.

52. Michael Heseltine, BBC Radio 4, 2 August 2016, in Hennessy and Shepherd, *The Complete Reflections*, p. 300.

53. TNA, PREM 19/578, 'IT TOOK A RIOT', Heseltine to Thatcher, 13 August 1981.

54. Heseltine in Hennessy and Shepherd, *The Complete Reflections*, pp. 300–301.

55. TNA, CAB 128/71–8, Cabinet Conclusions, 16 July 1981.

56. TNA, PREM 19/578, 'IT TOOK A RIOT'.

57. Timmins, *The Five Giants*, p. 369.

58. TNA, PREM 19/578, 'IT TOOK A RIOT'.

59. Peter Hennessy, *Whitehall* (Pimlico, 2001), p. 124.

60. Ibid.

61. Ibid.

62. Michael Heseltine interview for the Brook Productions Channel 4 Television series *All the Prime Minister's Men*, 17 April 1986.

63. Heath, *Social Progress in Britain*, p. 17.

64. Richard Wilkinson and Kate Pickett, *The Spirit Level: Why Equality is Better for Everyone* (Allen Lane, 2009).

65. House of Commons Select Committee on Health, Third Report *Health Inequalities*, (House of Commons, 26 February 2009), Chapter 2 point 16

https://publications.parliament.uk/pa/cm200809/cmselect/cmhealth/286/28602.htm

66. Alison L. Weightman et al., 'Social Inequality and Infant Health in the UK: Systematic Review and Meta-Analyses', *BMJ Open* vol. 2, no. 3 (2012): e000964.

67. Heath, *Social Progress in Britain*, p. 39.

68. Ibid., p. 37.

69. Timmins, *The Five Giants*, p. 507.

70. BBC Radio 4, *Rethinks*, discussion chaired by Amol Rajan, 23 June 2020.

71. Jan Tinbergen, *Income Distribution: Analysis and Policies* (North-Holland, 1975).

72. Heath, *Social Progress in Britain*, p. 18.

73. Timmins, *The Five Giants*, p. 456.

74. Ibid., p. 463.

75. Kenneth Baker, BBC Radio 4, 23 August 2016, in Hennessy and Shepherd, *The Complete Reflections*, p. 392.

76. Ibid., pp. 393–4.

77. *Woman's Own*, 31 October 1987.

78. Thatcher, *The Downing Street Years*, p. 626.

CHAPTER 5: SOCIAL MARKET

1. Major, *The Autobiography*, p. 246.

2. *World at One*, BBC Radio 4, 22 June 2020.

3. Alastair Campbell, *The Alastair Campbell Diaries*, vol. 2: *Power and the People, 1997–1999* (Hutchinson, 2013), pp. 249–50, diary entry for 5 January 1998.

4. James Meade Memorial Lecture, 8 May 2000, quoted in William Keegan, *The Prudence of Mr Gordon Brown* (Wiley, 2003), p. 256.

5. David Cameron, *For the Record* (Collins, 2019), pp. 3–4.

6. Major, *The Autobiography*, pp. 200–201.

7. Moore, *Herself Alone*, p. 738.

8. Private Information.

9. Hennessy, *The Prime Minister*, p. 439.

10. John Major, BBC Radio 4, 13 August 2014, in Hennessy and Shepherd, *The Complete Reflections*, pp. 120–21.

11. William Waldegrave, 'Three Prime Ministers', paper delivered to the Twentieth Century British History Seminar, Institute of Historical Research, 10 December 1997.

12. Major, *The Autobiography*, pp. 247–8.

13. Ibid., p. 248.

14. *The Citizen's Charter: Raising the Standard*, Cm. 1599 (HMSO, 22 July 1991).

15. *Competing for Quality: Buying Better Public Services*, Cm. 1730 (HMSO, 1991).

16. Moore, *Herself Alone*, p. 220.

17. Major, *The Autobiography*, p. 215.

18. Ibid., p. 273.

19. Ibid., pp. 286–8.

20. Moore, *Herself Alone*, pp. 801–2.

21. Ibid., p. 801.

22. 'Unemployment Rate (Aged 16 and Over, Seasonally Adjusted)', Office for National Statistics, 17 August 2021; www.ons.gov.uk/employmentandlabourmarket/peoplenotinwork/unemployment/timeseries/mgsx/lms, accessed 6 September 2021.

23. Denman and McDonald, 'Unemployment Statistics from 1881 to The Present Day'.

24. Timmins, *The Five Giants*, p. 496.

25. Heath, *Social Progress in Britain*, p. 27.

26. 50 Years of English Housing Survey, Department for Communities and Local Government, November 2017, p. 5; https://assets.publishing.service.gov.uk/government/uploads/system/uploads/attachment_data/file/658923/EHS_50th_Anniversary_Report.pdf, accessed 27 August 2021.

27. Ibid., p. 12.

28. Timmins, *The Five Giants*, p. 503.

29. 'UK Homelessness: 2005 to 2018', Office for National Statistics, 17 September 2019; www.ons.gov.uk/releases/ukhomelessness2005to2018, accessed 6 September 2021.

30. Anthony Harrison and John Appleby, 'The War on Waiting for Hospital Treatment: What Has Labour Achieved and What Challenges Remain?', King's Fund, 4 August 2005, p. xi; www.kingsfund.org.uk/sites/default/files/field/field_publication_file/war-on-waiting-hospital-treatment-labour-full-report-john-appleby-anthony-harrison-kings-fund-4-august-2005.pdf, accessed 3 September 2021.

31. Ruth Thorlby, Tim Gardner and Catherine Turton, 'NHS Performance and Waiting Times: Priorities for the Next Government', The Health Foundation, 22 November 2019, p. 4; www.health.org.uk/sites/default/files/2019-11/nhs-performance-and-waiting-times-priorities-for-the-next-government-geo2-.pdf, accessed 3 September 2021.

32. Harriet Harman, BBC Radio 4, 24 August 2017, in Hennessy and Shepherd, *The Complete Reflections*, pp. 486–92.

33. Campbell, *Diaries*, vol. 2, p. 309.

34. Timmins, *The Five Giants*, p. 362.

35. Ibid., p. 564.

36. Ibid.

37. John Rentoul, *Tony Blair, Prime Minister* (Little, Brown, 2001), p. 374.

38. Conversation with Frank Field, 10 July 2020.

39. Timmins, *The Five Giants*, p. 573.

40. Keegan, *The Prudence of Mr Gordon Brown*, p. 265.

41. Ibid. Nigel Lawson's 'tease' can be found in the *Financial Times*, 5 October 2001.

42. Ibid., p. 585; Rentoul, *Tony Blair*, p. 381.

43. Timmins, *The Five Giants*, p. 585.

44. Ibid., p. 652.

45. Ibid., p. 596.

46. www.gov.uk/government/collections/households-below-average-income-hbai--2, Table 1.4a, accessed 4 July 2021.

47. www.gov.uk/government/collections/households-below-average-income-hbai--2, Table 1.4b, accessed 4 July 2021.

48. Keegan, *The Prudence of Mr Gordon Brown*, p. 243.

49. J. K. Galbraith, *The Affluent Society* (Hamish Hamilton, 1958).

50. Timmins, *The Five Giants*, p. 594.

51. Frank Field and Andrew Forsey, *Not for Patching: A Strategic Welfare Review* (Haus, 2018), p. viii.

52. John Hills, *Good Times, Bad Times* (Policy Press, 2017) p. 261.

53. Keegan, *The Prudence of Mr Gordon Brown*, p. 279.

54. Timmins, *The Five Giants*, p. 601.

55. I am grateful to the House of Lords Library for collecting these figures.

56. David Cameron, *For the Record* (Collins, 2019), p. 279.

57. Sir Nicholas Stern, *The Economics of Climate Change* (HM Treasury, 30 October 2006).

58. 'Summary of the Key Provisions of the Climate Change Act 2008', NHS Sustainable Development (Department of Health) undated.

59. Timmins, *The Five Giants*, p. 655.

60. Iain Duncan Smith, BBC Radio 4, 21 August 2018, in Hennessy and Shepherd, *The Complete Reflections*, pp. 649–50.

61. Cameron, *For the Record*, p. 188.

62. Timmins, *The Five Giants*, p. 699.

63. Ibid., pp. 699–70.

64. Cameron, *For the Record*, p. 471.
65. 'Legal Aid: The Review of LASPO', Part 1, House of Commons Library Briefings, 7 May 2020.
66. House of Lords Select Committee on the Constitution, *Covid-19 and the Courts*, HL Paper 257 (HMSO, 30 March 2021).
67. Tom Bingham, *The Rule of Law* (Penguin, 2010).
68. Timmins, *The Five Giants*, pp. 708–9.
69. Ibid., pp. 600, 605, 676–7.
70. Ibid., p. 604.
71. Peter Hennessy, *The Kingdom to Come: Thoughts on the Union Before and After the Scottish Referendum* (Haus, 2015), pp. 9–10.
72. Ibid., p. 54.
73. BBC News, 23 July 2020.
74. Peter Clarke, *Hope and Glory: Britain 1900–90* (Allen Lane, Penguin Press, 1996), p. 322.
75. Tom Nairn, *The Break Up of Britain* (NLB, 1977), pp. 182–7.
76. www.royal.uk/silver-jubilee-address-parliament-4-may-1977, accessed 9 July 2021.
77. Winston S. Churchill, *The World Crisis* (Macmillan, 1923), p. 112.
78. Michael Marmot et al., 'Health Equity in England: The Marmot Review 10 Years On: Executive Summary', Institute of Health, www.instituteofhealthequity.org/resources-reports/marmot-review-10-years-on/the-marmot-review-10-years-on-full-report.pdf, accessed 24 August 2021. Quotes taken from, pp. 5, 37, 40–41, 50, 63, 65, 111 and 115.

CHAPTER 6: THE BREXIT EFFECT

1. Jean Monnet, *Memoirs* (Collins, 1978), pp. 451–3.
2. Richard Ritchie (ed.), *Enoch Powell: A Nation or No Nation* (Batsford, 1978), pp. 43–4.
3. Intelligence and Security Committee of Parliament, *Russia*, HC632, 21 July 2020, pp. 9–14.
4. Ibid., p. 10.
5. Ibid., p. 28.
6. Enoch Powell, *Byline*, BBC1, 3 July 1989.
7. TNA, CAB 128/35 Part 1, CC (61), 22nd Conclusions, 20 April 1961.
8. Conversation with Lord Wilson of Dinton, 2 October 2008. He originally advanced his 'anaesthetic' interpretation to my MA students at Queen Mary University of London during a seminar on Cabinet government.

9. Peter Hennessy, *Distilling the Frenzy: Writing the History of One's Own Times* (Biteback, 2012), p. 14.

10. Quoted ibid., p. 255.

11. The late Lord Dahrendorf used the phrase more than once in conversation with the author.

12. Susan Barnes, *Behind the Image* (Cape, 1974), pp. 235–6.

13. I first heard Lord Patten use this phrase in the discussion after his Ditchley Foundation Lecture, 8 July 2005.

14. www.gov.uk/government/speeches/the-governments-negotiating-objectives-for-exiting-the-eu-pm-speech, accessed 6 September 2021.

15. www.gov.uk/government/speeches/pms-florence-speech-a-new-era-of-cooperation-and-partnership-between-the-uk-and-the-eu, accessed 6 September 2021.

16. www.gov.uk/government/speeches/pm-speech-on-our-future-economic-partnership-with-the-european-union, accessed 6 September 2021.

17. www.gov.uk/government/publications/the-future-relationship-between-the-united-kingdom-and-the-european-union, accessed 6 September 2021.

18. John Bercow, *Unspeakable: The Autobiography* (Weidenfeld and Nicolson, 2020), pp. 371–2.

19. Ibid., pp. 272–3.

20. Ibid., pp. 373–4.

21. House of Commons Library Briefing Paper 7639, 29 June 2016 European Union Referendum 201629, June 2016, p. 7.

22. House of Commons Library Briefing Paper 7327, 1 October 2019, Deprivation in English Constituencies, 2019, Frontispiece. The data is based on index of multiple deprivation calculated for 2015/16 (Deprivation is calculated differently in Scotland, Wales and Ireland).

23. Anthony Seldon with Raymond Newell, *May at 10* (Biteback, 2019), pp. 4–5.

24. Ibid., p. 3.

25. *The United Kingdom Internal Market* (CP 278), July 2020, p. 17; www.gov.uk/government/publications/uk-internal-market, accessed 20 August 2021.

CHAPTER 7: PATHOGEN BRITAIN
AND ITS LESSONS?

1. Richard Feynman, Appendix to the Rogers Commission Report on the Space Shuttle *Challenger* accident, 6 June 1986. Elizabeth Knowles (ed.), *The Oxford Dictionary of Modern Quotations* (Oxford University Press, 2002), p. 113.

2. Professor Sarah Gilbert and Dr Catherine Green, *Vaxxers: The Inside Story of the Oxford AstraZeneca Vaccine and the Race Against the Virus* (Hodder, 2021), p. 5.

3. Jeremy Farrar with Anjana Ahuja, *Spike: The Virus vs the People – the Inside Story* (Profile, 2021), p. 231.

4. Michael Rosen, *Many Different Kinds of Love: A Story of Life, Death and the NHS* (Ebony Press, 2021), pp. 181–3.

5. Cabinet Office, *National Risk Register of Civil Emergencies*, https://assets.publishing.service.gov.uk/government/uploads/system/uploads/attachment_data/file/644968/UK_National_Risk_Register_2017.pdf (2017 edn); https://assets.publishing.service.gov.uk/government/uploads/system/uploads/attachment_data/file/419549/20150331_2015-NRR-WA_Final.pdf (2015 edn); https://assets.publishing.service.gov.uk/government/uploads/system/uploads/attachment_data/file/211867/NationalRiskRegister2013_amended.pdf (2013 edn); https://assets.publishing.service.gov.uk/government/uploads/system/uploads/attachment_data/file/211858/CO_National-RiskRegister_2012_acc.pdf (2012 edn); https://assets.publishing.service.gov.uk/government/uploads/system/uploads/attachment_data/file/211853/nationalriskregister-2010.pdf (2010 edn); https://assets.publishing.service.gov.uk/government/uploads/system/uploads/attachment_data/file/969213/20210310_2008-NRR-Title-PAGE_UPDATED merged-1-2.pdf (*National Risk Register*, 2008), all accessed 3 August 2021.

6. Public Health England, *Exercise Cygnus Report, Tier One, Command Post Exercise, Pandemic Influenza*, 14–20 October 2016; https://assets.publishing.service.gov.uk/government/uploads/system/uploads/attachment_data/file/927770/exercise-cygnus-report.pdf, accessed 3 August 2021.

7. Lynn Barber, 'I'm plagued by worries of Disaster', *The Spectator*, 7 August 2021.

8. Farrar, *Spike*, pp. 134, 185.

9. Prime minister's press conference, 12 May 2021.

10. Prime minister's press conference, 17 March 2020.

11. 'Public Trust in UK Ministers Plummets', *Guardian*, 2 June 2020. See also Geoffrey Hosking, *Trust: A History* (Oxford University Press, 2014).

12. www.royal.uk/christmas-broadcast-2020, accessed 20 August 2021.

13. Captain Tom Donations: What Was the £33 Million Spent on? BBC News, 3 February 2021; www.bbc.co.uk/news/uk-52758683, accessed 20 August 2021.

14. www.theplayerstribune.com/posts/dear-england-gareth-southgate-euros-soccer, accessed 20 August 2021.

15. www.royal.uk/address-her-majesty-queen-75th-anniversary-ve-day, accessed 20/08/21.

16. Rudyard Kipling, 'The Lesson 1899–1902'; www.poetryloverspage. com/poets/kipling/lesson.html, accessed 17 August 2021.

CHAPTER 8: A NEW CONSENSUS AND A NEW BEVERIDGE?

1. Peter Medawar, review of Arthur Koestler's 'The Act of Creation', *New Statesman*, 19 June 1964, reproduced in P. B. Medawar, *The Art of the Soluble* (Pelican, 1969), p. 11.

2. George Soros, 'Rethinks', *The World at One*, BBC Radio 4, 25 June 2020.

3. George Mackay Brown, 'Healer', in Bevan and Murray (eds.), *Collected Poems of George Mackay Brown*, p. 300.

4. Jack Straw, *Last Man Standing* (Macmillan, 2012).

5. 'What's Your Problem, Social Care? the Eight Key Areas for Reform', King's Fund, 5 November 2019.

6. 'How Covid-19 Has Magnified Some of Social Care's Key Problems', King's Fund, 25 August 2020.

7. *With Respect to Old Age*, Report of the Royal Commission on long-term care, Cm. 4192 (HMSO, 1999).

8. 'Social Care: Forthcoming Green Paper (England)', House of Commons Library Briefing Paper 8002, 13 May 2019.

9. House of Lords Economic Affairs Committee, *Social Care Funding: Time to End a National Scandal*, HL Paper 392, 4 July 2019, p. 12.

10. Ibid., p. 5.

11. Timmins, *The Five Giants*, p. 605.

12. House of Lords Economic Affairs Committee, *Social Care Funding*, p. 5.

13. Ibid., p. 4.

14. Robert Booth, Denis Campbell, Heather Stewart, 'PM warned £12 bn gamble will not fix care crisis', *Guardian*, 9 September 2021.

15. Jessica Sargeant, 'Social Housing: Case for Increased Provision', Lords Research Briefing Housing, 24 January 2019, p. 1.

16. John Harris, 'The End of Council Housing', *Guardian*, 4 January 2016; www.theguardian.com/society/2016/jan/04/end-of-council-housing-bill-secure-tenancies-pay-to-stay, accessed 6 September 2021.

17. Sergeant, 'Social Housing', p. 1.

18. Ibid.

19. Timmins, *The Five Giants*, p. 680.

20. Ibid., p. 182.

21. Mark Brown, *Symbolic of Society: Grenfell Testimonies Distilled for the Stage*; "'It's a powerful allegory": Grenfell Inquiry Gets Verbatim Theatre Treatment', *Guardian*, 5 July 2021.

22. Ibid.

23. The Charter for Social Housing Residents, *Social Housing* (HMSO, 17 November 2020), p. 11.

24. Hennessy, *Never Again*, p. 163.

25. Ibid., p. 171.

26. 'Coronavirus: Support for Rough Sleepers (England)', House of Commons Library Research Briefing 9057, 14 January, 2021; https://commonslibrary.parliament.uk/research-briefings/cbp-9057/, accessed 6 September 2021.

27. *Report of the Endowed Schools Commission 1868*, House of Commons 1868, vol. 28, part I, p. 80.

28. Hennessy, *Winds of Change*, pp. 452–4.

29. Timmins, *The Five Giants*, p. 615.

30. Nerys Roberts, Philip Loft, Robert Long and Shadi Danechi, 'University Technical Colleges', House of Commons Library Research Briefing, 27 July 2020, p. 3.

31. *Skills for Jobs, Lifelong Learning Opportunities for Opportunity and Growth*, CP338 (HMSO, January 2021), pp. 10–11.

32. *Independent Panel Report to the Review of Post-18 Education and Funding* (HMSO, May 2019, p. 11 https://assets.publishing.service.gov.uk/government/uploads/system/uploads/attachment_data/file/805127/Review_of_post_18_education_and_funding.pdf accessed 13 July 2021.

33. Andy Powell and David Foster, 'T Levels: Reforms to Technical Education', House of Commons Library Research Briefing, 16 December 2019.

34. A. M. Turing, 'Computing Machinery and Intelligence', *Mind*, vol. 59 (1 October 1950), pp. 433–60.

35. House of Lords Select Committee on Artificial Intelligence, *AI in the UK: Ready, Willing and Able?*, HL paper 100, 16 April 2018, p. 17.

36. Ibid., p. 18.

37. Department for Business, Energy and Industrial Strategy, *Industrial Strategy: Building a Britain Fit for the Future* (HMSO, November 2017), p. 37.

38. House of Lords, *AI in the UK*, p. 14.

39. Ibid., p. 21.

40. Paul Nurse, *What Is Life? Understand Biology in Five Steps* (David Fickling Books, 2020), pp. 208–9.

41. House of Lords, *AI in the UK*, p. 77.

42. Ibid., p. 85.

43. Quoted ibid., p. 63.

44. Mark Carney made these remarks during the Q and A session that followed the delivery of his third 2020 Reith Lecture, 'From Covid Crisis to Renaissance', BBC Radio 4, 16 December 2020.

45. 'Fiscal Risks Report', Office of Budget Responsibility, 6 July 2021, p. 6; https://obr.uk/docs/dlm_uploads/Fiscal_risks_report_July_2021.pdf, accessed 6 September 2021.

46. John Browne, *Make, Think, Imagine: The Future of Civilisation* (Bloomsbury, 2020), p. 177.

47. 'Paul Crutzen: Seer of the Anthropocene', *The Economist*, 13 February 2021, p. 62.

48. Hennessy, *Never Again*, pp. 101–2.

49. Rob West, 'Investing for an Energy Transition', Thunder Said Energy, 13 October 2019. I am grateful to John Browne for bringing this paper to my attention.

50. Browne, *Make, Think, Imagine*, p. 145.

51. Mark Carney, 'From Climate Crisis to Real Prosperity', delivered on BBC Radio 4 on 23 December 2020.

52. Ibid.

53. Bill Gates, *How to Avoid a Climate Disaster: The Solutions We Have and the Breakthroughs We Need* (Allen Lane, Penguin Press, 2021), p. 189.

54. *The Economics of Biodiversity: The Dasgupta Review* (HM Treasury, 2021), p. 4.

55. *Build Back Fairer, The Covid-19 Marmot Review* (UCL, December 2020), p. 202.

56. She was speaking on BBC Radio 4's *The Life Scientific* on 15 September 2020.

57. *The Path to Net Zero* (Climate Assembly UK Full Report, 10 September 2020), chapter 11; www.climateassembly.uk/report/read/about-climate-assembly-uk.html#about-climate-assembly-uk, accessed 6 September 2021.

58. Ibid., 'Statement'; www.climateassembly.uk/report/read/executive-summary.html#executive-summary, accessed 6 September 2021.

CHAPTER 9: THE ROAD TO 2045

1. Adam Smith, *The Theory of Moral Sentiments*, 2nd edn (Andrew Millar of London and Alexander Kincaid of Edinburgh, 1761), p. 146.

2. R. H. Tawney, *Equality* (Allen and Unwin, 1938[1931]), p. 39.

3. Ben Pimlott, *The Queen: Elizabeth II and the Monarchy*, (Golden Jubilee edn, HarperCollins, 2001), pp. 446–7.

4. Lytton Strachey, *Queen Victoria* (1st World Library Literary Society, 2006[1921]), p. 265.

5. Hennessy, *The Kingdom to Come*, p. 119.

6. 'Queen Breaks Her Silence Over Scottish Independence', *Daily Telegraph*, 15 September 2014.

7. David Cameron, *For the Record* (Collins, 2019), pp. 551–3 (where he discusses his actions on the referendum and the Queens remark).

8. *The Cameron Years*, episode 2, BBC2, 26 September 2019.

9. Hennessy, *The Kingdom to Come*, p. 111.

10. Andrew McDonald, *Changing States, Changing Nations: Constitutional Reform and National Identity in the Late Twentieth Century* (Hart, 2021), p. 227.

11. Linda Colley, *The Gun, The Ship and the Pen: Constitutions and the Making of the Modern World* (Profile, 2021), pp. 13–14.

12. I am grateful to Ava Mayer and Dan Weedon of the House of Lords Constitution Committee for compiling this chart from figures produced by Her Majesty's Courts and Tribunal Service. Email from Dan Weedon, 17 September 2020.

13. House of Lords Select Committee on the Constitution, *Covid-19 and the Courts*, House of Lords Report 257, 30 March 2021, p. 35.

14. Ibid., p. 38.

15. Ibid., p. 79.

16. Ibid., p. 9.

17. Farrar, *Spike*, p. 227.

18. John Maynard Keynes, *Essays in Biography* (Royal Economic Society, 1972[1933]), pp. 173–4.

19. *The IFS Deaton Review of Inequalities: A New Year's Message* (IFS, 2021), p. 1.

20. J. M. Keynes, *The General Theory of Employment, Interest and Money* (Macmillan, 1936), p. 161.

21. Wilkinson and Pickett, *The Spirit Level*, pp. 4–5.

22. 'The Introduction of a Universal Basic Income. House of Commons Library Debate Pack', DPO 096, 8 October 2020, p. 2.

23. Jay (ed.), *The Oxford Dictionary of Political Quotations*, p. 156.

24. 'The introduction of a universal basic income', p. 4.

25. 'Citizen's Income', HC793, House of Commons, 28 April 2017, p. 3; https://publications.parliament.uk/pa/cm201617/cmselect/cmworpen/793/793.pdf.

26. Anna Coote, 'Universal Basic Services and Sustainable Consumption', Sustainability Science, Practice and Policy, vol. 17, no. 1 (2021), published online December 2020, p. 34.

27. Ibid., p. 35.

28. 'Social Prosperity for the Future: A Proposal for Universal Basic Services', Institute for Global Prosperity, University College London, 2017, p. 11.

29. Ibid., p. 25.

30. Ibid., pp. 51–2.

31. Ibid., p. 31.

32. Ibid., p. 34.

33. Nicholas Macpherson to the author, 'Some Thoughts of Where We Go From Here', 17 February 2021 (I am very grateful to him).

34. Sir Keir Starmer, 'A New Chapter for Britain' speech, 18 February 2021, https://labour.org.uk/press/full-text-of-keir-starmer-speech-on-a-new-chapter-for-britain/, accessed 6 September 2021.

35. '"It's difficult on Zoom, I haven't spoken to a room of people as Labour leader", Sir Keir Starmer in conversation with Stephen Swinford and Eleni Courea', The Times, 13 February 2021.

36. Starmer, 'A New Chapter for Britain'.

EPILOGUE: 'WOULDN'T IT BE NICE?'

1. R. H. Tawney, 'A National College of All Souls' first appeared in The Times Educational Supplement, 22 February 1917. It is most easily consulted in R. H. Tawney, The Attack and Other Papers (Allen and Unwin, 1953), pp. 29–34. This quotation is on page 34.

2. Ibid., p. 30.

3. Michael J. Sandel, The Tyranny of Merit: What's Become of the Common Good? (Allen Lane, Penguin Press, 2020), p. 224.

Index